Marian Barry

SUCCESS

International English Skills

for Cambridge IGCSE®

Student's Book

Third edition

CAMBRIDGE
UNIVERSITY PRESS

University Printing House, Cambridge CB2 8BS, United Kingdom

Cambridge University Press is part of the University of Cambridge.

It furthers the University's mission by disseminating knowledge in the pursuit of education, learning and research at the highest international levels of excellence.

Information on this title: education.cambridge.org

First published by Georgian Press (Jersey) Limited 1998
Second edition 2005
Reprinted and published by Cambridge University Press, Cambridge 2010
Third edition 2015
Reprinted 2015

Printed in the United Kingdom by Latimer Trend

A catalogue record for this publication is available from the British Library

ISBN 978-1-107-49594-4 Paperback

Contents

Contents chart

To Judith Brown,

for her unique skills, clear vision and dedication to this material which have provided immeasurable support over two decades.

Introduction

Dear Student,

In this book you will find all the support and information you need to help you prepare for the Cambridge IGCSE in English as a Second Language (E2L).

This suite helps you develop each skill you will need for success in your course – whether it is note-making, summary writing, reading comprehension, composition writing, listening or speaking. You will learn to communicate effectively and make good sense.

The IGCSE in E2L has two levels, known as Core and Extended. This book covers both levels, but aims to stretch and challenge you to reach a higher level than you perhaps thought possible.

As you use the book, what is expected of you is made very clear. You will always understand what you are doing and why you are doing it. The units are structured to build up the skills gradually, starting with the easier aspects of learning, such as recognising and understanding information. For example, you might have to write an article for a teenage magazine. Before you start, you will be given lots of help with vocabulary and the style to use, so when it is your turn to write independently you'll be able to do so confidently and easily. The **Unit focus** at the end of each unit explains the skills you have practised.

This suite is topic-based, and you will be practising your language skills while deepening your understanding of a range of contemporary issues. The exam can include questions on topics of international relevance. Students often feel unable to talk or write knowledgeably about such topics, but there is no need to feel like this. The book provides the factual information and ideas you might need, as well as helping you to think about them in a straightforward way. As your thinking skills develop, your ability to analyse new ideas naturally increases, so you will feel ready to tackle the topics you might meet in the exam.

As you progress through each unit of the book, you will enjoy having interesting themes to explore at the same time as improving your language techniques. You will pick up new vocabulary and structures quite painlessly.

Students sometimes have lots of good ideas in their heads but they struggle to get them down on paper. The exercises in this suite will help you overcome that kind of frustration because each topic is broken down into small bits. This means you can get each part of an exercise clear in your mind before moving on to the next part. In the end, you'll have an overview of a whole topic, and will find you can produce an excellent letter or article, or present an impressive talk to your group.

On the subject of talking, this book provides many opportunities for you to share your ideas in English with your group. Discussion is a great way to get your thoughts straight, bounce your ideas off other people, take a concept a stage further or get ready for an interesting listening or reading exercise. Don't forget to use the photographs in the book to get your ideas going too.

Mature self-expression is an important goal of the course. There are several exercises which show the difference between a simple, basic way of writing and a more mature style which is appropriate for a young adult. Achieving a mature writing style involves various language and personal skills, but the results are well worth the effort of learning the techniques.

During the course, you will be helped to evaluate your progress so you can see what you need to do next to keep extending and developing yourself. I hope you will use the **Key advice** at the end of each unit, as this will help you reflect on what you have achieved in the unit. It also gives ideas for further progress, as well as advice on exam techniques. At the end of each unit there are **Exam-style questions** for you to practise.

When the time for the exam comes, I am sure you will feel well prepared and confident of achieving your best.

Finally, the secret of successful learning is not being born with a superior brain. It's making up your mind to achieve something and sticking with it!

All the best,

Marian Barry

1

Unit 1:
Happiness and Success

1.1 What is happiness?

1 Quiz

Do this quiz in pairs to find out how happy you are. Don't worry about individual words – just try to understand the main ideas.

1 Which statement best summarises your feelings about your education?

   a My talent is unrecognised.

   b I'm very clear about what way of working suits me.

   c Other people's approval is very important.

2 How do you feel about relationships?

   a I think people should accept me for who I am.

   b I know what I have to give, but sometimes I fail.

   c I try hard to be an ideal son/daughter/friend.

3 Which statement best describes your relationship with your closest friend?

   a Our relationship is so good we never argue.

   b We do argue, but we make up afterwards.

   c We like to get every niggle off our chests.

4 Which statement best describes your feelings about your home?

   a It's a place to rest my head.

   b My heart lifts when I come home.

   c I feel proud when I tell someone my address.

5   You've got a chance to redecorate your bedroom. Do you
    a   let your parents choose the colour scheme and carpet, etc?
    b   go for something outrageous or soothing – whatever makes you feel good?
    c   select something stylish you saw in a magazine?

6   What are your feelings about other people?
    a   I believe there is usually an ulterior motive in people's behaviour.
    b   I give individuals the benefit of the doubt.
    c   I trust people and then feel let down.

7   You've been invited to a big party. All your friends will be there. You hate parties. Do you
    a   tell everyone you're going but don't turn up?
    b   explain your feelings in a light-hearted way?
    c   go anyway and feel miserable?

8   You're feeling proud of a new outfit. A 'friend' makes a hurtful remark. Do you
    a   give a sharp reply/say something nasty back?
    b   ignore it?
    c   vow never to be seen in it again?

9   How do you choose your clothes?
    a   I go for classics.
    b   For comfort and personal taste – favourite colours, cuts and fabrics.
    c   I like to be fashionable.

10 What are your feelings about family and personal relationships?
    a   I believe that I have a duty to others.
    b   I'll make sacrifices, but I know my limits.
    c   I believe I must be happy in whatever I do.

11 What is the most important part of your home?
    a   Main reception room.
    b   Bathroom, kitchen, bedroom or 'den'.
    c   Front entrance.

12 How do you deal with difficult situations?
    a   I avoid situations that might hurt me.
    b   I remove myself from any situation that keeps causing me pain.
    c   I persevere in situations that are hurting me.

13 How would you describe your life?
    a   I've no time to pursue personal goals.

    b   I've a clear sense of meaning and purpose.
    c   I'm over-committed and I feel all over the place.

14 Which best describes your friendships?
    a   I'd like to have more.
    b   I choose my friends.
    c   My friends choose me – I'm liked and accepted.

15 You're relaxing at home after a hard day when a friend phones. Do you
    a   get someone to tell her you're out?
    b   get someone to tell her you'll call back?
    c   take the call?

See the end of the book for quiz scores.

2 Discussion

A   The quiz suggests the happiest people are those who live life in their own way. They know what they want and don't feel the need to do things just because others want them to. How far do you agree with this interpretation?

Do you think living like this can make people selfish? Does everyone have a right to happiness? Try to explain your ideas to your group.

3

B What makes you happy? Read some comments made by students.

'Finding a £5 note in the pocket of my jeans when I thought I was broke.'
'Going to a football match and seeing my side win.'
'A surprise long-distance call from a really close friend.'

Now add your own ideas. Be specific!

_____

_____

C Share your ideas around your group.

D What can you do when you feel unhappy?

Study these comments.

'I ride my horse down to the river and just sit and think. It's my real place to escape.'
'I talk to my dad and he tells me how he coped in a similar situation.'

Discuss your ideas with your partner or keep them private.

3 Formal and informal styles

Here is some informal or colloquial language from the quiz. Match it to the more formal equivalents.

1 I feel all over the place.
2 We like to get every niggle off our chests.
3 I go for classics.
4 You're waiting for life to come and dish out the happiness.
5 You've hardly got off the launch pad.
A I prefer clothes that will not go out of fashion.
B I lack a clear sense of my goals in life.
C You aren't taking responsibility for making yourself happy.
D You haven't started moving.
E We always tell each other our bad feelings even if they are about something unimportant.

4 Spelling patterns and speech sounds

You've just completed a quiz. In English spelling, *q* is always followed by *u*. *Qu* is a spelling pattern. The speech sound is /kw/.

Can you guess the following words, each containing the pattern *qu*? Use your dictionary to check that your spelling is correct.

1 The king is married to her.
2 He started the essay with words from his favourite poem.
3 This is the sound a duck makes.
4 A celebration meal which a very large number of people attend.

Ph is another spelling pattern, and sounds like /f/. It's in **ph**one, **ph**otograph and **ph**rase.

What other sounds and spelling patterns do you know?

5 Approaches to spelling

Tick the strategies you use to help you spell.

☐ I remember how the word looks on the page (visual recall).

☐ I use spelling rules.

☐ I link spelling patterns with speech sounds (e.g. *q+u* is a pattern and sounds like /kw/).

Everyone makes spelling mistakes! To improve your spelling you need to use a combination of all these approaches. One method which is particularly useful and quick to learn is called the 'look, say, cover, write, check' method, described below.

6 Look, say, cover, write, check

This method concentrates attention on each letter group in a word so you won't miss any letters out. It also stops you putting letters into a word which don't belong there – even if they sound as if they do! It can be used with other strategies such as spelling rules and linking speech sounds to spelling patterns.

Break into syllables

To help you remember how a word looks, break it into syllables. For example, *quality* has three syllables: qua/li/ty.

Qualification has five syllables: qua/li/fi/ca/tion.

Break these words into syllables:

quota
question
automatic
quarrel

Take a mental photograph

Cover the word with a piece of paper. Then move the paper so that you can see the first syllable only. Study the syllable carefully, 'photographing' it in your mind and saying the syllable to yourself. Then move the paper along so that you can see the next syllable. Repeat the process, until you have mentally 'photographed' the complete word.

Test yourself

Cover up the whole word. Write it from memory. Then check your spelling with the original. If your spelling was correct, write out the word three times from memory to reinforce the visual recall. If you didn't get it right, repeat the whole process until you are sure you can spell the word accurately.

7 Tricky words

Here are some words students find hard to spell correctly. Make sure you understand the meaning of each one. Can you pronounce it properly? Say it aloud to your partner to check.

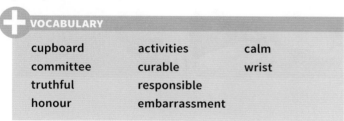

VOCABULARY

cupboard	activities	calm
committee	curable	wrist
truthful	responsible	
honour	embarrassment	

How well can you spell these tricky words? Use the 'look, say, cover, write, check' method. Remember to break each word into syllables first. When you have mastered the spelling of each word, move on to the next. Finally, use each word in a sentence to show its meaning.

8 Why are words misspelled?

A Try this exercise in a pair or group of three.

Study each tricky word in exercise 7 again. Do you notice anything about the word which makes it extra hard to spell? Think about these questions.

Is the problem the fact that we do not pronounce some of the letters in the word? These are called **silent letters**.

Is the problem the **ending** of the word? Do we make mistakes because the sound of the ending is different from the correct spelling?

Is the problem the fact that the word is a **plural**? What happens to the word when it changes from singular to plural?

Is the problem the fact that there are **double letters** in the word? Do we make mistakes because we are not sure whether to use a double or single letter?

B When you have decided why each word is tricky, make a note.

Examples: *Cupboard* is tricky because you can't hear the *p*, so you might forget to put it in.
Activities is a tricky word because the singular is *activity.* You might forget to change the ending to -*ies* when you write the plural form.

C Write down examples of other words which have silent letters and -*ies* plurals.

Examples: *p* is not only silent in *cupboard.* You can't hear it in *receipt, raspberry* or *psychology.*

Dictionary, story and *memory* are other words which have -*ies* plurals. But words like *boy* and *railway* just add *s* to make the plural.

D When you have written as much as you feel you can, discuss your results with other pairs or groups.

9 How helpful is your dictionary?

Dictionaries give you the meaning of words and help you to spell. Does your dictionary also

- tell you how to pronounce the word?
- tell you the grammatical class (verb, noun, adverb)?
- tell you if the word belongs to more than one grammatical class (e.g. nouns that can be used as verbs)?
- tell you if a noun is countable or uncountable?
- give you example sentences?
- give you any idiomatic expressions using the word(s)?

If the answer to most of these questions is no, you need a new dictionary! Choosing a good dictionary is complex. Before you spend a lot of money, ask your teacher or your classmates for their ideas.

10 Getting organised

Have you got a spelling and vocabulary book? If not, start one now. Plan the layout carefully. Use columns, notes on pronunciation, space for translations and example sentences. Keep it nicely organised and you'll find it a great aid to memory. It will be an enormous help in understanding the patterns of English.

5

1.2 Happy not to be a high-flyer

11 Before you read

A Compare this description with the photograph.

Tina's short brown hair is cut in a boyish style with a fringe. She has a beaming smile and looks alert, confident and ready for anything.

Do you agree with the description? Would you change anything?

B You are going to read about Tina's way of being happy. Before you read, try to answer these questions.

Where do you think the text comes from?

What do you think the style is going to be – chatty and informal, or formal and serious?

Who do you think the article is written for?

Vocabulary check

Make sure you know the meaning of these words from the text.

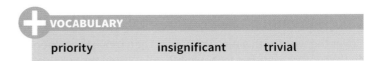

VOCABULARY

| priority | insignificant | trivial |

12 Comprehension check

Now read the article. Then answer the questions which follow.

Tina Barry, acquisitions assistant of a TV company, is happy standing still on her career ladder.

'My mum always wanted me to do well at school and to have a high-status job, but that sort of thing isn't a big priority for me. I did have the potential to do well and go to university, but I was just too busy having a good time. My relationships have always been far more important to me than academic or career success.

'My present job basically involves working as an assistant, and friends still insist I could have achieved more in my working life. When I was younger, I did feel I had to set myself goals and attain them within a certain period. I successfully ran my own business for a while, but having kids put life back into perspective.

'There have been times when I could have taken on a lot more responsibility at work, but I imagine that if I had a more senior role at work, another part of my life would have to give, and I'm not prepared to risk that. I'm just not the sort of person who can trample on others to get to the top. I find it satisfying to do a productive job because I like to feel I'm doing something useful, but I'm not into climbing the career ladder now.

'The biggest priorities in my life are my husband, David, and our young children – son Greg and daughter Fleur. If I'm ever fed up after a day at work, I just spend some time playing with the children, and the enjoyment I get from them makes me realise how insignificant and trivial my worries at work can be.

'Occasionally, I'm reminded of how tied down I am – if a friend goes off travelling, for example. But I suppose an important part of contentment is to accept life's limitations, and to learn to enjoy the things that you *can* do.'

6

1   Why do Tina's friends think her job isn't good enough for her?

2   What does Tina think is the most important part of her life?

3   Why is Tina not ambitious?

4   Describe Tina's attitude to life.

13 Principles of a happy life

Psychologists, analysing the ingredients for a happy life, have come up with the following dos and don'ts. Unfortunately, the words *do* and *don't* are missing.

Working with a partner, write *Do* or *Don't* next to each point.

_____   regret decisions you made in the past.

_____   hold resentment against your parents.

_____   value status and material possessions more than people.

_____   spend a lot of time envying other people.

_____   be realistic about how much you can achieve.

_____   choose a job which gives you real satisfaction.

Now discuss your opinions in groups.

14 Finding examples

Working in groups of two or three, look back at Tina's comments about her life. Try to find specific examples in what she says which illustrate the principles about happiness in the list above.

Example:
She says she had the potential to go to university but it wasn't a priority. She was too busy having a good time. This shows she doesn't regret decisions made in the past.

15 Sharing ideas

A   When your group has finished, check your examples with those of another group. Are there any differences? Make any corrections you need to. Include new, interesting ideas on your own list.

B   Suggest some 'happiness principles' to share with your group. Try to base them on your own experience.

Examples:
Do try to be tolerant of other people.
Don't be too self-critical.

16 Discussion

Tina says she's happy not to be a high-flyer. On the other hand, people say they get great fulfilment from being promoted to highly demanding jobs. Would you be prepared to make any sacrifices in your personal life in order to have a high-flying career? Why/Why not?

17 Goal setting

A   Tina says that, when she was younger, she set herself goals. Is goal setting a good idea? Does it help you achieve things, or should you take each day as it comes? Should you ever change your goals?

B   Have you any goals of your own? Take a few minutes to think and then write them down. Divide them into daily, medium-term and long-term goals. Share them with others or keep them private if you prefer.

Examples:
A goal for today is to tidy my bedroom.
A medium-term goal is to improve my fitness by swimming twice a week.
A long-term goal is to travel the world.

Daily goal   _____

Medium-term goal   _____

Long-term goal   _____

18 Figurative meanings

Tina says, 'I'm just not the sort of person who can *trample* on others to get to the top.'

The literal meaning of *trample* is to tread heavily on something in a way which damages it.

Example: *They trampled over the garden, ruining the new plants.*

Tina uses *trample* figuratively, meaning that she would not behave in a way which would hurt the feelings of others.

In each of the following sentences, one word is used figuratively. Underline the word, and then discuss its meaning with your partner. Finally, write sentences of your own to illustrate the meanings. Don't forget to use a dictionary when you need to.

1   I spent the day wrestling with our financial problems.

2   My heart lifts when I come home.

3   She was unhappy because her older sister always squashed her ideas.

4   We're fighting the authorities who want to close our village school.

5   His face broke into a smile when he heard the news.

6   I'm tired of battling with staff who refuse to accept different working conditions.

7   After his wife's death, he buried himself in his work.

8   She's crippled by shyness.

The English language is full of figurative uses of words. Reading and listening to authentic English will develop your awareness. Work towards including examples in your own vocabulary.

19   Homophones

Tina says that she doesn't want a more senior role at work. *Role* here means job.

Role has the same sound as *roll*, but each word has a different spelling and meaning. *Roll* can refer to a bread roll, or be used as a verb meaning movement, e.g. *roll the ball along the ground.* Words with the same sound but different spellings are called **homophones**. The following sentences are based on students' writing. Choose the correct homophone in each case. Can you explain the meaning of the incorrect one?

1   There's no plaice / place like home.

2   I was in terrible pane / pain when I broke my arm.

3   You need peace / piece and quiet for your work.

4   I read the hole / whole book in one evening.

5   We're not aloud / allowed to stay out late.

6   We have a pear / pair tree in the garden.

7   The wind farms will be a horrible site / sight.

8   Their / There are six people in my family.

9   I answered four / for questions.

10   He's got a saw / sore throat.

20   More homophones

Work in small groups to try to find a homophone for each of these words.

1	steal	6	bear
2	male	7	tail
3	your	8	sale
4	week	9	poor
5	hour	10	wail

Now put each word into a sentence to show its meaning.

1.3   The price of greatness

21   Before you listen

Name someone who you think deserves to go down in history for their work or achievements. Why do you think this person should be admired? Try to be specific.

Example: *Marie Curie – because her discoveries led to the development of X-rays and successful treatments for cancer.*

Make a few notes.

What do you know of this person's background and personal life? If you don't know very much, what picture do you have in your mind of it? Do you imagine a happy home life or one dominated by struggle and conflict? Why/Why not? Write down your ideas.

Share your ideas with the rest of the group.

22 Vocabulary check

Match the words which you are going to hear with their definitions.

1	genius	A	something which makes it difficult for you to do what you want
2	inner drive	B	inherited through your parents
3	genetic	C	reach an extremely high standard
4	setback	D	unhappy feelings, anxiety, depression
5	excel	E	average, not particularly good
6	psychological unease	F	a strong determination to achieve
7	mediocre	G	(a person of) exceptional ability

23 Listening: Radio interview 🔊

Listen to this radio interview and choose the best answer for each question.

1 According to Steve, the disadvantages suffered by great achievers when they were children
   a made it more difficult for them to reach their potential.
   b drove them to excel.
   c made the public more sympathetic to their achievements.
   d embittered them for life.

2 The interviewer's attitude to the information that suffering is a significant factor in great achievement is
   a doubtful.
   b amused.
   c horrified.
   d intrigued.

3 What, according to Steve, did great achievers need when they were children?
   a understanding
   b companionship
   c solitude
   d training

4 Steve's message to ordinary children who are hoping to fulfil their potential is
   a discouraging – you'll probably never make it as a real superstar.
   b supportive – everyone should develop his/her abilities.
   c cautious – try to achieve but take care not to get depressed.
   d excited – there's a wonderful future ahead of you.

24 Post-listening discussion

A According to the speaker, the greatest thinkers had unhappy lives. Does this surprise you at all? Why/Why not?

B Do you agree that being very successful is '5 per cent talent and the rest hard work'? Explain your views.

25 Apostrophes (1)

These sentences come from the script of the radio interview. Why are the apostrophes used, do you think? Discuss your ideas with your partner.

1 Steve's been reading an absolutely wonderful book.
2 You can't just pick out one or two factors.
3 It's a very complex web.
4 They've probably suffered from depression.
5 I wouldn't say you ought to stop trying to achieve your potential.
6 You mightn't be the next superstar.

Pronunciation

Practise saying the contracted forms to your partner. Try to make the contraction smooth and natural-sounding.

26 Apostrophes (2)

With a partner, study the exact position of the apostrophes in these sentences.

1 Someone's stolen the doctor's bag.
2 He got a parents' guide to zoos.
3 All the passengers' luggage goes in the hold.
4 There are no men's toilets on this floor.
5 Give me Brendan's shoes.
6 I spoke to the children's favourite teacher.
7 Can I introduce Maria's husband?

9

What conclusions can you come to about using apostrophes? Write down your ideas.

_____

_____

_____

_____

_____

27 Correcting sentences

Now correct the following sentences by adding apostrophes where they are necessary.

1   The teachers listened to Carols views.
2   Theyve bought a new car.
3   I went to my mothers office.
4   Please dont touch the babies clothes.
5   Its hard to explain the programmes success.
6   She works in the womens ward of the hospital.
7   Hes training to be a ladies hairdresser.
8   Youll find her in the teachers workroom – all the staff go there.
9   He mightve become the next Einstein.
10 She couldnt understand why her cat had lost its appetite.

Practise saying the sentences aloud to your partner.

28 Speculating about a photograph

Study this photograph with a partner. Read how three students have described the person in it. Which comments do you most agree with? Try to explain why.

A

He looks big and heavy-set. He's got a warm, humorous expression and a rugged, outdoor appearance. He could be a farmer or a sailor.

B

He has a pleasant expression and friendly smile. He looks confident and also trustworthy. He could be a lawyer or a businessman.

C

He's fair-skinned with bushy eyebrows and swept-back hair. He's rather sensitive-looking. He could be an artist or a ballet dancer.

The photograph is of Alexander Garcia, a high-flying entrepreneur who started his own business selling mobile phones at 17, and became a multimillionaire at the age of 21. He has decided to share his business skills and help others start small businesses. He particularly supports applications from people who want to start a business in an area of high unemployment.

29 Describing personal qualities

Here are some comments people have made about Alex. Study them with a partner. Make sure you understand each one.

When he's deciding whether to invest in a business idea he gets negative comments such as, 'It's not worth it, Alex, that project is a waste of money. The applicant is too uneducated to do well.' But he doesn't think like that. He believes everyone deserves a chance to succeed.

He has invested in small businesses with no guarantee of success, but he says that it was worth it because now, all over the world, people are running a business they are proud of.

He thinks there are still huge economic problems and a lot of poverty. But he reminds us that if we make the world a fairer place, everyone will benefit.

When he hears about an exciting project he's filled with enthusiasm. He relies on friends saying, 'Wait a minute Alex, you've got to do this or do that to avoid disaster.'

He believes that encouraging people to believe in their future is vital. Even if others think he is too optimistic, he just has to do what he thinks is right.

His work involves constant travel, which can be exhausting, and business ventures do not always prosper. What has kept him going is having good friends who share his ideals.

After reading people's comments about Alex's life, do you think it is right to draw the following conclusions about him? Answer yes or no.

He has

1 the courage to take risks.
2 benefited from positive advice.
3 bad memories he cannot forget.
4 accepted stress as part of his life.
5 support from people around him.
6 trouble trusting others.
7 self-belief.
8 a positive outlook.
9 determination.
10 difficulty adjusting to change.

30 Discussion

1 Alex might be successful, but is he happy? What are your views?
2 Is there anything about Alex's approach to life you would choose for yourself? Try to explain why.
3 Do you think Alex is a good example to younger people? Could he be a role model (a person who inspires others to copy them)? Why/Why not?
4 Does Alex share any qualities with your own personal heroes or heroines?

31 Drafting a paragraph

Write a paragraph of about 75 words describing the kind of person you think Alex is. Try to give reasons for your opinions.

When you've finished writing, show your paragraph to a partner. Does he/she think you should change anything? Do you agree? Make a second draft, putting in the changes you both agreed on.

1.4 Obstacles and challenges

32 Expressing fears and giving reassurance

In pairs, read the following dialogue.

A: I've got to recite a poem in front of the whole school.
B: How do you feel about it?

A: To tell you the truth, I'm a bit worried about it.
B: Don't worry. You'll be fine. Everyone thinks you're great!

When people want to express fears, they use these expressions. Tick the one(s) which sound most fearful.
I feel sick every time I think about it.
To tell you the truth, I'm a bit scared about it.
I'm not really sure I can cope.
To be honest, I'm not sure I'll be able to do it.
The thought of it bothers me.
I'm terrified!

Here are some expressions you can use to calm someone's fears. Which do you prefer?

There's nothing to worry about. You'll do a wonderful job.
You'll be fine. Nothing can go wrong.
Things will be all right. We're all supporting you.
Don't get too upset. It'll all go well.

Practice

Practise expressing fears and giving reassurance in pairs. A should explain what he/she has to do. B should give reassurance. Then swap over. Base your dialogues on these situations.

- a fear of taking an exam
- a fear of competing in a race
- a fear of giving a talk in front of the school
- a fear of going to the dentist

33 Pre-reading discussion

You are going to read about Monica, a woman who didn't learn to read until she was an adult. Discuss the following questions.

1 What everyday problems do you think not being able to read would present?
2 Why might someone who was unable to read not try to get help to learn?
3 What effect do you think not being able to read might have on him/her?

34 Vocabulary check

Make sure you know the meaning of these words from the text. Use a dictionary if necessary.

VOCABULARY		
taunted	illiterate	volunteer

35 Reading: Textual organisation

Read the text carefully and match each paragraph with one of these headings.

A   Effects on Sally's education

B   Hiding the problem

C   Unhappy school days

D   Qualifying as a parent-educator

E   Sally's birth

F   Monica's work today

G   Learning to read

Facing the Fears

Monica Chand's childhood memories are of crippling stomach aches each morning before school, of missing lessons through illness and falling so far behind that she understood little but did not dare to ask for help, of silent misery as other children taunted her as 'stupid'. She says, 'I spent all those years feeling I had failed at school, but now I think school failed me, and when I had Sally, 17 years ago, I was determined it would not be the same for her.' She is sitting in her immaculately tidy flat in south London. Sally, a rangy, striking teenager, joins us – at first shy, then exchanging memories with her mother.

Monica is describing how it feels to be unable to read and write, to be illiterate in a world where just about everything we do, how we are judged, depends on our literacy skills. Few people, she says, realise what it means to be unable to read a road sign, safety instructions or the contents of a food packet, when every form you have to fill in, every note you need to write, is an impossible task. Monica remembers it very clearly: 'I felt so conscious of not being able to join in the life other people were living.' Nor do many people realise the elaborate charades people put on to disguise this inadequacy. Monica explains, 'I would have the names of places I wanted to go to written down, and then I'd show this and ask someone to help, explaining that I'd left my glasses at home or some such story. I'd carry a book or paper around and pretend to read it. You get good at fooling other people, but you can't fool yourself. It makes the world a scary place.'

Her husband Ravi, who died earlier this year, was unaware of her secret. She says, 'I'd just ask him to do the things I couldn't cope with and he accepted that. But it really came home to me when Sally was born. I felt very insecure as a mother, and as she grew up everyone around me was saying, 'You must read to her.' I felt so stupid because I couldn't.' Even then she did not tell Ravi, although she smiles now and says, 'I think he must have known in his heart of hearts, but he was such a sweet man he never let on. I made sure he did the reading with Sally – I'd say I had to cook dinner and that it was a good way for them to be close.' Sally remembers, 'Sometimes Mum would sit with us and seem to join in. I never realised she wasn't actually reading.'

Things changed when Sally went to primary school and Monica became a volunteer, helping with the children. One morning the head said they wanted to offer her a paid job as a helper. 'I just froze. I knew that would involve reading and writing – the things I'd avoided so far. But the head had recognised my problem. She took me under her wing and did reading with me every day so that I could take the job. As I learned, she put me in with older children and I realised I could read and write. It was like a miracle.'

That was the beginning. When the present head took over he set up a parents' group and Monica was part of it. He asked them to write a book for parents teaching their children. Monica says, 'My first reaction was, "Ooh, I can't do that," but then I realised I could contribute. And I wanted to because I realised there were other parents "in the closet", as I had been, and that I could help them.' By now she was doing a training course to become a parent-educator. 'The day I got my certificate – the first in my life – Sally and I went out for a really nice meal to celebrate.'

These struggles are in the past. Monica now works in several different schools and has just returned from a conference in Cyprus where she gave a presentation on involving parents in reading. Her delight is obvious. 'Learning to read has made the world a different place. Suddenly I feel there are so many things I can do. But the most important thing is that Sally hasn't been held back.'

Sally pulls a face. 'Mum was very pushy about studying and homework. She'd find fault with everything because she was so keen I should do well.' But Monica is unapologetic. 'Perhaps I pushed harder than other parents because I knew what failing feels like, and I suppose I was living my life through her. But we were both bursting with pride the day she did really well in her GCSEs. I was in tears in front of everyone at school because I was so proud.' Sally is no less proud. She is sitting on the arm of the sofa near her mother, listening, and her smile is overflowing with affection. She says, 'I think it was brave of Mum. She's also shown me how important it is to take opportunities when they come. If she hadn't done that, she wouldn't have become the person she is now, with a great future.'

36 Comprehension check

1 Why did Monica dislike school? Give two reasons.
2 How did she hide from other people the fact that she couldn't read? Give two examples.
3 Explain how Monica felt when she was offered paid work by the headteacher.
4 What has Sally learned from her mother's experiences?

37 Vocabulary: Odd one out

The following groups of adjectives each contain a word which doesn't describe Monica. Cross it out.

1 Monica as a child:

anxious   robust   delicate   tense   shy   sensitive

2 Monica as a young mother:

secretive   insecure   abrasive   gentle   worried

3 Monica now:

fulfilled   timid   cheerful   understanding   frank

38 'Bird' idioms

Monica explains that the headteacher 'took me under her wing' (paragraph 4) when she was learning to read. This image comes from birds. What does it mean, do you think?

Now try to complete the sentences, choosing a suitable expression from the box to fill each space.

> **+ VOCABULARY**
>
> | | |
> |---|---|
> | a bird in the hand is worth two in the bush | kill two birds with one stone |
> | a bird's-eye view | a hen party |
> | took her under her wing | an ugly duckling |

1 He's seven years old and has just lost his front teeth. He's going through _____ phase.
2 We climbed to the top of the tower to get _____ of the town.
3 She had _____ on the night before she got married.
4 I decided to take the job I was offered rather than wait for the results of my next interview. After all, _____.
5 Eleni was nervous when she joined her new school but one of the older girls _____.
6 I went home to visit my mother. She told me my old friend Ahmed had moved into the area, so I decided to _____ and go and see him as well.

39 Post-reading discussion

A Monica accepted the challenge of learning to read as an adult. Why are challenges important? What challenges do you have in your own life?
B Monica says 'I suppose I was living my life through her' (paragraph 7). What bad effects might living your life through another person have?
C Some people feel they will be happy if they have success, achievement, material things. Other people claim happiness comes from inside you. Where does Monica's happiness come from? Try to explain your views.

How far do you think literacy is important to the progress of a country?

Do you have any idea of the literacy rates in your own country? If you don't know, try to find out.

13

Nearly 17 per cent of the world's population are illiterate. Two-thirds of illiterate adults are women.

Globally, 122 million young people are illiterate.

UNESCO believes education is the best means of breaking the connection between illiteracy and poverty, unemployment and ill-health. Currently UNESCO is operating global literacy programmes particularly targeting the education of young people and girls.

40 Describing people

Sally is described as a *'rangy, striking teenager'* (paragraph 1). *Rangy* means tall and very slim with long, slender limbs. What does the adjective *striking* tell us about her appearance?

The writer uses only two adjectives before the noun. Do you think this is enough? How well do you think he/she manages to convey the impression Sally makes?

The writer tells us that as Sally listens to her mother *'her smile is overflowing with affection'* (paragraph 7). What kind of person does Sally seem to be? What is her relationship with her mother like? How does the language used emphasise warmth and closeness?

41 Using a wide range of adjectives

When you are trying to describe the impression a person makes, you can refer to their appearance and their character. Try to use adjectives which are fresh and individual.

You can use:

- specific single adjectives: *striking, sensitive, charming*
- adjective compounds (adjective + noun + *-ed*): *broad-shouldered, fair-skinned, good-natured*
- compounds with *-looking: stern-looking* (instead of saying 'He looked as if he were a stern person.')

Compounds with *-looking* usually refer to a person's inner qualities: *capable-looking, studious-looking, miserable-looking. Good-looking* is an exception.

42 Adjective collocations

Study the adjectives in the box. Divide them into four groups, under the four headings. Work with a partner

and use a dictionary to help you. Find translations if you need to.

Appearance   Hair   Voice   Character

VOCABULARY

deep	well-proportioned	luxuriant
wavy	quiet	gentle
tight-fisted	self-centred	rangy
grating	dreamy	elegant
straight	plump	scruffy
genial	ill-mannered	argumentative
husky	altruistic	overweight
shy	balding	curly
placid	high-pitched	skinny
ambitious	burly	bad-tempered
melodious	rugged	close-cropped
slim	generous	domineering
tolerant	well-dressed	frank
wispy	considerate	bushy
absent-minded	outgoing	humorous
tender-hearted		

43 Positive and negative

You might not mind being called *slim*, but you probably wouldn't like to be called *skinny*! *Slim* has a positive connotation, whereas *skinny* is negative.

Study your word groups in exercise 42 again. Tick (✓) the words you think are definitely positive, and mark with a cross (✗) the ones you think are definitely negative.

44 Negative prefixes

Make the character traits below into their opposites by adding one of these prefixes:

dis-   im-   in-   ir-   un-

VOCABULARY

responsible	trustworthy	happy
loyal	contented	honest
mature	reliable	
secure	efficient	

Now put the words into sentences to show their meanings.

45 Colour

Colour is a big part of people's appearance. You could write *'He had black hair and blue eyes'*. However, your writing will get a better response if you say what shade of blue and what kind of black you mean.

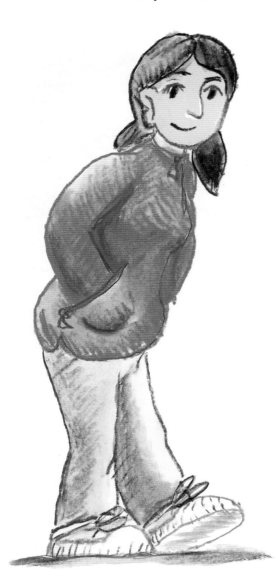

Using an image from the natural world helps identify an exact shade of colour and produces more vivid writing.

Examples:
Her eyes were sapphire-blue.
His hair was jet-black.
She was wearing a raspberry-pink fleece.

Write sentences about people's appearance using these colour images.

 VOCABULARY

chestnut-brown	emerald-green
chocolate-brown	lime-green
cherry-red	jet-black
rose-pink	sky-blue
strawberry-blonde	lemon-yellow

Being creative

Make up some other associations of your own by linking colours to natural objects. Think about the people and colours around you.

Examples:
He's wearing a leaf-green jacket.
She was carrying a banana-yellow shopping bag.

46 Developing a more mature style

Try to avoid stringing lots of adjectives together. Using clauses beginning with *which/that …* and phrases beginning with *with …* makes your descriptive style more mature. Underline the examples in these descriptions.

> *He had straight, dark-yellow hair and milky blue eyes that made him seem dreamy and peaceful.* (Anne Tyler, *The Ladder of Years*)

> *She was a tall, fragile-looking woman in a pretty blue hat that matched her eyes.* (Barbara Pym, *An Unsuitable Attachment*)

> *He was a tall, melancholy man with curly hair, rather romantic-looking in his long, sewer-man's boots.* (George Orwell, *Down and Out in Paris and London*)

Conjunctions such as *but* introduce a contrast:

> *He had grown to be a large-boned man, but his face was still childishly rounded, with the wide eyes, the downy cheeks, the delicate lips of a schoolboy.* (Anne Tyler, *Dinner at the Homesick Restaurant*)

47 Conveying character traits

Study this example again:

He had straight, dark-yellow hair and milky blue eyes that made him seem dreamy and peaceful.

15

Now look at this explanation of the way the writer achieves her effect. Do you agree with it?

> We get a clear picture of the impression this man makes because of the writer's carefully chosen adjectives. She describes his eyes vividly as milky blue. Milk is associated with innocence and childhood. Using an unusual expression like milky blue emphasises the gentle, trusting qualities of the man. Choosing adjectives such as dreamy and peaceful strengthens the impression the man gives of being accepting and placid.

Choose one of the other examples from exercise 46 and try to write about it in the same way.

48 Writing your own description

Each of us is unique. No one has exactly the same face, hands, hair, body or voice as anyone else. Even identical twins are said to have different ears!

Choose a friend to describe. Don't try to describe everything about him/her. Concentrate on a few special characteristics which convey your friend's uniqueness. For example, he/she may have beautiful, well-shaped hands, a melodious voice, sparkling eyes. Try to link physical characteristics to character traits.

Remember, use adjectives and colour images selectively. Don't overdo them. Use clauses to make your writing more mature.

Write about 75 words.

Feedback

Read your description aloud to your group. Listen carefully to the feedback. (Criticisms should be positive!) Are there any changes you would like to make after hearing the comments?

1.5 Someone I admire

49 Example description

Read this article which was sent to a teenage magazine running a series called 'Special Friends'.

How did the writer meet Simon? As you read, underline any words you don't understand.

My special friend

I'd like to describe my friend Simon. Simon is a complex mixture of frankness and reserve. He is small, slight and rather studious-looking. His gentle, golden-brown eyes are hidden behind a large pair of black-framed glasses. Simon is very neat and particular in everything he does. Even his books and pencils are always arranged in perfect order on his desk!

I admire Simon because he used to be painfully shy. He's never been interested in sport or smart clothes and he often shops in secondhand shops. The other students used to think he was scruffy and gave him the nickname 'ugly duckling'. One day, however, he decided he wasn't going to let his shyness crush him. He had to try to be himself. He began to open out and make friends.

Simon is a very trustworthy and straightforward friend. When I was worried about an operation I had to have, he helped me talk through my fears. I gradually got the confidence to ask the doctors for a proper explanation. I learned from Simon that it is better to face your fears than to hide them.

I know I'm really a lucky person because I have a good friend on whom I can always rely.

Comprehension check

1   What impression does Simon make?
2   Why was he unhappy at school?
3   How do you know Simon is a determined person?
4   Why does the writer value Simon's friendship?

Format

A good description shows what the person is like by giving:

- key details about appearance
- examples of behaviour
- reasons why this person is unusual or valued.

Underline the key phrases which provide insight into Simon as a person and as a friend.

What comments can you make about the structure of the sentences? Think about clauses, descriptive vocabulary and expressing reasons.

Beginnings and endings

What sentence is used to begin the article?

How is the article brought to a conclusion?

50 Comparing two styles

The following description was written by a student, Manos, as a first draft. What would you like to change to make the style more mature?

I am 16 years old and I would like to describe my father. My father is a nice man. You can talk to him. He will not get angry. My friends like him. He's tall and big and not very fat. He is about normal size. He's got brown eyes, black hair and a nice face. His black hair has some white hairs in it. He makes a lot of things at home. He made a cabinet for me. It is for my DVDs. The cabinet is made from pine. I like my cabinet very much. It is very nice. I look after it all the time. He has made me a good desk. The desk is for my computer. He always wears a grey suit to work. He doesn't like his suit. It is not comfortable for him. He always likes jeans. He wears jeans a lot.

Manos showed his work to his partner. They discussed how he could improve his style. Are the changes an improvement, do you think? Why/Why not?

My father's a friendly, approachable person who is popular with all my friends. He's a genial-looking, tall man of medium build with dark brown eyes and coal-black hair, streaked with grey. He's very practical and confident with his hands. He made me a pine cabinet for my DVDs which I treasure, and an attractive computer desk. He has to dress formally for work in a smart suit, but he prefers casual dress and feels most comfortable in jeans.

51 Rewriting with more sophistication

Try to rewrite the following description in a more mature style.

My friend is a good person. Her eyes are big. They are green. They are nice eyes. She has short hair. It is very, very short. The colour is blonde. She smiles a lot. She has a nice smile. She shows her white teeth. Her clothes are nice. Her style of her clothes is different from other people. She looks at other people's clothes. She can see their character from their clothes. She is a very good student. Her work is always good. She gets high marks. She is kind. She helps me do my work too.

When you have finished, compare your draft with someone else's. What differences can you find, and what similarities?

52 Writing from notes

A   Have you heard of Joseph Lister? Write down any facts you know about him.

B   Now try to write the following description of Joseph Lister in full. You will need to change some words and add others.

17

I want / describe Joseph Lister. He be / surgeon who / be born / 1827. In those days / many patients die / after operations because their wounds / become / badly infect. Lister wonder if / bacteria / air / which make / meat decay / also make / wounds septic.

Lister decide / clean / everything which touch / patient's wounds / carbolic acid. Carbolic acid / destroy / all germs. As a result / these precautions / patients recover quickly / operations. The rate / infection / fall dramatically.

Lister develop / safe, antiseptic operations / which be / major medical advance. He receive / many awards

/ his work. I admire him because / he be dedicated / unselfish. He take / great personal risks / make this discovery. Surgery / use to be / highly dangerous. People be / terrify / surgeon's knife. Lister change / all that. Modern surgery be / lifesaver.

Vocabulary

bacteria: organisms which cause disease

septic: badly infected

decay: go bad, rot

precautions: actions taken to avoid danger

GRAMMAR SPOTLIGHT

Present simple and continuous

One of the uses of the **present simple** is to describe facts that are usually or always true:

> **I avoid** *situations that might hurt me.*
> I **choose** *my friends.*

Look at the quiz in **exercise 1** and underline five more examples of the present simple.

The **present continuous** is used to talk about things that are happening at this moment:

> Monica **is describing** *how it feels to be unable to read and write.*
> She **is sitting** *in her immaculately tidy flat in south London.*

Look at the final paragraph of the text in **exercise 35** and underline three more examples of the present continuous.

Some verbs do not usually take the continuous form:

> I don't **understand**. *Can you explain that again?*

Verbs like this include: *believe, belong, contain, know, like, love, mean, own, prefer, seem, suppose, understand, want, wish.*

Complete these sentences using the correct present tense of the verb in brackets.

1 That's strange – Josh _____ with his friend Ken. He never normally _____ with anyone. (*argue*)

2 You _____ very quiet this morning. Are you OK? (*seem*)

3 Tanya is very kind-hearted. Helping other people _____ her happy. (*make*)

EXAM-STYLE QUESTIONS

Writing

1   A famous person who was born and grew up in your town has died recently. The local council wants to erect a memorial to him or her, and has asked people to suggest suitable memorials. Write a letter to the newspaper in which you say:

   - why the town should remember this person and feel proud
   - the kind of memorial you would like to see erected
   - suggestions for other ways to celebrate the life of this person.

   Write about 150–200 words (or 100–150 words for Core level).

2   Write an article for a teenage magazine describing someone you are close to. In the article you should:

   - describe the person's special qualities
   - give examples of his/her behaviour
   - explain why the relationship is important to you.

   Write about 150–200 words (or 100–150 words for Core level).

3   You have joined a penfriend organisation. You receive this email from your new penfriend.

Dear …

Thank you for your lovely letter telling me all about your home, your family and your school. I was just a little bit disappointed, however, because you didn't explain what I really want to know which is … what makes YOU tick! Tell me what makes you happy or sad. What do you want to achieve in your life? What are your most important goals? Please hurry! I can't wait to hear from you.

Best wishes,

Kim

Write Kim a letter of reply, describing your approach to life and your personal goals. Write about 150–200 words (or 100–150 words for Core level).

Speaking

1 Becoming happier

Many young people say they are unhappy and feel negative about their lives. Why do you think this is? How could they develop a more positive approach? Try to explain your views.

You might consider such things as:

   - the opportunity to enrich your life by doing more things which bring pleasure
   - the advantages (or disadvantages) of planning your life and setting goals
   - the value of role models in inspiring young people
   - the idea that voluntary work with disadvantaged people develops our gratitude.

You are free to consider any other related ideas of your own. You are not allowed to make any written notes.

2 The importance of people's names

Our first or given name is often very important to people. Discuss this topic with the assessor. You could use the following ideas to help develop the conversation:

   - how you came to be given your own name
   - names that are popular in your culture and any special meanings they have
   - whether the name people have affects their personality and the way people treat them
   - the advantages and disadvantages of nicknames
   - the idea that calling everyone by their first name is a good thing.

You are free to consider any other related ideas of your own. You are not allowed to make any written notes.

KEY ADVICE

1　Use a special combination of visual recall (look, say, cover, write, check method), speech sounds, spelling patterns and spelling rules to **learn new spellings**.

2　When you learn a language, it helps to have a good memory. **Improve your memory** by:
- highlighting key ideas
- studying new vocabulary regularly and memorising it
- reading through your class notes frequently
- drawing pictures to illustrate words or concepts
- linking new words to words you already know
- using new words and phrases in your speech and writing
- learning something by heart because it means something special to you (e.g. a poem or pop song).

3　Find time each week to **organise your course notes**, to make it easy to find work from previous lessons. A lot of the work you'll be doing is sequential. This means you'll often have to look back at notes you made earlier.

4　**Draft your written work** two or three times. If you can't think of what to write, get something down on paper anyway. If you have nothing written, you have nothing to change. Show your written work to a friend. Listen to advice about improvements you could make.

5　Be prepared to work in groups and to be an active participant, but take responsibility for working alone at times too.

6　**Practising your English outside class** will help your progress. Here are some ways to do this.
- Get an English-speaking penfriend.
- Watch or listen to English programmes, films, videos, pop songs, YouTube, etc.
- Make an arrangement with a friend who also wants to learn English, and practise speaking together once or twice a week.
- Read widely in English: books, magazines, newspapers, etc.

Exam techniques

7　When you **describe a person**, remember that a physical description is not usually enough to fully answer the question. You may also have to describe character and give reasons, examples and evidence to support your views.

UNIT FOCUS

In this unit you have produced short answers to questions on detailed reading texts.

You have listened to a discussion and answered **multiple-choice questions**.

You have learned skills and language structures for **describing a person's appearance and qualities**.

Unit 2:
You and Your Community

2.1 Home town

1 Interview: Introduction

'Home Town' is the title of a regular feature appearing in a magazine. It aims to give personal insights into people's home lives, so the interviewees are encouraged to talk as openly as they can.

Imagine that you are involved in writing or being interviewed for a 'Home Town' article. You will need to divide into two groups: Group A (Journalists) and Group B (Interviewees).

2 Group A: Journalists

You are going to interview one of your classmates about their home town and family life.

You need to achieve an insightful, revealing interview which really gets below the surface of your interviewee's life. Asking your interviewee for personal anecdotes, their opinions and attitudes will get the in-depth interview you are looking for.

Tick off any points you would like to raise in the interview.

Neighbourhood and home life

☐ some good points about the neighbourhood and its atmosphere

☐ a favourite family activity

☐ a happy family memory

☐ a special quality of his/her parents

☐ a value he/she has learned from his/her family

Personal information

- [ ] his/her pet hates
- [ ] a challenge or problem he/she is proud of overcoming
- [ ] the strangest experience he/she has ever had
- [ ] his/her personal goals

What else would you like to find out? Add any other points to the lists.

Being flexible

You obviously can't know how your interviewee is going to answer. Be prepared for 'dead end' answers. If your question leads nowhere, have an alternative up your sleeve.

Examples:
How does your family usually celebrate holidays / religious festivals / other special occasions?
What are your brothers and sisters like? What do you quarrel about?
Tell me about your own bad habits (!)

If your interviewee has left home, change your questions to the past tense. Or your interviewee may prefer to talk about his/her life now. Let him/her decide.

Getting good descriptions

Remember to use open questions.

Examples:
What is/are your … like?
What do you … about …?
How do/does …?
Tell me about …
Tell me more about …

Explore the answers you get by asking *Why?, In what way?*, etc.

3 Group B: Interviewees

Before being interviewed, spend a few quiet minutes thinking about your home life. Visualise the street you live in, your house, your family, things you enjoy doing at home, what you like about your locality. If you have moved away from your home town, you can talk about the way you live now. You decide.

Dealing with personal questions

Personal questions can be intrusive. You have the right to avoid answering a question if you prefer. You can say things like:

That's personal. I'd rather not say, if you don't mind.

or

I can't answer that.

Being flexible

If you are flexible when answering questions, it will help the interviewer. For example, you can say *I'd rather not answer that but I can tell you about my …*

You can adapt a question by saying *I'm afraid I don't know much about that, but I can tell you about my …*

Getting more time

If you need more time to think, you can say:

Let me think about that for a moment.

or

Well, let me see.

4 Honest feedback

Did you both feel the interview was successful? Why/Why not?

Remember, interviewing and being interviewed are real skills which even professionals have to develop. Don't be afraid to say what you would change next time round.

After the feedback, it is useful to record your decisions like this:

Next time I'm taking part in an interview, I'll …

5 Reading

You are going to read an article about Chris Brown, a biochemist from England, who now lives in Seattle on America's Pacific coast.

As you read, number the following events in the order in which they happened.

a He went cycling around Leyland.

b He studied at university.

c He worked at a cancer research centre.

d He learned more about fishing from his uncle.

e He got a job with a pharmaceuticals company.

f He went to live in the United States.

Home Town

For our Home Town feature this month, the spotlight is on British newcomer and research scientist Dr Chris Brown.

5 Chris lives a long way away from the small terraced house in Leyland, in the north-west of England, where he grew up – thousands of miles away, in fact. He now lives in the vibrant city of 10 Seattle, where he works as a biochemist in a pharmaceuticals company. Like many newcomers, Chris still misses his home town.

Chris says, 'Even though there is 15 so much I love about America, I still miss seeing my family and friends back home. I Skype my parents every weekend – it's a good way to keep in touch. My parents are very sociable. 20 When I Skype Mum and Dad, I'll often have a word with a friend who has just dropped in for a bite to eat.'

In his mind, Leyland stands for the carefree days of his childhood. He 25 remembers playing with his sister and other children in the street after school.

And he recalls sunny afternoons in the local park, building dens in the woods or fishing with a child's fishing rod in 30 a muddy river.

'I was quite adventurous from a young age. I loved exploring the surrounding countryside on my bike. I was never really sporty, though, and 35 didn't mind being alone sometimes, which is maybe why I've always liked fishing. One summer, when I was 16, I was allowed to travel to Ireland on the ferry on my own, to stay with my 40 Uncle Pete. He lived near a lake and took me out fishing in a rowing boat. It was magical to be on water that was like polished glass. The only sounds to be heard were the birds calling to 45 one another. He taught me a lot too – you have to be patient, for example, to be a good angler, and have the right equipment as well.

'After I finished my postgraduate 50 studies, I applied for a job at a cutting-edge cancer research centre here in Seattle, and amazingly I got it! But it was hard at first to get used to a new culture. Life in America was 55 more different from England than I'd expected. People found my British accent quaint, which was a surprise. I'm always being asked to repeat things I've said, but it isn't rudeness – 60 they're just being curious. My work here has worked out well, but I still

feel homesick at times for the little things, like my mum's home-made Irish stew.

65 'When I was feeling low, my parents always encouraged me to give it time, not to give up. My mum left Ireland when she was a teenager to train as a nurse, and my dad left school at 14 to 70 work in a factory, although he got more qualifications later. They are both go-ahead and they persevered to achieve what they wanted, but they really love having fun and enjoying themselves 75 too.

'Gradually, I've made good friends here. I have inspiring work colleagues who have mentored me. In my neighborhood*, the warmth of 80 the people reminds me of home. They invite me round for barbecues or on hiking trips – they've been really kind.

'I've lived in Seattle for nearly two years now and I've now moved to a new 85 job with even better career prospects and research opportunities. Seattle is also a great city for the arts, which I love, and for the outdoors. There are fascinating exhibitions and concerts right on my 90 doorstep. If I want fresh air, I can be out of the city in no time, indulging in my favorite* hobby of hiking in the foothills of Mount Rainier.

'Will I live permanently in Seattle? 95 Well, I'm considering it, but it's still early days. I'm not absolutely sure yet.'

* US spelling

23

6 Discussion

In general, what do you think of the journalist's interview skills? Have you gained insight into the factors which have shaped Chris's personality? Why/Why not?

7 Detailed comprehension

Try to answer the following questions in full sentences.

1 What evidence is there that Chris enjoyed being independent when he was younger? Give two details.

2 People in Seattle find Chris's accent strange, but he does not mind having to repeat himself. What does this tell us about his personality? Give two ideas.

3 How did Chris's parents help him adapt to his new life?

4 How do we know Chris has easy access to the countryside?

5 How would you describe the tone of Chris's response to the interviewer?

   a He sounds enthusiastic and positive – he is enjoying his new experiences.

   b He sounds neutral – he does not mind where he lives or works.

   c He sounds disappointed – America has not met his expectations.

6 What were the benefits to Chris's career of his move to Seattle? Make four points.

Vocabulary

Find words in the text that mean the same as:

a drugs, medicines

b without worries

c small shelters made of branches and leaves

d a boat that takes passengers across a river, lake or sea

e a person who fishes for a hobby

f charming and old-fashioned

g unhappy because you are living away from home

h didn't give up

i advised, guided

j the countryside and nature

8 Describing Chris

From what Chris says in the article, what kind of person do you think he is? Circle the appropriate adjectives, checking in a dictionary if necessary.

VOCABULARY

thoughtful	timid	persistent
academic	courageous	appreciative
lazy	antagonistic	adventurous
open-minded	sociable	curious
resilient	sporty	impatient

9 Describing Chris's family

Can you pair up adjectives of similar meaning from the following lists? Using a dictionary and checking with a partner will help clarify unfamiliar items. When you've made the pairs, tick those that describe Chris's family and neighbours. What clues in the text help you decide? Be prepared to justify your decisions!

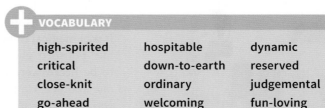

VOCABULARY

high-spirited	hospitable	dynamic
critical	down-to-earth	reserved
close-knit	ordinary	judgemental
go-ahead	welcoming	fun-loving
reticent	supportive	

10 Colloquial words and phrases

Chris uses some colloquialisms (informal words and expressions). You can often guess their meaning by analysing the context in which they are used. For example, he says that 'I'll often *have a word* with a friend who has just *dropped in for a bite to eat*.'

Do you think *have a word* is likely to mean a formal conversation or a friendly chat? Has someone who has *dropped in* arranged the visit in advance? Would you expect *a bite to eat* to be a large meal or a snack?

Match these colloquialisms from the text with the more formal expressions.

1	the little things	A	too soon to know
2	on my doorstep	B	very quickly
3	in no time	C	matters which are small but significant
4	early days	D	very near to where I live

11 Translation

What colloquialisms do you use in your own language? Can you think of any direct equivalents in your language for the colloquial expressions in the text in exercise 10?

12 Discussion

A Chris describes his parents in this way: '*They are both go-ahead and persevered to achieve what they wanted, but they love having fun and enjoying themselves.*' Could Chris himself be described like this? Why/Why not? How far do you think children acquire their parents' characteristics?

B Chris attributes a lot of his present success to his close-knit family. How far do you think early family life influences your chances of success later on? Apart from your family, where else can you find support and encouragement to help you achieve your goals?

C What do you think of Chris? Do you admire him? Why/Why not? In your own culture, can you think of someone who has done well and whom you find inspiring? Share your ideas with your partner.

13 Idioms

Can you work out the meaning of the following common sayings about family life from their context?

1 I gave the job to my nephew rather than my neighbour's boy. After all, *blood is thicker than water.*

2 She gave the police evidence against him, even though he was *her own flesh and blood.*

3 My job doesn't pay much but it does *keep the wolf from the door.*

2.2 Favourite places

14 Discussion

Most of us have one or two places nearby we especially like visiting. When you want relaxation and pleasure, where do you go? Do you head for wide, open spaces, relishing the thought of glorious sunsets, freedom and natural beauty? Or do you prefer urban environments and the intimate atmosphere of coffee shops and social clubs?

15 Reading and vocabulary

Read about the way one student likes to spend her time. What does she do? Does the place sound inviting? Would you like to go there? Why/Why not?

When I've got some free time, I love visiting our local market. It's a large, outdoor market by the seafront. Even if I'm not going to buy anything, I really like the light-hearted, bustling atmosphere and the cheerful sounds of stallholders calling to each other.

I'm usually tempted by the brightly coloured array of fruit and impressed by the gorgeous cloth on sale. As the market is quite near the seafront, the pungent, fishy odours mingle with the fragrant smells of herbs, plants and vegetables. There's a secondhand stall I browse through too, unable to resist the chance of finding something valuable. I once bought a wonderful old Chinese candlestick for just 50 cents! When I'm at the market I forget all about my everyday problems. I can just relax, unwind and enjoy the sights and scenes around me.

Read the text again and underline the descriptive phrases. Then group them according to:

Size and location: _____

_____

Atmosphere: _____

_____

Smells: _____

_____

Sounds: _____

_____

Colours: _____

_____

Emotions: _____

_____

Opinions: _____

_____

16 Writing

Now close your eyes and imagine yourself in a favourite place of your own. Are you alone, or with family or friends? What are you doing? Let the sights, colours, sounds and smells of the place wash over you. Think about the way you feel when you go there.

When you're ready, try to write down your ideas on paper. Be prepared to make one or two drafts before you get the description just right. Use a dictionary to help. Don't forget to explain why this is one of your favourite places.

Descriptive phrases

To help complete your writing, choose from the descriptive words and phrases below. Don't forget, however, the importance of correct collocations (word combinations). Check with a dictionary or a partner that the words you have chosen are appropriate for what you are describing.

Smells

fragrant   perfumed   sweet-smelling   scented   fresh pungent   smoky

Sounds

cheerful sound of talk and laughter   peaceful not a sound   noisy   silent   sound of birds calling

Colours

colourful   vibrant   bright   shining   rich   gorgeous glowing   radiant   soft   muted

Atmosphere

light-hearted   bustling   tranquil   intimate sophisticated   safe   warm and friendly   lively awe-inspiring   cosy   invigorating   eerie   civilised comfortable   appealing   relaxing   dimly/brightly lit mysterious   unspoilt

Where is it?

off the beaten track   right in the centre of town only five minutes away   isolated hard to get to but worth the effort

Expressing feelings

When I'm there I …

… feel close to my family or friends / revel in the solitude / enjoy my own company.
… relax and unwind / forget my everyday problems.
… feel excited/happy/contented/secure/exhilarated.
… experience the beauty of nature / find it spiritually uplifting / marvel at the wonderful things people have created.

17 Reading aloud

Everyone sees things differently, so it can be nice to share your thoughts and feelings with others and to hear why they might enjoy going to a favourite place. Without writing your name on the paper, drop what you have written into a box. The papers can then be shuffled and you can take turns in selecting one and reading it aloud to your group.

18 Showing enthusiasm

Listen to the following descriptions of places. Notice how the most important words which show strong, definite feelings are stressed.

1   What an **amazing** place! It would make a **great** change from life in the city.

2   What a **lovely** place! I'm sure I'd appreciate the special **atmosphere**.

3   What **fun**! It would be a **superb** place to relax on holiday.

4   How **fascinating**! My friends and I **love** wildlife. We **must** go there.

5   How **interesting**! Now I'll see it through **new eyes**!

Practise saying the sentences to your partner. Make sure you sound enthusiastic. Stress the important words which show your attitude.

19 Order of adjectives

Study this sentence from the text in exercise 15.

*I bought a **wonderful** old Chinese candlestick for just 50 cents.*

Which type of adjective comes first: opinion, origin or age?

A sequence of adjectives before a noun usually has a certain order in English:

personal opinion/judgement, size/height/shape, age, colour, origin, material, purpose (what it's used for)

Put these adjectives into the sentences according to the rules above.

1   I've lost a bag.   *(sports canvas red)*

2   We stayed in a house.   *(three-bedroomed Swedish quaint)*

3   The new boss is a woman.   *(friendly Egyptian middle-aged)*

4   I want to buy a jacket.   *(leather good-quality black)*

5 I've bought a coat. *(warm tweed winter)*

6 Thieves stole a teapot. *(oriental silver priceless)*

7 On holiday I enjoyed trying the food. *(Indian vegetarian tasty)*

8 How do you remove coffee stains from a rug? *(silk Chinese expensive)*

20 Developing a more mature style

Using too many adjectives before a noun is confusing. Three is usually enough. You can 'break up' a long description by adding a clause instead. This creates a more mature style.

Examples:
Adjectives + noun + **with** (extra details)
*He decided to wear a cool white cotton shirt **with short sleeves**.*

Adjectives + noun + **made of** (material)
*He was wearing an amazing, long, purple cloak **made of velvet and silk**.*

(Note that commas are sometimes used between adjectives in longer sequences.)

Adjective + noun + **which** (a variety of information)
*She was wearing an Italian gold watch **which looked very expensive**.*
*He has a reliable old scooter **which he doesn't mind lending to people**.*

Practice

Combine each group of sentences into one longer sentence. Use the correct adjective order and a clause where appropriate. When you've finished, compare your answers with a partner's. Do you both agree that the order sounds natural and the style is elegant?

1 He gave her a box. The box was made of wood. It had a picture of a famous story on the lid. It was Russian. It was an unusual box.

2 She was wearing a brown suit. It was wool. It looked too warm for the weather.

3 The television is portable. It's white. It's Japanese. It has 100 channels.

4 It's a frying pan. It's copper. It's heavy. It's French. It has a lid.

5 Someone's taken my mug. It has my name on it. It's blue. It's a pottery mug. It's used for coffee.

6 He has lost a coat. It's polyester. It's a school coat. It has his name on the inside.

7 Rosanna decided to wear a long dress. It was green and white. It was made of silk. She had bought it in America.

2.3 Improving your neighbourhood

21 Discussion

A Have you ever campaigned to make your neighbourhood a better place to live in? What did you do? Were you successful? How proud do you feel of your achievement?

B How would you like to improve your neighbourhood for teenagers? Would you like to see improved facilities for education and training, more varied sports and leisure amenities, or better-lit streets and safer public areas? Discuss your ideas in your groups.

22 Before you listen: Vocabulary check

You are going to listen to a discussion between two officials, John and Pamela, about the best way of converting a disused warehouse for the benefit of local teenagers.

Before you listen, make sure you know the meaning of these words and phrases:

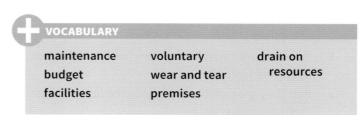

VOCABULARY		
maintenance	voluntary	drain on resources
budget	wear and tear	
facilities	premises	

23 Listening for gist 🔊

Listen to the conversation for general meaning first, and find answers to the three questions.

1 What facility does the woman want?

2 What facility does the man want?

3 What does Pamela say which shows she is changing her mind?

24 Detailed listening 🔊

Now listen for detail and choose the correct ending for each statement.

1 Pamela has already

    a thrown away inappropriate applications.

    b decided which applications are worth considering.

    c contacted people whose ideas she preferred.

2 Pamela feels a study centre would

    a be inexpensive to operate.

    b be cheap to run but unpopular.

    c only be used at weekends.

3 John thinks the public library is

    a very popular with students.

    b very busy but well staffed.

    c well resourced and efficient.

4 Pamela believes leaving school with good qualifications is

    a more important for teenagers than good social facilities.

    b a guarantee of entry to a good job or further study.

    c less relevant for modern teenagers than it was in the past.

5 John thinks a youth club would be

    a a place where all students could make friends.

    b fair to both academic and less academic students.

    c a way to help teenagers prepare well for the future.

6 John mentions the way teenagers raised money for charity in order to show

    a that they are capable of good behaviour and self-discipline.

    b that they are capable of understanding the needs of disabled people.

    c that they are capable of obeying the instructions given by a supervisor.

7 John thinks it would be possible to pay a supervisor a salary for

    a more than one year.

    b six or seven months.

    c up to one year.

8 Pamela agrees to the youth club because

    a so many local people want one.

    b she knows a capable supervisor will be in charge.

    c there have been so many teenage tragedies.

25 Follow-up

Inference

You had to use **inference** to answer questions 1 and 3. Try to explain your thinking.

In general, whose views do you sympathise with – John's or Pamela's? Why?

Idioms

People sometimes say *I'm digging my heels in* or *I'm sticking to my guns* when they refuse to change their minds, despite pressure. Could these idioms be applied to John or Pamela? Why?/Why not?

26 Persuading: Stress and intonation 🔊

In their discussion, John and Pamela use the following polite phrases to persuade each other to listen to their point of view. Listen again and tick each one as you hear it. Notice how the words in **bold** letters are stressed. Do the phrases generally have a rising or a falling pattern?

☐ Do you **really** think it's a good idea …?

☐ (That) sounds all right in **theory**, but in **practice** …

☐ I take your **point, but** …

☐ (That's) all very well, **but** …

☐ That's true, **but** …

☐ Look at it **this** way, …

Practise saying these phrases aloud to each other. How could you complete each one?

27 Role play: Spend, spend, spend

Your family has won $20,000 in a competition. You all took part in the competition, so you're having a family conference to discuss how to spend the money.

In groups of three or four, choose from the roles below. Your aim is to persuade the family that your ideas for spending the money are best. Use the phrases from exercise 26 to show you're listening to what they have to say but that you want to express a different opinion.

Mum

You think it is important to spend the money on something sensible and practical which will bring lasting benefits. You want to spend it on new furniture, curtains, carpets, and a new washing machine.

Dad

You want to save the money for the future. Eventually the family will need money to move house, for the children's education or for retirement. It is silly to rush into spending the money without being sure of the best way to use it. A good investment account will earn high interest on the savings so the money will be worth more in the future.

Daughter

You want the family to build a swimming pool in the garden. There is no swimming pool near your home and you are a keen swimmer. It would be a good way for the whole family to get exercise and to cool off after school/work in the summer.

Son

You think the money should be used for an exciting holiday of a lifetime that would be impossible to afford otherwise. You want the family to have a safari holiday in Kenya. You've always wanted to see wildlife in its own habitat, and everyone would learn so much from it.

2.4 Making a difference

28 Pre-reading discussion

Some people can't stand the idea of going into hospital, even if they need treatment. Why do you think this might be?

Have you ever visited a friend in hospital? Did you bring a gift? What was it?

How did your friend feel about being in hospital?

What did you notice about the hospital atmosphere? Did the patients seem relaxed and comforted? Share your ideas with your group.

29 Reading for gist

You are going to read about Dolores who has worked to improve the experience of teenagers and children having treatment at her local hospital.

Read the article for general meaning. Has Dolores been successful?

The Woman who Put Comfort into Caring

Dolores Albertino is proof that sometimes finding yourself in the wrong job can have wonderful consequences. Several years ago, the former nurse and mother of two teenage sons returned to work at her local community hospital, but this time as a receptionist. 'The trouble is I was absolutely rubbish at the job,' says Dolores with a smile. Phones went unanswered, and she never did master the computer, but that was because she spent time away from her desk chatting to and comforting the parents of sick children and the children themselves. 'I found it very frustrating that a child would ask for a simple thing, such as ice cream, but because it was not meal time, they could not have it. I also knew that the families could benefit from meeting each other but, because of confidentiality, I could not pass on anyone's details.'

Dolores had never imagined starting a charity, but when she spoke to one of the doctors about these problems, he offered to help. He suggested putting together a plan and said he would support her. She enlisted the help of two families whose children were ill and they spent hours sitting around her kitchen table filling in charity forms. 'It was incredibly hard work, but I've never regretted it,' she 35 says. To date, Dolores, the 'hopeless' receptionist, has raised millions of dollars. 'I am very practical,' she says. 'I rolled up my sleeves and made it happen.' She believes the key reason 40 the charity has been successful is that 'everyone knows where every penny is going. The money does not disappear into one big pot.'

Since the project began, the 45 atmosphere of the children's unit has changed beyond recognition. Children asked for a place to play outdoors so Dolores developed a neglected area in the hospital 50 grounds and transformed it into a beautiful garden and play space. After children said that they didn't like walking down the sterile corridor to the ward, the corridor was given a 55 makeover too, with magical mosaics designed by the patients. There is now a common room for teenagers, equipped with trendy furniture,

internet access and a fridge full of 60 snacks and fresh juices.

Parents, who are often very apprehensive when their children develop a health problem, were not forgotten either. The formerly drab 65 ward kitchen has been spruced up and parents can help themselves to coffee, tea, chocolate biscuits and crisps.

Dolores also organises family liaison groups so parents can give each other 70 mutual support. 'The children need their parents or grandparents to be rocks – you see them looking into their eyes for help and support.' The whole community has worked to 75 make the dream come true. Getting local schools to raise funds has been surprisingly easy. The community has also pulled together by organising street parties, sponsored walks, sky 80 dives, car washes, picnics and concerts. Joanna, the mother of 16-year-old Antoine, who is receiving treatment at the hospital, says, 'Dolores is not working to a template. You see her 85 listening, talking to the medics and getting on with it. The charity brings comfort and much-needed fun to the children's unit. Everyone benefits.'

Seeing her work spread nationwide 90 is Dolores's dream. 'People everywhere will donate when they can see good results. Coping with illness is a challenge, but children should not feel as if they are being punished because 95 a doctor is sending them to hospital.'

30 Vocabulary

Match these words from the text with their definitions.

1	confidentiality	A	managing to deal with a difficult situation
2	neglected	B	treated harshly for doing something wrong
3	sterile	C	clinical, not homely
4	apprehensive	D	dull, lacking colour
5	drab	E	nervous, worried
6	template	F	not passing on private information
7	coping	G	ignored, lacking necessary attention
8	punished	H	a pattern to follow

Can you guess the meaning of the words *ward* (line 54) and *liaison* (line 68) from the contexts?

31 Post-reading discussion

Share your views on the following questions in your groups.

Tone

How do you think people reading the magazine article would feel at the end? Would they feel:

a   saddened? (It is depressing to think of children having health problems.)

    or

b   positive? (The story is an example of human kindness and strength of purpose.)

Author's main aim

Do you think the MAIN aim of the article is to:

a   explain how to develop medical techniques for treating children?

b   tell the reader what caring for sick children is like from a nurse's viewpoint?

c explain why sick children and their families need comfort, and how to achieve this?

d convey the viewpoints of everyone involved in caring for sick children?

Structure

Which is the best description of the structure of the article?

a It is a mixture of long and short sentences. There are several short paragraphs as well as long ones.

b The sentences are mainly long and complex. The article is composed of a few long paragraphs.

Style

Is the style chatty, technical, formal or neutral?

32 Comprehension check

1 What evidence is there that Dolores was not effective as a receptionist? Give two examples.

2 Why did Dolores want to make changes at the children's unit? Give two details.

3 How has she helped the children and teenagers? Give two details.

4 How has she helped parents? Give two examples.

5 What have schools and the local community done to help? Give two examples.

6 In about 40 words, describe Dolores's attitude and say why she has been successful.

33 Further discussion

A Dolores says children and teenagers need the support of their families when they are ill. Do you think support from their friends is just as important as family support?

B Dolores has raised money to make a stay in hospital more comforting for patients and their families. Some people might say the money would be better spent on the latest medical technology, not a play space or furniture. What are your views?

C Have you ever taken part in fundraising for charity? Explain what you did and why. If you have not taken part in fundraising, would you consider doing so? What sort of charity would you choose to support? Discuss your ideas in your groups.

D Some people claim that money for health care should be provided by the government and not by charities. What are the advantages and disadvantages of using charities to support health care?

34 Colloquial language in context

With a partner, study these colloquial expressions from the text. Try to work out their meaning from the context.

1 I was *absolutely rubbish* at the job.

2 I *rolled up my sleeves* and made it happen.

3 The money does not disappear into *one big pot*.

4 The corridor has been given *a makeover*.

5 The children need their parents, or grandparents, to be *rocks*.

Try to find another colloquialism in the text and decide on its meaning.

35 Spelling: Doubling consonants when adding suffixes

Suffixes are word endings, such as:

-ed -ing -er -est -ish -y -able

Adding a suffix can change a verb tense, make a comparative or superlative form, change nouns into adjectives, etc.

Look at these verbs from the magazine article with their endings:

*sit**ting** chat**ting** meet**ing** work**ed** send**ing***

Notice how the final consonant of *sit* and *chat* has been doubled, but not those in the other verbs. Can you say why?

> The rule for adding suffixes to one-syllable words is: double the final consonant if the word ends in one vowel + one consonant.

Examples:

cut	*cutting*
sun	*sunny*
spot	*spotty*
red	*reddish*
big	*bigger*
wet	*wetter*

31

Exceptions are one-syllable words which end with **w**, **x** or **y**.

Examples:
buy   buying
few   fewer
box   boxing

> We do NOT double the consonant if a one-syllable word ends in either two vowels + one consonant, or one vowel + two consonants.

Examples:

n**ee**d	needing	needed	
w**ai**t	waiting	waited	
ada**pt**	adapting	adapted	adaptable
dou**bt**	doubting	doubted	
ta**lk**	talking	talked	

Practice

Look carefully at the one-syllable words in the sentences below. Check the pattern of the ending (one vowel + one consonant, one vowel + two consonants, or two vowels + one consonant). Add suitable suffixes to complete the words, doubling the final consonant where necessary.

1 When I arrived home I could hear the phone ring_____.

2 Yesterday was the hot_____ day of the year.

3 Ibrahim has stop_____ smoking.

4 We really enjoy_____ our day out yesterday.

5 That's the sad_____ news I have ever heard.

6 Let's visit the new shop_____ centre.

7 Stop chat_____ and do some work!

8 The baby is already walk_____.

9 We are send_____ our son to boarding school.

10 I bought these apples because they were much cheap_____ than the other ones.

11 Zena got tired of wait_____ and left.

12 He is always ask_____ for money.

13 Don't go look_____ for trouble.

14 Our school has a new swim_____ pool.

36 Adding suffixes to multi-syllable words

There are some longer words in the article which double the final consonant when adding a suffix:

forgot**ten**   regret**ted**

Others do not: offer**ed**   listen**ing**

Do you know why?

> The rule for adding suffixes to words of two or more syllables is: double the final consonant if the last syllable is stressed and it ends in one vowel and one consonant.

Examples:

for**get**	for**getting**	for**gotten**
pre**fer**	pre**ferring**	pre**ferred**

So, we do NOT double the final consonant if the stress is on the first syllable:

offer	**off**ering	**off**ered
listen	**lis**tening	**lis**tened

or if the last syllable contains TWO vowels before the consonant, or one vowel and two consonants:

exp**lai**n	exp**lai**ned
retu**rn**	retu**rn**ed

Practice

Add suitable suffixes to complete the words in these sentences, doubling the final consonant if necessary.

1 Theo regret_____ leaving his job, but it was too late.

2 Smoking is not permit_____.

3 The accident occur_____ last night in thick fog.

4 I reason_____ with him about his aggressive behaviour.

5 He has commit_____ a serious crime.

6 The earthquake happen_____ in the evening.

7 She explain_____ the begin_____ of the story to them.

8 I've always prefer_____ travelling by train.

37 Look, say, cover, write, check

Understanding how grammar and pronunciation work helps you understand English spelling. You can also reinforce your understanding by using a visual strategy. Learn these commonly misspelled words through the 'look, say, cover, write, check' method. Why not ask a friend to test you when you are confident you have learned them correctly?

＋ VOCABULARY

beginning	swimming	travelled
preferred	shopping	dropped
occurred	happening	development
occurrence	happened	permitted

38 Words from different languages

Liaison is a French word which has come into English. English has a fascinating history of borrowing words from a vast number of languages. Many words came from invaders, colonisers and international trade.

With your partner, try to match the common 'loan' words in the box below with their language of origin. Use a dictionary to check the meaning of unfamiliar words.

＋ VOCABULARY

athlete	bungalow	patio
tea	caravan	villa
cuisine	chocolate	ski
sofa	opera	karate

ARABIC _____ ITALIAN _____

AZTEC _____ JAPANESE_____

CHINESE _____ LATIN _____

FRENCH _____ NORWEGIAN _____

GREEK _____ PERSIAN _____

HINDI _____ SPANISH _____

Can you guess why the word might have come from that language? Think about the climate, way of life, food, etc.

Check your pronunciation of the words with your partner. Finally, use each word in a sentence of your own.

Comparing languages

What English words do you use in your own language? What words in your language come from other languages? Share your knowledge with your group.

2.5 Welcoming an exchange visitor

39 Reassuring your guest

In order to learn more about other cultures, many young people take part in exchange visits with students of their own age. They take turns going overseas to stay with each other's families. By doing so, they improve their understanding of another culture and way of life, improve their skills in a foreign language and have a pleasant holiday at the same time.

Imagine that your family is going to take part in an exchange visit. Your guest, who you have not met before and is about your age, is coming from overseas to stay with you for three weeks. How do you think he/she might be feeling? Nervous, excited, apprehensive?

In a letter, how could you put your guest at ease and make your home and your local area sound inviting? Make a few notes under the following headings.

Positive things about my home and family

_____

_____

_____

_____

Enjoyable things to do together

_____

_____

_____

_____

Exciting places to visit

_____

_____

_____

_____

What aspects of your home life or area would you NOT want to draw attention to (if any)? Why?

_____

_____

_____

Beginnings and endings

How would you like to begin your letter? Look at some sentences students have used and choose the appropriate ones. Which sentences are unsuitable? Why?

a   I am very sorry that this is my first letter to you.

b   I wish to write you a letter to inform you about my background.

c   It is my generous attitude which invites you to my home.

d   What a pleasant surprise to hear from me in this friendly letter.

e   This is a quick line to welcome you to my home.

How would you like to close the letter?

f   It will be a great joy for me on the day I see you.

g   My friend, we are all waiting for you.

h   We can't wait to meet you.

i   Surprisingly, you will enjoy your life with me.

j   I am happy I wrote you this letter today.

40   Example letter

Now read this example letter. Underline the phrases used to welcome the visitor.

Dear Jacob,

I'm really pleased you're coming to stay with us soon. My family consists of my mum, dad and my younger sister Betty and my pet cat Rufus. We're an easy-going, ordinary family and my parents are very approachable. They let us do more or less what we like as long as we tell them about it first.

We live in a three-bedroomed house with a small front and back garden. It's about ten minutes' walk away from the town centre, which has a wide choice of modern shops, three cinemas, lively clubs and a weekly market. We also have a superb new swimming pool in town, so I hope you'll bring your swimming things. If you enjoy history, I'll show you our museum. It has some fascinating information about the history of my town.

I've made a list of the most interesting things to do and see in the area. I heard you are keen on watching football so I've booked two tickets to see a big match while you're here. I got my driving licence last month and dad has promised to let me use the car. We can explore the countryside and perhaps even camp for a night or two. The countryside won't be as spectacular as Kenya but it's very peaceful and we might even see some wild ponies.

Good luck with your trip!

Best wishes,
William

Comprehension

1   What is William's family like?

2   What kind of environment does he live in?

3   What has he planned for Jacob's visit?

Format

1   Do you think the letter sounds inviting or off-putting? Why? Underline the phrases which show that the writer has considered the feelings of his guest. Does he give reasons for the plans he is making? What are they?

34

2 Does William plunge straight into the topic of the exchange visit or is the beginning indirect? Do you think his approach is a good one? Why/Why not?

3 The letter has three main paragraphs. Do they follow each other in a smooth and natural way, or do they seem awkward and unconnected? Why?

4 Underline the opening and closing sentences of the letter. Are they appropriate? Why/Why not?

5 Overall, the letter is fairly short. Do you get a good enough picture of what the holiday is going to be like for Jacob? Why/Why not?

41 Achieving a suitable tone

In pairs, read the following sentences taken from students' exchange visit letters. If you were the recipient, which would make you feel at ease? Which might worry you? Put a tick against the sentences you like and a cross against the others.

As you work, discuss how any inappropriate expressions could be made more suitable. Correct any structural errors.

1 It'll be lovely to see you.

2 Unfortunately my father died seven years ago so you will not be able to meet him.

3 We're all looking forward to meeting you.

4 The food here will be rather distasteful for you.

5 At least when you are in the house try to behave with respect to my parents.

6 You'll be very welcome.

7 My friend, you can come and enjoy it but my family is very strict.

8 You'll soon feel at home.

9 The place itself is safety, you do not need to be afraid when walking, in case of thieves.

10 I would like to tell you that my parents are very good and they don't like people who drink too much.

11 Mostly, we will visit our countryside every day because here that is the only worth visiting place.

12 Mum and Dad always listen to our problems before giving their own point of view.

13 My family are selfishness and want someone to do things for them but I know such a thing will not inconvenient your visit to me.

14 We're going to have a wonderful time together.

15 We can go cycling through our beautiful countryside and have great parties on the beach.

16 As I already told you, this is a very small place, so don't think about hotels, theatres, cinemas and so on.

17 We can promise you the best time of your life.

18 Don't take chances if you cannot swim my friend, you will not survive.

Rewriting

Choose three of the sentences above which don't sound right and rewrite them to make a more appropriate impression. Try them out on a partner. Does he/she agree that they sound more inviting?

42 Correcting mistakes

This letter is from Jacob, who is writing to thank William for his holiday. Can you find the mistakes and correct them? The mistakes are to do with:

- prepositions
- missing words
- tenses
- punctuation
- spelling
- paragraphing
- vocabulary
- articles
- grammar

There are also two sentences in the letter which are inappropriate in tone. One of these can be deleted. You'll need to write a different sentence for the other one.

Finally, rewrite the whole letter correctly.

Dear William,

It is a great honour for me to write you this letter. Thank you for your kindness in the visit I make to your family last month. I am haveing many happy memorys of your family especially your mother. She is the best cooker in the world? I was very surprised of your town. It is extremely pleasant and not so industrial that I expected. I also liked your neighbours and I not forget familiar university students. I enjoyed the activities we done and I send you the best photographs of our camping trip in my next letter. Please come to a holiday in my family. Our house is standing in a lake. My father will let you to borrow his little boat. Beaches here are wonderful and now is becoming summer so we can go swimming which I know you enjoy. In cloudy days we can visit huge shoppings which are very popular for tourists. I'm expecting your letter with a cheerful heart.

Love,
Jacob

43 Sentence completion

Most of us find some aspects of our home life less than wonderful. You might wonder how a complete newcomer will fit in. If you want to give a realistic idea of your home life and still sound welcoming, it's a good idea to balance a negative idea with a positive one.

Try to complete these sentences positively.

1   Even though he is a nuisance at times, my little brother …

2   Despite being too dangerous for swimming, our local river …

3   Although we're a long way from the bright lights of the city, …

4   My parents are a tiny bit strict yet …

5   You'll probably find our way of life just a little strange at first, but …

6   We don't have a perfect house but …

Reassurance

When English people are trying to reassure someone about something, they sometimes use expressions like '*a tiny bit* awkward', '*just a little bit* difficult'. What do you say in your language?

44 Surprise party: Tone and register

You recently arranged a surprise party for your parents' wedding anniversary. You went to a lot of trouble to make the party a success. Unfortunately, your cousin was ill and unable to attend.

Which of the following would you say to your cousin? Why?

1   Where were you? Everyone expected you to come.

2   Why didn't you arrive? You should have been there.

3   It was such a shame you couldn't make it.

4   You disappointed us very much.

45 Reordering

The following letter describes a surprise party. It is written to a relative who missed the celebration. First, reorder the sentences and decide on the correct

sequence of paragraphs. What overall impression do you think the letter will make on the recipient?

Dear Ella,

a   As you know, Mum and Dad didn't know anything about it.

b   Just before the end, Uncle Steve let off lots of fireworks in the garden.

c   She had decorated the house beautifully.

d   Perhaps the DVD I'm sending you of the occasion will be a little compensation.

e   However, everyone understood that you were still feeling weak after the operation.

f   So you can imagine their surprise when, instead of going to the Blue Fountain, we arrived at Auntie Susan's house.

g   Hope you feel better soon.

h   No one looked tired or seemed inclined to go early.

i   It was a great shame you couldn't come.

j   Although most of the guests must have been over 50, the party went on until the early hours.

k   Despite the fact that we all missed you, we had a lovely day.

l   This was a wonderful way to round off the occasion.

m   Once again, I know how disappointed you were not to be there.

n   Just a short letter to let you know about Mum and Dad's anniversary party.

o   They assumed I was taking them to a restaurant to celebrate.

Lots of love,

Krystyna

46 Writing

Your cousin went to live abroad with her family when she was only two or three years old. Her parents have asked if she can stay with your family for a holiday. You have never actually met before. Write a letter to your cousin in which you:

- introduce yourself
- describe your family and background
- tell her about enjoyable things to do together
- describe interesting places to visit.

Write about 150 words.

36

The world's most widely spoken languages, by numbers of native speakers and as a second language, are Mandarin Chinese, English, Spanish, Hindi and Arabic.

Linguists say that more than 6,000 languages exist, though some are spoken by relatively few people. Sadly, hundreds of minority languages throughout the world are dying from lack of use. In Europe, for example, Breton, Scottish Gaelic and Romani are just three examples of scores of languages in danger, and Karaim, a Turkic language of Lithuania, has fewer than 50 speakers left.

Experts predict this decline will continue and, by the year 2030, there will be fewer than 3,000 languages spoken in the world.

What do you think might cause people to stop speaking a particular language?

The chart shows the numbers of languages spoken in selected African countries.

1 In which African countries are more than 100 languages spoken?

2 Does the information in the chart surprise you? Why/Why not?

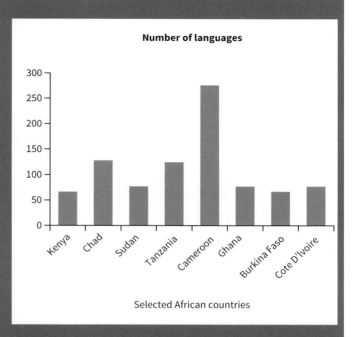

Number of languages

Selected African countries

3 What could help preserve endangered native languages?

GRAMMAR SPOTLIGHT

Gerund or infinitive?

A Certain verbs are followed by an **infinitive**:
*I was allowed **to travel** to Ireland.*
*I'm always being asked **to repeat** things.*
Can you find another example in paragraph 6 of the text in exercise 5?
Verbs like these include: *allow, ask, want, would like, promise, warn, remind, expect, decide, make, agree, refuse, offer, help, encourage, manage, tend.*

B Certain verbs are followed by a **gerund** (*-ing* form):
*I didn't **mind being** alone.*
Can you find another example in paragraph 4 of the text in exercise 5?
Verbs like these include: *finish, hate, avoid, like, dislike, love, risk, imagine, deny, postpone, recall, enjoy, imagine, mind, miss, suggest.*

C There are a few verbs that can take **either** the gerund **or** the infinitive, depending on the meaning:
*He **remembers playing** with his sister.*
BUT
***Remember to take** your dictionary with you.*
Verbs like these include: *remember, forget, need, try, stop, continue, go on.*
Discuss the difference in meaning between:
Her neighbour was in a hurry and didn't stop to talk.
Her neighbour didn't stop talking.

D The gerund is used after certain expressions, such as *can't stand, spend/waste time*:
*Some people **can't stand going** into hospital.*
*She **spent time chatting** to the parents of sick children.*

E The gerund, because it is like a noun, can be used as the subject of a sentence:
***Getting** local schools to raise funds has been easy.*
Can you find two more examples like this in the last paragraph of the text in exercise 29?

EXAM-STYLE QUESTIONS

Writing

1   The following note from your headteacher appears in your student newsletter.

Some new students will be joining us next term. They and their families are new to this area and I have decided to put together a 'Welcome' pack telling them about the school and neighbourhood. I would like to include articles about local places which you enjoy visiting. Please submit your articles by 10th December.

Write an article aimed at the new students. In the article you should:

- describe **one** local place of interest
- say why you enjoy visiting it (the atmosphere, scenery, etc.)
- explain why you think the new students will enjoy it too.

Write about 150–200 words (or 100–150 words for Core level).

2   You are interested to read the following announcement.

The Queen's Trust Newsletter wishes to hear from individuals or community groups about a project they have been involved in which has resulted in improved facilities for their school or neighbourhood. We have a number of prizes which will be given for the best entries.

Write an article for the newsletter describing a project you have been involved in. Explain why the improvement was needed and how it has benefited your school or neighbourhood.

Write about 150–200 words (or 100–150 words for Core level).

3   You recently took part in a fundraising activity in your community to raise money for charity. Write an email to a friend in which you:

- describe the aims of the charity
- explain how you raised funds for the charity
- encourage your friend to take part in a fundraising activity.

Write about 150–200 words (or 100–150 words for Core level).

4   Your school recently held a Community Day, aimed at elderly people who wanted to improve their skills with computers, the internet, etc.

Write an article for your school newsletter in which you:

- describe how you helped
- explain how you think elderly people benefited from the day
- explain what you think you learned from helping.

Write about 150–200 words (or 100–150 words for Core level).

Speaking

1 Building a community

A community can be defined as a group of people who share similar values and common interests. Some people say the happiest societies are built on a solid community foundation. Discuss this topic with the assessor.

You may wish to use the following ideas to help develop the conversation:

- how you feel about the community you belong to
- whether a strong community really makes people happier and more neighbourly and reduces crime
- the advantages and disadvantages of belonging to online communities
- whether some communities are restrictive and limit personal freedom
- whether globalisation has a positive or negative impact on community life.

You are free to consider any other related ideas of your own. You are not allowed to make any written notes.

2 Improving neighbourhoods

Neighbourhoods can be very diverse. While some are comfortable for residents of all ages, others lack basic amenities. There are a number of things that can be done to improve such neighbourhoods. Discuss this topic with the assessor.

You may wish to use the following ideas to help develop the conversation:

- how noise, litter or pollution could be reduced
- how places of entertainment could be developed
- whether wireless internet access in cafés and similar places would be helpful
- the value of parks and pleasant, open spaces for everyone to enjoy
- the importance of public transport facilities.

You are free to consider any other related ideas of your own. You are not allowed to make any written notes.

KEY ADVICE

1   Enlarge your understanding of **tone and register** by listening as much as possible to people speaking English. Notice the words they use to express their feelings in different situations (breaking bad news, expressing pleasure, complaints, reservations, annoyance, etc.).

Think also about the 'music' in their voices, the different **intonation patterns** that are used to show feelings, and try to imitate it. Listening to English radio plays (if you can) is a delightful source of tone, register and intonation, as is watching television dramas or going to the English-speaking theatre.

Joining a drama club and putting on English plays is an exciting and fun way to extend your spoken English skills.

2   **Spelling and the grammatical system** go hand in hand. Understanding how words are spelled will help you understand more about grammar and vice versa. Knowledge about grammar will expand your range of strategies for word building (turning nouns into adjectives and so on) and for identifying the logic of irregular-looking spellings.

3   **Proofread** your work for mistakes. You can do this during the writing process when you feel like a break from composing, and at the end. Use the dictionary as a spell-checker when proofreading. Your dictionary is your friend. The more you use it, the quicker and more efficient with it you will become.

4   If you use a computer to help you learn English, there are many interesting and entertaining spelling programs you can use to back up your learning.

5   Some kinds of dictionary are a brilliant fund of information about the history of the English language. Have fun browsing through a dictionary, investigating the numerous 'borrowings' from a huge number of other languages.

Exam techniques

6   Reading comprehension questions don't always have to be answered in your own words. You can answer some questions by **using words from the text**.

39

UNIT FOCUS

In this unit you have taken part in formal and informal conversations about yourself, your neighbourhood, your community and your family.

You have **listened to a dialogue** about a community project for teenagers and answered **multiple-choice questions**.

You have practised detailed reading skills.

You have developed skills for **writing about yourself, your family and background and places of local interest**.

You have studied tone and register and learned how to **welcome and reassure** an overseas guest.

Unit 3:
Sport, Fitness and Health

3.1 Is sport always fun?

1 Note-making and summaries: Sharing ideas

In this unit you will be learning how to make notes and write summaries. To help you, the skills will be broken into small stages.

In some exercises, you will be asked to read a text, make notes on it and then join your notes into a connected summary. This is because note-making practice is treated as one of the stages in learning to write a summary. In Paper 1 (Core) of the exam, the same texts are used for the note-making and summary questions. In Paper 2 (Extended), different texts are used.

Making notes

With a partner, tick off the aspects of note-making you find most challenging.

☐ reading quickly and absorbing a lot of information

☐ deciding what to select from the text

☐ finding some words and phrases of similar meaning, where possible

☐ presenting notes clearly so they can be followed by someone who has not seen the original text

In an exam, your notes don't have to be in your own words. However, it's a good idea to try to find some words and phrases of similar meaning rather than copying out chunks of texts.

Summarising

Summarising involves the note-making skills in the list above. However, unlike notes, summaries must be presented in connected grammatical prose. In Paper 1 (Core), you have to write a summary based on the notes you completed. Your summary should be about 70 words and must not be longer than 80 words.

In Paper 2 (Extended), your summary should be about 100 words and must not be longer than 120 words. You must use your own words wherever possible.

What difficulties, if any, do you find in:

- connecting ideas grammatically and in your own words?
- keeping to a strict word limit?

2 Discussion

Which sports on your school curriculum do you particularly like? Why?

3 Quiz

Work with a partner to complete the quiz about what you have learned from doing sport at school or college. (If you've left school, look back at your experiences.)

Sport at school has taught me …

(Put a ✓ in the box for Yes, and a ✗ for No.)

	MYSELF	MY PARTNER
1 to enjoy healthy competition.	☐	☐
2 self-confidence.	☐	☐
3 self-discipline.	☐	☐
4 to enjoy team work.	☐	☐
5 to improve my concentration and coordination.	☐	☐
6 how enjoyable exercise is.	☐	☐
7 to think positively about carrying on with sport in adult life.	☐	☐
8 ways to relax and unwind when I feel tense.	☐	☐
9 how to approach sport safely, e.g. using the right clothing and equipment.	☐	☐
10 to appreciate fair play and the need for rules.	☐	☐

4 Is sport always fun?

How far do you agree with these comments about sport at school? Work with your partner and rank them from **0 (disagree totally)** to **3 (agree completely)**.

	MYSELF	MY PARTNER
1 'I hate sport at school. It's so competitive and only fit children can do well.'	☐	☐
2 'I don't mind things we can do at our own pace like swimming or gymnastics, but I hate being forced to take part in races.'	☐	☐
3 'It's usually too hot or too cold to enjoy being outside.'	☐	☐
4 'I dread the time when we get picked for the team. I'm always the last one to be selected.'	☐	☐
5 'There's so much standing around on the playing field waiting for something to happen. Sport is just boring!'	☐	☐
6 'At my school we're forced to do the traditional sports our parents did. Why can't we do more up-to-date activities?'	☐	☐

41

5 Pre-reading discussion

'Sports day' in many schools is a competitive event in which all children take part. Parents may attend to watch their children perform. Do you have a similar event in your school? Do you enjoy it? Why/Why not?

6 Predicting content

Predicting content is part of getting the right mental attitude to reading.

You are going to read an article in which the writer criticises the sports day at her son's primary school (a school for children aged 5–11). What specific things about sports day do you expect the writer to criticise? Tick as many of the following points as you think could be relevant.

- [ ] the value of the prizes
- [ ] the competitive aspect of the day
- [ ] the bad effect competitive sport has on some children
- [ ] the skills of the teachers
- [ ] her child's poor performance
- [ ] the time of year sports day is held
- [ ] the fact that sports day takes time away from academic subjects
- [ ] the young age of the children taking part

7 Reading with concentration

Now read the article as fast as possible, trying to absorb as much information as you can. This means reading fast any sentences which are easy to understand. Read more slowly the sentences which are difficult or which you think contain key ideas.

Try, where you can, to work out the meaning of unfamiliar words from the context. Use a dictionary if this technique doesn't help **and** the word seems important to the key meaning. However, don't worry too much about each word. **You don't need to understand every word to understand a text well.**

8 Comprehension check

Try to answer these questions without looking at the text, if possible.

1 What symptoms do children who are afraid of sports day show?

2 Where was the sports day held?

3 Why do some of the children who like running still find sports day traumatic?

One afternoon in the last week of term, I saw three children from my son's school in tears being comforted by teachers. That morning, my 11-year-old had stomach pains and had been retching into a
5 bowl. Talking to other mothers, I heard about other children with stomachache or difficulty sleeping the night before.

What caused so much distress? Sports day –
not sports day at a highly competitive independent
10 school, but at a large village primary. For the children who can fly like the wind, it causes no problem. For those who are poorly coordinated, overweight or just not good at sport, it is a nightmare. Even for those who enjoy running, but who fall halfway down the
15 track in front of the entire school and their parents, it can prove a disaster.

Why do we put our children through this annual torment? Some may say competition is character-building; or it's taking part that's important, not
20 winning; or that it's a tradition of school life. I just felt immense pity for those children in tears or in pain.

Team games at the end of the 'sports' produced some close races, enormous enthusiasm, lots of
25 shouting – and were fun to watch. More importantly, the children who were not so fast or so nimble at passing the ball were hidden a little from everyone's gaze. Some of them also had the thrill of being on the winning side.
30 I wish that sports day could be abandoned and replaced with some other summer event. Perhaps an afternoon of team games, with a few races for those who want them, would be less stressful for the children and a lot more fun to watch.

4 What does the writer feel for young children who are upset by sports day?

5 How did the children feel about the team games played after the races?

6 What alternative to sports day does the writer suggest?

Finding the main ideas

Match the following main ideas to the relevant paragraphs (1–5) of the article.

A   How team games produced a positive atmosphere on sports day

B   The reasons why sports days are still a part of school life

C   An alternative to the traditional sports day

D   The explanation for the children's illnesses and fears

E   The physical symptoms that fear of sports day produces

9 Checking predictions

How many of the points you ticked in **exercise 6** were mentioned in the article?

What did the writer say that you did not predict?

10 Choosing a headline

Reading the title or headline of a text you are going to summarise is important because it gives an overall idea of what the text is going to be about.

Which of these headlines do you prefer for the article you have just read? Be prepared to explain your choice.

> It is time that sports were banned from the school curriculum
>
> Sports day torment
>
> It is essential that protests are made about the unfair ways young children are treated on their school sports day
>
> Mum raps sports day
>
> Sports day: How one school has upset many of its pupils

11 Note-making practice

Here is an exam-style note-making question, based on the article in exercise 7:

Read the newspaper article about a school sports day. Then write a set of notes based on the article, using the headings below.

Reasons for having a sports day

_____

_____

_____

The negative effects of sports day

_____

_____

_____

Sports day: possible improvements

_____

_____

_____

Underlining relevant parts of the text

Re-read the article and underline the parts which are relevant to the question. When you've finished, compare your underlined sections with your partner's. Do you both agree on what is relevant?

Making notes and checking your work

Make notes under the headings given. Use short, relevant words and phrases from the text, or adapt phrases from the text, using some words of your own. Don't just copy out large parts of the original. You do not need to write complete sentences.

In pairs or threes, compare your notes.

Check the **content**:

Do you need to add anything or leave anything out? Is there any repetition?

Check the **language**:

Have you managed to avoid copying out large chunks of the text? Are your notes clear and concise?

Check the **presentation**:

Have you written the correct points under the correct headings?

12 Comparing two summaries

Summarising requires you to write in grammatical, connected prose. The following two summaries, based on the article, were written by students. Analyse them by answering these questions.

1   Which summary 'lifts' from the text?

2   Which summary uses the student's own words as far as possible?

3   Which summary uses two linking words incorrectly?

4   The summaries have one mistake in common. What is it?

5   Which summary seems to show the best overall understanding of the text? Why?

43

Summary 1

Many reasons are given for having a sports day, such as the competition is character-building, or it's the taking part that is important, not the winning, or that it's a tradition of school life. Moreover, sports days can be a nightmare for those who are poorly coordinated, overweight or just not good at sport. Despite for those children who enjoy running but fall down on the track in front of the entire school it can prove a disaster. It is said that sports day should be abandoned and replaced by an afternoon of team games with a few races for those who want them but I think that would spoil a nice summer event.

Summary 2

Sports days at school are said to be valuable because they're a school custom, the competition is healthy, it develops character and the main point of the event is the enjoyment of playing. However, sports days can be traumatic, especially if the pupils are not slim, agile or capable at sport. Even the confident, athletic ones can be very upset if they fall over before a large audience. An afternoon of team games, with a few races for those who are interested, should be offered in the summer instead of sports day. I believe most parents would prefer this to a competitive sports day.

3.2 Enjoying sport safely

13 Compound nouns

Like *sports day*, many compound nouns are a combination of two nouns (or a gerund plus a noun, e.g. *running shoes*). By avoiding the need for a preposition, as in 'a day of sports' or 'shoes for running', compound nouns can help you write more concisely.

Some of these words can follow the word *sports* to make common compound nouns. Write **sports** in the spaces as appropriate.

_____ bag   _____ drink
_____ car   _____ enjoyment
_____ child   _____ equipment
_____ centre   _____ hobby
_____ club   _____ instructor

_____ man   _____ time
_____ person   _____ woman

Practice

Form compound nouns by writing suitable words from the box alongside these words. In each case more than one combination is possible.

swimming _____   skating _____
football _____   leisure _____

VOCABULARY

match	programme	stick
bat	centre	field
costume	rink	pool
shorts	boots	shirt
players	hat	
team	trunks	

hockey _____   cricket _____
fitness _____

What other compound nouns do you know? Make a list with a partner.

14 Pre-listening discussion

Do you ever go to a sports centre? What facilities do you use? Do you enjoy it? Why/Why not?

If you don't go to a sports centre, would you like to visit one? Why/Why not? What facilities do you think you would see there?

15 Listening to a recorded announcement 🔊

You are going to hear some recorded information about facilities available at a sports centre. Listen first for general meaning and try to complete the list of compound nouns, putting one word in each space.

1 open-air swimming _____
2 coin- _____ locker system
3 _____ rooms
4 _____ court
5 _____ tennis
6 cheap-rate _____

44

7   sports centre _____

8   application _____

9   reception _____

10 keep-fit _____

Now listen again and complete the diary. How much does membership of the sports centre cost?

Sports Centre Diary

Monday

A.M.   9–11 Swimming in the open-air pool
         (i)   Need _____

P.M.   (ii) Sports centre _____

Tuesday

A.M.   10–11.30 Badminton court open
         (iii) Bring _____

P.M.   Open for schools only

Wednesday

A.M.   9–11.30 Table tennis
         (iv) Ask supervisor for _____

P.M.   (v)   Gym _____
         (vi) Must wear _____

Thursday

A.M.   (vii) Collect application form from _____

P.M.   (vii) Senior citizens' _____

16 Marking the main stress

John and Ella are watching Poland and Finland play football. Ella is unsure about some things. Listen to the dialogue while you read. Why is the main stress marked in this way?

Ella: Is Poland playing in the **blue** and **green**?

John: No, Poland's playing in the **yell**ow and green.

Ella: Did you say **Fin**land was in the yellow and green?

John: No, I said **Po**land was in the yellow and green.

Ella: Is Poland playing **France** this season?

John: Poland plays France **ev**ery season.

Ella: Did Poland win a **few** of their matches last season?

John: They won **all** their matches last season!

Now practise reading the dialogue in pairs, putting the main stress as indicated. Why is a different word stressed in each answer?

Practice

With a partner, decide where the main stress falls in the following dialogue and mark it. Then practise the dialogue together.

A: Were you surprised about Kelly's behaviour on the field last night?

B: I'm never surprised about Kelly's behaviour!

A: Did you think the referee acted fairly?

B: No one thought the referee acted fairly.

A: Is anybody from your family going to see the game tomorrow?

B: Everybody's going to see the game tomorrow.

A: Do you think the match will be as exciting?

B: I don't think any match could be as exciting.

17 Analysing headlines

To save space in headlines, and to be dramatic, newspapers invent unusual word combinations like **TRAGEDY BOAT**. Such 'compound nouns', although very creative, can be difficult to understand. This is particularly true if several nouns are strung together:

BOMB HOTEL HORROR PROBE

Underline the key words in the following newspaper report. Make sure you understand the meaning of *collision* and *compensation*.

Crash woman rejects deal

A female student who was seriously injured when she was involved in a collision with a Kuranda bus in October today rejected the compensation offered by Kuranda Bus Company.

How does the headline convey the key elements of the story? What compound noun is used? Do you think this is an invented compound or one in normal use?

Verb tenses

As in many headlines, the present simple tense is used. Why is this, when the report describes the rejection in the past tense?

45

Vocabulary

Why do you think the headline refers to *crash* and *deal*, when the report uses *collision* and *compensation*?

Articles

The report refers to **a** *collision* and **the** *compensation*. Why does the headline not use the articles?

18 Expanding headlines

Read the following headlines and answer the questions.

> # COMA BABY HOPE: US SURGEON TO OPERATE

1 Read *coma baby hope* backwards. Does this provide clues to understanding?
2 How is the future expressed? Why?
3 Why is the colon used?
4 Try to rewrite the headline as a complete sentence.

> # TRAIN BLAZE: CHILD FOUND 'UNHURT'

5 Why is the compound *train blaze* used rather than 'big fire on train'?
6 How is the passive voice of the present perfect tense conveyed in the headline?
7 Why is 'unhurt' in inverted commas, do you think?
8 Rewrite the headline as a complete sentence.

19 Noun or verb?

The following short words are common in newspaper headlines. Sometimes they are used as nouns, and sometimes as verbs. Choose one word from the box to complete each pair of headlines.

VOCABULARY		
AID	CUT	JAIL
ARM	HEAD	VOW

1 a REFUGEES TO GET FRESH _____
  b CHARITY SHOPS _____ HOMELESS

2 a JUDGE TO _____ MURDER INQUIRY
  b CRASH VICTIM DIES OF _____ INJURIES

3 a BABY'S _____ SAVED IN MIRACLE OP
  b POLICE CHIEF _____S CITY POLICE

4 a FATHER _____S REVENGE ON KILLER
  b PRESIDENT BREAKS ELECTION _____

5 a GOVERNMENT TO _____ WORKING HOURS
  b MORE EDUCATION _____S ON WAY

6 a JUDGE _____S TRAIN ROBBER
  b CONDITIONS IN WOMEN'S _____S 'SHOCKING'

20 Comparing languages

How does the newspaper language of your own language compare with English? Do you find any similarities? Or do you feel it is plainer?

21 Discussion

What do you think has happened to the sportsperson in the picture?

How can you get hurt when you play sport? If you are hurt, what should you do?

Have you ever suffered an injury whilst taking part in sport? How did it happen? What helped you recover?

22 Rewording

When you write summaries, you need to use your own words without altering the meaning. For example:

If you carry out weight training, you would be well advised to do this in a gym under expert supervision.

could become

You should do weight training in a gym under the care of a qualified supervisor.

In groups of two or three, try to rewrite the following sentences about sports injuries, using your own words where you can. Can you also make the sentences more concise?

1 Many acute injuries to the body are accompanied by bleeding, swelling and pain.

2 In the first 24 hours, ice (or alternatively a packet of frozen peas) should only be used for short periods of ten minutes at a time.

3 Ice should never be applied directly to the skin because of the danger of burns.

4 In the early stages when there is a great deal of swelling and pain, you would be well advised to rest the injured area.

5 Nevertheless, you must begin gentle movement and exercise of the injured part as soon as possible.

6 Where possible, it is important that any exercise of the injured area is carried out under the supervision of a physiotherapist.

7 Your doctor may prescribe painkillers or anti-inflammatory tablets when your injury is painful or the swelling is marked.

23 Writing a short summary

Read the introduction to a leaflet entitled 'Avoiding Sports Injuries'. In your own words, write a paragraph of about 45 words explaining how you can avoid getting injured when you play sport. Approach the task in a methodical way, as you did earlier in the unit.

When you have finished, ask a partner to check that you have:

- kept to the question set
- used your own words where possible
- left out unnecessary words and details
- left out opinions of your own
- connected the summary grammatically
- kept to the word limit.

24 Expressing warnings

You have just read some warnings in written language. When we speak, warnings are expressed very directly.

In pairs, read the following mini-conversations giving warnings about the possible dangers of sport and physical exercise.

1 *A:* I've just started to play cricket.

   B: Take care to use protective shin pads. They can stop you getting a nasty injury.

   A: Thanks. I'll remember that.

2 *A:* My brother is only three but he wants to learn to swim.

   B: Make sure he wears armbands, even in shallow water. He could easily lose coordination.

   A: You're right. I'm glad you told me.

Avoiding Sports Injuries

Active sports are becoming ever more popular. Whether for relaxation and as a way of reducing stress, or for weight control, or to improve health and fitness, greater numbers of people of all ages are taking part in various active sporting pursuits.

However, as more people take part, sports injuries are becoming more common. Fortunately, these injuries are seldom too serious, and if treated properly and promptly, get better quickly – never to return. Nevertheless, if you are planning to start a fitness programme, you need to be aware of the ways injuries can be prevented in the first place.

You need systematic and sensible physical preparation to get fit for sport. Besides training for strength and stamina, you should ensure that you get proper rest. It is essential never to try to train when you are tired, as tiredness itself can cause injury. It is also vital to use an appropriate technique when doing sport. Not only is it obviously very helpful in achieving success in your chosen sport, but it can also greatly reduce the chance of sustaining an injury.

Protective equipment, such as helmets, gum shields, shin pads and other items, including comfortable and supportive footwear, will improve your performance and help prevent unnecessary injury.

3 A: We're going sailing in Hinton Bay on Saturday.

B: Watch out for rocks in that area. You can easily run aground.

A: That's true. I'll tell the others too.

Warnings

Take care to / Be careful to (take precautions)

Make sure you (take precautions)

Watch out for / Look out for (unseen danger)

Responses

Thanks. I'll remember that/I'll do that.

That's true. I'm glad you told me.

You're right. I will.

Practice

Create mini-conversations with a partner around the situations below, using the following pattern.

Student A: Talk about plans.

Student B: Give a warning.

Student A: Show you've understood the warning.

1 start jogging / need good running shoes to protect feet

2 lift weights at the gym for first time / proper supervision from instructor

3 hill walking alone / tell someone where you are going

4 swimming in sea on holiday / jellyfish sting you

5 mountain biking in a new area / lots of rain recently, ground muddy and slippery

3.3 Motivation through sport

25 Pre-reading discussion

Would you enjoy teaching other young people how to play your favourite sport? Would you be good at it? What do you think are the qualities of a good sports coach?

26 Predicting content

You are going to read an article about a sports project which brings together young people from different countries who have dropped out of school. The project teaches them sports and communication skills. What points might you expect to find in this article? Complete the list.

- Why communication skills are linked with sports
- _____
- _____
- _____
- _____

27 Vocabulary check

Before you read the article, try to match these words with their meanings.

1	truancy	A	face-to-face argument
2	top	B	non-attendance at school without permission
3	confrontation	C	people of the same age as one another
4	context	D	piece of clothing worn on the upper part of the body
5	peers	E	conditions and circumstances

28 Reading with concentration

Read the article as quickly as possible but with full concentration. Adapt your reading speed to your comprehension of what you are reading. Don't worry about trying to understand every word.

29 True/false comprehension

Are the following statements true or false?

1 The minimum age for joining the project is 17.

2 Young people from any country can participate.

3 The main aim of the project is to teach young people new sports.

4 Participants have all had personal problems.

5 Participants learn how to coach each other in the skills.

48

All 70 participants at the four-day course run by the European Association of Second Chance Schools (E2C) are 16- to 25-year-olds in danger of social exclusion. They have no qualifications and all have had a mixture of difficulties – family problems, truancy and crime.

The participants are from Italy, France, Sweden, Germany, England and Ireland and they have gathered at the South Leeds Sports Stadium in England to learn organisational and communication skills. The focus of the project is to help the young people acquire these skills through sport: first by learning how to play a variety of games, and then by learning how to coach each other in racket skills, athletics, netball, cricket or football.

The sessions are run by professional coaches who show the groups the basic skills of each sport and then demonstrate how to teach others the same skills.

Seventeen-year-old Nadia is a typical participant. She won't talk about her past except to say she had 'the usual' problems. Nevertheless, professional coach Riley says she has done particularly well at teaching football, learning to project her voice and taking command of the group with firm and clear requests. Nadia says, 'I'm enjoying the project as I'm learning new skills. When I go home, I'm going to get qualifications so I can get a job working with children.'

On the badminton courts, a group of youngsters from Spoleto, in northern Italy, is shown how to grip the rackets and practise with easy-to-control balls. The tutor accompanying them, Stefania Rosati, watches carefully to see how her students cope. 'They are enjoying the experience of being here as most of them haven't been abroad before. One of the most useful things for them is learning more self-discipline.' In the Italians' second session, pairs of them are asked to coach the rest of their group. Badminton coach Brian Harrison is impressed. 'Some are well-coordinated and find it easy, while others are finding it hard, but no one is getting impatient – they are working together,' he says.

But it isn't all so positive. During the next session, one of the boys loses interest in being coached by his peers and wanders off. The participants leading the session ignore his behaviour in order to avoid a confrontation. Afterwards, though, they discuss it and suggest ways it could have been tackled sensitively and effectively. They also discuss other difficult situations, such as what to say to a participant who turns up in a fashionable top instead of the correct sportswear.

Meeting other nationalities at the events is an important element of the programme which the participants enjoy. Although nationalities are not mixed for the coaching sessions, the sporting context gives the youngsters an opportunity to see how other cultures differ. Phillipe Marco, a tutor from Marseille whose group are all originally from North African countries, says, 'They love discussing ideas with young people from other countries. It is opening their minds, and they are able to explain their beliefs to others. The sport and social events are helping to break down barriers.'

The youngsters are given diaries to record their thoughts and experiences every day. Their comments reveal their enjoyment of meeting people from different backgrounds but with similar problems. 'All of us had challenges and barriers. I think we worked well as a team to overcome them,' and 'I have learned there is more to sport than the obvious activities,' are typical of the responses.

One Swedish tutor sums up the experience of many of his colleagues with a report on a girl who attended the project. 'Before, she had been quite self-centred. During the course she has stopped focusing on herself and has really enjoyed everything.'

49

6 The project gives people an opportunity to compare cultures.

7 There is an emphasis on competition and trying to win.

8 Nationalities are kept separate for coaching.

9 The participants write their thoughts in a daily journal.

30 Checking predictions

How much of what you expected to read about was actually mentioned in the article?

31 Writing a headline

With a partner, write a headline for the article and suggest a suitable picture. Look back at the guidelines earlier in the unit to help you.

32 Post-reading discussion

What are your feelings about this kind of social project? Do you think the positive effects it has on young people will make a permanent difference to them? Or do you think the benefits will be forgotten when they return to their normal lives?

33 Making notes

Write a set of notes based on the article about the sports project, using the headings below.

Aims of the project

_____
_____
_____

What participants learn

_____
_____
_____

Reasons the project is popular

_____
_____
_____

Look at the approach suggested in exercise 11 and apply that method here. When you've finished, ask your partner to check the following:

Content: Is it all relevant? Should anything be left out?

Language: Is your language clear and precise?

Presentation: Have you put the right points under the right headings?

34 Correcting a connected summary

Study this exam-style question.

Read the article about the European Association of Second Chance Schools and then write a summary describing the aims of the project, what the participants learn to do and the reasons why they enjoy taking part. Write about 100 words, and use your own words as far as possible.

Here is one student's attempt to answer the question. Some of the information in the answer is unnecessary, making the answer too long. Cross out the unnecessary information.

The aim of the European Association of Second Chance Schools project is to encourage young people from European countries who have not succeeded at school to improve their ability to communicate and organise themselves. Sport is used as the medium for this. I think this is a very unusual idea and we should start a project like this in my country. Participants are taught a range of skills needed for a variety of sports and then they are expected to coach each other. Phillipe Marco came from Marseille in France with his students and he explained that his group liked telling the others about their views and beliefs which might be the first time they have had the chance to talk to people who listen properly to them. Participants also have to learn self-discipline, to take trouble doing things even if they don't feel like it and to cope with troublesome behaviour from some of the others. They enjoy learning new skills, teamwork, sharing cultures, and discovering that they are not alone with their problems. One 17-year-old girl whose name is Nadia explained, 'I'm enjoying the project. When I go home, I'm going to get qualifications so I can get a job working with children.'

35 Rewriting a summary

Now rewrite the summary correctly. Make sure you keep within the approximate word limit.

36 Expressions of measurement

The article says that participants go on *a four-day course*. This is a concise way of saying that the course lasts for four days. One of the participants is described as *17-year-old Nadia*, which is a more concise way of saying Nadia is 17 years old. Similarly, we can say that a hotel that has been awarded three stars for quality is *a three-star hotel*, or a walk that is five kilometres long is *a five-kilometre walk*. Notice how the plural *s* is not used in the hyphenated words.

Practice

Rewrite each of these sentences using a number + noun form.

1   She uses a fitness video which lasts for fifty minutes.
2   He made a cut which was six inches long.
3   Ali got a contract worth a thousand dollars.
4   They ordered a meal which consisted of six courses.
5   I need a coin worth ten cents for the phone.
6   The drive to work takes ten minutes.
7   Tanya gave birth to a baby weighing seven pounds.
8   I'd like a bag of sugar weighing two kilograms.

37 Vocabulary: Using fewer words

In the article, the word used for 'people taking part in the course' is *participants*.

The following words are also taken from the article. With a partner, choose the correct one to replace the words in italics in the sentences.

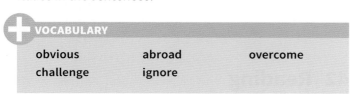

+ VOCABULARY		
obvious	abroad	overcome
challenge	ignore	

1   Learning to paddle the canoe was a *difficult and testing task* for Mario.
2   If you can *manage to control* your fear, bungee jumping is a thrilling experience.
3   If they behave like that again, you should *take no notice of* them.
4   The answer to the problem is *easy to see*.
5   Natasha's ambition is to go *to another country* to study.

Now put each word into a sentence of your own.

38 Redundant words

Extra words, which repeat what we have already said, often slip into our speech. Such repetition usually goes unnoticed in everyday conversation. In fact, the repetition is sometimes helpful. However, when we write, we should write concisely and try to avoid 'redundancy'.

Example:
The children stood patiently in a round circle and listened to the coach.

Round is unnecessary because a circle is always round.

With a partner, decide which words are redundant in the following sentences and cross them out.

1   When did you first begin to learn basketball?
2   Aysha bought new summer sandals for the children's feet.
3   He has some priceless old antiques in his house which are so valuable that it is impossible to say how much they are worth.
4   We received an unexpected shock on our return from holiday.
5   She was upset that the vase was broken as it was very unique.
6   Betty wasn't very helpful when I asked for some scissors to cut with.
7   He had to repeat himself many times, saying the words over and over again, before he was understood.
8   Since starting to play squash, Jeff has been unhealthily obsessed with winning every game.

51

INTERNATIONAL OVERVIEW

Work with a partner to test your knowledge of approaches to sport, health and fitness across the world.

1   The global 'rule' for the number of hours of sports practice required to reach world class standard is:

  1,000   3,000   10,000   15,000   20,000

2   In Ireland, pupils aged 5–12 can expect to do 37 hours per year of PE (physical education). How many hours can a pupil in the same age group expect to do in France?

  35   60   88   108   135

3   In which country can you expect to have the longest lifespan in good health?

  Switzerland   Argentina   Japan   Sweden

4   In which country can every child receive a nutritionally balanced free school lunch providing a third of the daily calories needed?

  India   Australia   Finland   Spain

3.4 Health, diet and fitness

39 Pre-reading discussion

Sport itself cannot make you fit. You have to get fit for sport. A healthy diet is an important part of getting and staying fit.

Discuss with your partner what, if anything, you do to make sure you eat a balanced, healthy diet.

40 Predicting content

You are going to read a magazine article about Shalimar, a digital artist, who changed her lifestyle habits. Using the title, picture and introductory paragraph to find clues, decide what particular things she might mention in the article.

Write four points.

1 _____
2 _____
3 _____
4 _____

Audience awareness

Who do you think this magazine is **mainly** aimed at – the medical profession, children, professional sports players, women, digital artists or elderly people?

What kind of language and style do you expect the writer to use? Do you expect to find a chatty style with lots of phrasal verbs? Or will the article be formal and use many specialised terms?

Writer's intention

What do you think the writer's intention is?

- ☐ To make people identify with Shalimar and change unhealthy habits
- ☐ To make people try harder to keep to fitness programmes
- ☐ To promote a particular diet and fitness programme

41 Vocabulary check

The following words connected with food and fitness are used in the article. Can you explain their meaning?

✚ VOCABULARY

| nibble | snack on | packed lunches |
| sluggish | | |

42 Reading

Read the article quickly and tick off these points as the story develops:

- ☐ what makes Shalimar accept she is unfit
- ☐ unhealthy work patterns
- ☐ after-work habits
- ☐ success on the programme
- ☐ new routines
- ☐ Shalimar today

NOW FEELING ON TOP OF THE WORLD

Digital artist Shalimar was so busy building her new own online gaming company she never noticed she was getting unfit – until the day she couldn't run for a bus.

Shalimar Lee was late for work one morning and, as her usual number 14 bus came around the corner, she put on a spurt. As she climbed aboard, her heart was beating so fast she could hardly speak to the driver. She thought she might be going to collapse. This finally made her face the fact that she was seriously unfit and she did not like it.

'I used to be very fit and played tennis and basketball at school. But when I went to university I gave up sport completely. Don't ask me why! After completing my degree, I got a great opportunity as a digital artist. Within a few years I had started my own computer games company. I gave everything to my job, but I paid a price and that was my health. The bus incident proved my problems had got out of hand and suddenly I couldn't stand it.'

For Shalimar, however, the idea of going on a fitness regime was inconceivable. 'I simply didn't think I had the time. Even when I wasn't at work, I was thinking of new story lines for my games, researching, or updating my blog.' Her online games, which are internationally known, centre around a family of penguins, and Shalimar has already achieved the status of a minor celebrity in the blogosphere.

'I got so immersed in work, I never took a meal break and worked ridiculously long hours. I would sip high-energy drinks all day long and nibble biscuits. When I got home, I'd slump in front of the TV, and, rather than cook a proper meal, I snacked on toast and chocolate spread. There was never anything much in the fridge anyway.' Not surprisingly, she didn't sleep well and would wake up feeling as if she needed another eight hours. 'I felt sluggish all the time, but I couldn't imagine how to change things.'

No one ever mentioned that Shalimar seemed exhausted. No one, that is, until her mum decided to pluck up the courage. 'I was visiting my family one weekend. Mum waited until I was relaxed after lunch and then plunged in. She had read that a new gym in the neighbourhood was starting up a fitness programme which not only included exercise, but offered information on developing a healthy lifestyle. Mum persuaded me that we should both give the programme a try.' Shalimar wasn't exactly thrilled but felt she ought to go. After the very first class, she was hooked.

'I got fitter immediately. The exercises were good fun. Gabrielle, our instructor, was so motivational and gave us loads of encouragement. She also told us about easy ways to replace bad habits with healthy ones, such as getting off the bus a stop earlier, and making time to shop for fresh ingredients. I used to leave feeling on top of the world.'

Shalimar explains that the programme focuses on making small changes that you can fit into your lifestyle. This, she feels, is the key to its success. 'I'm strict with myself now. However busy I am, I make up my packed lunch every day and leave the office to eat it in a park down the road.' Her office is on the fourth floor and she now uses the stairs as much as possible instead of the lift. She also keeps clear of fizzy drinks and drinks tea or water instead. 'I didn't need to go crazy to get healthy. Just a few simple, sensible changes have made all the difference.'

It's hard to believe Shalimar was ever so unfit she couldn't run for a bus. 'I'm still busy but I don't feel exhausted anymore. I'm sure eating properly has also given my brain a boost because I find it so much easier to conjure up new ideas for my games. I've got rid of my old habits for good and they are never coming back!'

Shalimar's business is also going from strength to strength. Her new computer game about a cute baby giraffe is about to be launched onto the market. 'The team and I are so excited. I think this is going to be our most successful product yet.'

43 Post-reading discussion

A In your culture, how do you define a healthy lifestyle?

B Shalimar's mother persuaded her to attend the fitness classes. Do you think her mother was right to do this, or was she interfering?

C Shalimar explains that the programme succeeds because it helps you make small changes that you can fit into your lifestyle. Do you agree that this approach would really work, or do you think bigger changes are necessary for people who are unfit because of unhealthy habits? What motivates **you** to have a healthy lifestyle?

D Shalimar feels a healthy diet has given her brain a boost. What evidence does she have? Do you feel nutritious food can make such a big difference to brain functioning?

Discuss your ideas in your group.

44 Writing a summary

Write a summary, based on the article, contrasting Shalimar's lifestyle before she began the fitness programme with her lifestyle now. Explain why she feels the fitness programme was particularly suitable for her. Try to use your own words as far as possible. Write about 100 words and not more than 120 words.

Approach

Approach your summary methodically: check key words in the question, underline relevant parts of the text, write notes in your own words and then connect them into a summary. You may need to make a few drafts before your summary is 'polished'.

When you have finished, compare your version with your partner's, and check that you have:

- included the relevant points
- put the points in the correct order
- left out unnecessary details
- left out your own personal opinions and ideas
- used suitable connectors
- written grammatically correct English
- used the appropriate number of words.

45 Vocabulary: Phrasal verbs

The following phrasal verbs were used in the article. Can you use them in an appropriate form in the sentences below?

+ VOCABULARY

give up	start up	plunge in
pluck up	conjure up	make up

1 He's trying to ＿＿＿＿＿＿ an after-school judo club for children in the village.

2 She knew mentioning the topic would be unpopular but she decided to ＿＿＿＿＿＿ anyway.

3 Antonio decided to ＿＿＿＿＿＿ doing overtime and see more of his family.

4 He ＿＿＿＿＿＿ the courage and asked Jane to marry him.

5 Although she didn't have much food in the fridge, Sally was able to ＿＿＿＿＿＿ a delicious meal.

6 They ＿＿＿＿＿＿ food parcels for people whose homes had been damaged in the flood.

46 Spelling: Adding suffixes to words with a final -e

In the text about Shalimar you saw these words with suffixes:

completing (complete + -ing)

encouragement (encourage + -ment)

Notice how the final -e of *complete* is dropped before the suffix, but the -e is kept in the word *encourage**ment***.

Can you explain why?

> A final -e in a word is usually dropped when adding a suffix beginning with a *vowel*.

Examples:
dance　　　　　*danc**ing***
educate　　　　*educat**ion***

> The -e is usually kept when the suffix begins with a consonant.

Examples:

hope	*hope**ful***
care	*care**less***
improve	*improve**ment***

There are some **important exceptions** to the above rule.

> The -*e* is usually kept before the suffix -*able.*

Examples:

notice   *notice**able***

> The -*e* is usually kept when it follows another vowel.

Examples:

see	*see**ing***
canoe	*canoe**ist***

Practice

Read this newspaper report about the teaching of traditional dance in schools. Add the correct suffixes to the words in brackets. Check your spelling with the rules above.

Choose from the following:

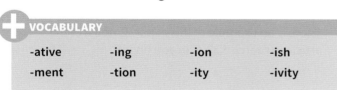

VOCABULARY

-ative	-ing	-ion	-ish
-ment	-tion	-ity	-ivity

More and more pupils are learning dance as part of their physical (educate) programme. It is a wonderful way of (have) fun and an (excite) way of keeping fit. Dance allows all pupils a chance to express their (create). Even the youngest pupils can learn simple (move) to music which act as an (introduce) to more complex traditional dance. Older pupils who lack (motivate) when it comes to competitive sport find traditional dance very (stimulate). Secondary school teachers say (participate) in such an enjoyable activity needs no (encourage).

Schools (achieve) a high standard may be selected for the Schools Dance Festival held each year. The festival is a wonderful (celebrate) of traditional dance. Last year, the (style) costumes, great (diverse) of dances, (imagine) approaches and wonderful music made the evening particularly special.

Discussion

Do you (or would you) enjoy watching or taking part in traditional dances? Explain your views.

47 Word building

Working with a partner, choose a suitable suffix from the box to add to each of the ten words below. Sometimes more than one is possible.

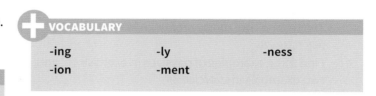

VOCABULARY

-ing	-ly	-ness
-ion	-ment	

1	time	**6**	involve
2	concentrate	**7**	ache
3	refine	**8**	state
4	exercise	**9**	unique
5	welcome	**10**	aware

Make sure your spelling is correct by checking with the rules for keeping or dropping the final -*e.*

Give each new word a grammar label (*noun, verb, adjective,* etc.). Refer to a dictionary if necessary.

Now use each word you have made in a sentence of your own.

48 Look, say, cover, write, check

Use the 'look, say, cover, write, check' method to learn these words, which are among those most frequently misspelled.

amaze	amazing	amazement	
argue	arguing	argument	
become	becoming		
excite	exciting	excitable	excitement
welcome	welcoming		
shine	shining		
invite	inviting	invitation	
surprise	surprising		
imagine	imaginary	imaginative	imagining
immediate	immediately		

✷ GRAMMAR SPOTLIGHT

Passives

A **Passives** are often used when we are reporting news, or explaining how something works:
A female student was seriously injured. (exercise 17)
The sessions are run by professional coaches. (exercise 28)
Find three examples of passives in exercise 10, and two examples in exercise 34.

B Verbs like *give, offer, lend* and *send* can have **two objects**, a person and a thing:

We sent Julio a birthday card.

When these verbs are used in the passive with two objects, we usually start with the person. This makes the sentence sound more pleasing:
Marianne was offered a place at Oxford University.
NOT *A place at Oxford University was offered to Marianne.*

There is an example of this in paragraph 8 of the article in exercise 28. Can you find it?

EXAM-STYLE QUESTIONS

Speaking

1 Fitness and exercise

In some countries many people suffer from a lack of exercise. Why is this happening, do you think? What can be done to raise people's awareness of the importance of staying fit? Discuss this topic with the assessor.

You may wish to use the following ideas to help develop the conversation:

- ways to develop a more energetic lifestyle in general, such as walking or cycling rather than using buses or cars
- the increased consumption of snack foods such as crisps and chocolate bars which are eaten quickly and do not satisfy hunger for long
- the fact that playing computer games, surfing the internet or watching TV can result in a lack of exercise
- the fact that in some countries children have less freedom to play outside than in the past
- the fact that increased use of washing machines and vacuum cleaners is reducing effort spent on keeping houses clean and comfortable.

You are free to consider any other related ideas of your own. You are not allowed to make any written notes.

2 Professional sport

Sport is popular all over the world and it is also big business. Top sports players are paid very large sums of money and are heavily in demand. Discuss this topic with the assessor.

You may wish to consider points such as:

- whether you personally enjoy watching professional sports games and matches
- the skills and abilities professional sports players require to become the best in their sport
- whether there should be stricter penalties for sports people who take drugs or cheat at sport
- the idea that international sports competitions create unpleasant rivalries that divide countries, rather than bring people of different nationalities together
- the view that professional sports people should not get involved in advertising commercial products.

You are free to consider any other related ideas of your own. You are not allowed to make any written notes.

Notes and summary writing

1   Read the following article about sleep and young people. Write a summary outlining why young people need more sleep than adults and the negative effects of lack of sleep on teenagers.

Your summary should be about 100 (and no more than 120) words long. You should use your own words as far as possible.

Sleep – Are You Getting Enough?

According to recent studies, many children and teenagers get less sleep than they did 30 years ago. Lifestyle changes may be to blame, including online gaming, late-night TV and parents, who, arriving home from work late in the evening, let children stay up later so they can enjoy quality time with them.

In clinical studies, nearly half of children up to the age of 12 were found to be having less than seven hours' sleep a night, when the recommended amount is ten hours. Many modern teenagers in the studies were getting just over six hours' sleep, rather than the nine hours they are thought to need. Using newly developed technological tools, scientists have been able to measure the impact loss of sleep has on young people. Their findings suggest a lack of sleep can cause worrying changes in teenagers' brain structure.

Throughout the night, everyone enters different stages of sleep. There are stages of light sleep, stages of dreaming sleep, called 'REM', and stages of deep or 'slow wave' sleep. However, the stages do not necessarily follow on one after the other. Instead, it is more accurate to think of the stages as being like the steps on a staircase – we move up and down the steps in different types of sleep all night long. The sleep researchers discovered that young people's sleep is different in quality from adult sleep because they need to spend 40 per cent of their time asleep in slow wave sleep. The slow wave stage is the time when the brain carries out its development and healing functions. Teenagers need to be asleep for long enough in order to get sufficient amounts of this slow wave sleep. In contrast, adults spend only 4 per cent of their time in slow wave sleep and much more time in the lighter stages.

Dr Avi Salem, a sleep researcher whose work has been published internationally, has spent many years studying the effects of lack of sleep on teenagers and has come to some very interesting conclusions. Using performance tests, Dr Salem and his team of researchers found that the 15-year-old volunteers who had insufficient sleep performed less well on tests of mental ability, often only reaching the standard of a typical 13-year-old, which is highly significant for the age group.

MRI brain scans show that sleep loss decreases the body's ability to extract sugar from the bloodstream, which makes the brain less alert and therefore less able to take in information. It also means that sleep-deprived young people find it more difficult to fulfil a goal that has been set for them, or to imagine the possible consequences and negative effects of foolish or impulsive behaviour.

Sleep has always been considered to be important and there are many references in literature praising the unique, health-giving qualities of sleep and lamenting the dire effects of lack of it. However, there is now more scientific evidence to support this age-old wisdom and to prove just how much sleep matters. Studies confirm the idea that having enough good-quality sleep is essential, especially for children and teenagers. Dr Salem explains the role of sleep in helping learning. For instance, if a teenager is studying a foreign language during the daytime, his or her brain needs sufficient slow wave sleep in order to encode new words that were studied earlier into the long-term memory. This process is required for the retention and recall of new language. Emotional experiences are also processed by the brain during sleep.

Many adults manage on too little sleep, and seem to find ways to cope, but when it comes to young people whose brains are not yet fully formed, can we afford to take the risk?

2   Read the following article about people's fear of swimming and then complete the notes.

Fear of Swimming

To what extent can you force children to cope with situations they find scary?

A concerned parent writes:
How seriously should you take a child's fear of the water? My son has a weekly swimming lesson at school which, for us, has become a nightmare scenario. His initial reluctance to swim has developed into a fear that seems little short of a phobia. We feel very strongly that it is important that he learns to swim, but each week, as the day of the lesson dawns, our son gets into a real state, which is emotionally exhausting for all of us. Should we give in to his extreme reluctance to swim or, as we have been doing, force him to go ahead with his lessons?

A professor of child psychiatry replies:
This little boy's fear of water is a very natural and healthy response, but on the other hand, children are much safer if they are able to swim.

A lot of children find group swimming lessons difficult to cope with for various reasons. School pools can be cold and noisy, with lots of people shouting and splashing, which is very off-putting for someone who doesn't feel in control of the situation. So it is easy to see why this could be a nasty experience.

Fear or dislike of group lessons is understandable given the situation, so these parents first need to teach their son to like water, probably in a pool which is warm rather than cold (presumably he doesn't have a problem in the bath, so the fear is probably not of water *itself*).

Choose a smallish, quiet pool, where the water is warm. Take it slowly and base it around having fun rather than focusing on getting on with swimming. He should get used to going underwater – it is much easier to start swimming while submerged.

His parents should not continue exposing him to repeated traumatic experiences, so they should speak to the teachers and see if they can take him out of his lessons until he feels that he is ready to rejoin the class. It really is not helpful to force him; his parents should work on his reluctance to swim outside the context of school and build up his confidence and skills.

A tutor at a swimming school replies:

I would suggest that this little boy would benefit from one-to-one tuition. Obviously something is happening in school – maybe someone has ducked him or splashed him in the pool and he doesn't like it. His parents should try to find out if something specific has happened to cause this problem.

In a situation like this, pushing him won't help at all, but they mustn't give up on him. Solo lessons should help. Perhaps the parents should take him swimming at the weekend and make sure it is fun, or get a teacher just for him.

It might be a good idea to leave the school lessons for a while. At the pool, they should forget the swimming aspect and just encourage him to enjoy the water.

At the swimming school we get a lot of adults who have been put off at a young age by being ducked or splashed, being taught to swim with a rope tied around the waist or a pole pushing them, and so, perhaps unsurprisingly, they have given up. Of course, there are people with a real fear of water, but they are more unusual.

We find that the main thing is helping individuals to become accustomed to getting their face wet. Bearing this in mind, perhaps bathtime would be a good time for the boy's parents to try this. They should also get him to put his mouth in the water and blow bubbles, and pour water over his head starting at the back so that it is not too startling. A lot of people really hate getting their heads wet, but if he can surmount the problem in a non-threatening environment such as the bath, he will be off to a good start.

At the pool, wearing good goggles might make a difference to him; it really is worth investing in a decent pair.

At our children's weeks, I advise parents of children who are petrified of water not to put the pressure on and to be happy with whatever their children can actually achieve in the water.

You are going to give a talk to your school sports club about the fear of swimming. Prepare some notes to use as the basis for your talk, using the headings below.

a Why some children fear learning to swim:

- *Fear of water is a natural response*
- _____
- _____

b Ways of overcoming a fear of swimming:

- _____
- _____
- _____

c How some adults were put off learning to swim:

- _____
- _____
- _____

3 Your teacher has asked you to write a summary of your talk for the school sports blog. Look at your notes from the previous exercise. Using your notes, write a summary about the fear of swimming.

Your summary should be about 70 words (and no more than 80 words) long. You should use your own words as far as possible.

KEY ADVICE

1 Before you start to read

Many students say they find it hard to 'get into' a newspaper or magazine article. The following strategies will help you get into reading more easily.

Ask yourself:

- What is this text likely to be about?
- What do I already know about the topic?
- Who is this written for? (young people, the general public, children, specialists in a profession, people with a particular hobby?)

This will orientate you to the likely style (technical, formal, chatty) and structure (long sentences and paragraphs, or short, simpler sentences and paragraphs).

Think about the author's main aim (to advise, warn, give technical information, entertain, give opinions, etc.). This will help you see the difference between the main points and background information.

Skimming headlines, subheadings and photos, diagrams or charts will also help to give you a quick idea of what the text is about.

2   Most students would like to read faster but still absorb what they read. **Adjust your reading speed to your reading needs**. You can skim-read sentences which are easy to understand or less relevant. Slow down (as much as you need to) over the parts which are more complex or which contain key points.

Keep a pen or a highlighter with you to mark important parts of the text.

After you have finished reading, ask yourself:

■   What were the main points of this text?

Make a short list. Check your list against the original text.

3   **Summarising** is a useful skill that can spill over into other areas of your life. It's a practical study skill for all parts of the curriculum.

When you summarise informally (plots of films, sports matches, social events), you are practising important intellectual and sequencing skills. Use these opportunities to improve your skills.

4   Feel proud of your progress with summarising. You are achieving in a tricky area which uses all your language resources and intellectual abilities.

Summarising is very challenging but don't be afraid of it. Tell your unconscious mind that you enjoy it, and as you become more at home with the skills you really will become more expert.

Exam techniques

5   Exam **summary questions** are usually 'guided'. You are asked, for example, to outline the advantages and disadvantages / trace the history of / explain the importance of something.

a   Underline key words in the question.

b   Look carefully at any headline, pictures, charts or subheadings to get a general idea of what the text is about before you start to read.

c   Read quickly with as much concentration as possible.

d   Underline or highlight key words and phrases.

e   Make a rough draft of the key words and phrases in connected prose. Use your own words as far as possible.

f   Count the words. Make corrections to the grammar and spelling as required.

g   Write a final draft using the word limit in the question as a guide.

h   Proofread your summary for mistakes.

6   For **note-making questions,** in examination use the above method as far as **d**.

Present your notes clearly, under the headings and bullet points provided. Write one point for each bullet. Full sentences are not needed.

Although a word limit is not given, your notes must be brief and concise.

7   Where the note-making and summary exercises are based on the same text, you should write your notes using the strategy above.

The summary you write will be based on the notes you have already made. The summary should be in full sentences, using your own words as far as possible, to show that you have a good range of vocabulary.

UNIT FOCUS

In this unit you have practised **making notes** from a text.

You have learned and practised the strategies you need to **summarise** a text.

You have also practised listening to a recorded announcement and completing a diary.

Unit 4:
Our Impact on the Planet

4.1 Transport then and now

1 Pre-reading discussion

A Apart from the car, what is the preferred mode of transport in your country? Do you feel it is a safe and comfortable form of transport? Give reasons for your views.

B Have you ever travelled by train? What did you like about it? If you have never been on a train journey, would you like to? Why/Why not?

Brainstorming

You are going to read about the coming of the first railways in the nineteenth century, and how life changed as a result. How do you think people at that time might have felt about the idea of such a different, and strange, form of transport? What would they have wanted to know? What do you think they worried about? Brainstorm your ideas, then share them in your group.

2 Vocabulary check

Before you read, check the meaning of these words.

VOCABULARY		
passenger	rigorously	novelty
suspicions	immobilised	

Early Train Travel

Trains and railway stations are such a common sight nowadays, it is strange to remember that at one time they did not exist. Before the passenger train was developed, the only ways to travel – if people travelled at all – were on foot, by boat, on horseback or camel, or by horse-drawn carriages or carts.

The earliest railways consisted of wagons pulled along rails by horses and were used for transporting raw materials and goods. The invention of the steam engine changed things dramatically, and in 1830, the Liverpool and Manchester Railway was opened, the world's first passenger railway as we know it. The Railway Age had begun.

People's objections

The first railways were fiercely opposed by many people who believed passengers might die from heart attacks caused by the extreme speed. There were also widespread fears that noisy trains would destroy the beauty and gentle pace of life in the countryside. Furthermore, farmers opposed the idea of railways cutting through their farmland, as they believed that the smoke and steam would destroy crops and scare their animals.

Safety concerns

There were many accidents on the first railways, which further increased people's distrust. When an accident happened, it made front-page news because people were eager to have their suspicions confirmed. As a result, people's fears of travelling by train grew even more intense. Those who were brave enough to travel on trains registered numerous complaints about lost luggage, delays and breakdowns.

When there was evidence, however, that safety concerns were being addressed, train travel became increasingly popular. A standardised clock giving the same time across the country was introduced to coordinate timetables and to avoid near misses on the tracks. Regulations controlling the building of the tracks, bridges and tunnels were improved, and trains were rigorously checked. If a problem was found, then the train was immobilised until it was judged to be safe.

Although the travelling public could never be given a guarantee of total safety, the accident rate declined. Moreover, people gradually became reassured that train travel was not likely to cause health problems. People of all ages and across all sections of society slowly began to experience the excitement and novelty of travelling by train.

Wider horizons

Before the Industrial Revolution, most people worked in the village or town where they were born. Train travel increased opportunities because people could travel easily to take up a wider variety of jobs in different parts of the country. This also gave them the chance to learn new skills and find out about a different way of life.

Finally, railway construction itself generated many new kinds of employment. Although the labourers who maintained the tracks were poorly paid, getting a job as a skilled railway engineer was highly prized as it meant a good salary and prospects.

3 Reading

Now read the article above about early train travel. Are any of the ideas you thought of here?

4 Making notes

Make very brief notes on the text using the headings and bullet points below.

Fears of effects on rural life

- _____
- _____
- _____
- _____

Safety improvements

- _____
- _____
- _____

Impact on employment

- _____
- _____
- _____

5 Post-reading task

1   What, in your view, was the **main** benefit of the train to people in the nineteenth century and what was the **main** disadvantage?

2 Imagine that you are living about 150 years ago. What factual things could you point out to someone who is afraid of travelling by train?

Example: *There is no evidence that travelling by train causes heart attacks.*

3 Some people today are afraid of flying. Do you think it would help them to know how people used to feel about train travel?

6 Language study: Logical reasoning

A Study these sentences from the article again with a partner. Underline the words you think are used to express reasoning.

When an accident happened, it made front-page news because people were eager to have their suspicions confirmed. As a result, people's fears of travelling by train grew even more intense.

The writer uses *because* to express reason and *as a result* to express consequence. Can you replace *because* and *as a result* with words of similar meaning? Use commas if necessary.

B Here is another sentence from the text. Study it carefully and underline the words that express a logical connection. Notice where commas are used.

If a problem was found, then the train was immobilised until it was judged to be safe.

C Which word in the following sentence is an alternative to *In addition*?

Furthermore, farmers opposed the idea of railways cutting through their farmland, as they believed that the smoke and steam would destroy crops and scare their animals.

7 Completing a text

Read this extract from a newspaper published in 1865 about the problems experienced by train passengers. With a partner, try to fill the gaps with words expressing reasoning and logical connection.

Many of our readers are increasingly concerned about those passengers who, with no apology, bring live chickens, ducks and even lambs with them on train journeys, _____ these animals seriously disturb the comfort of others on the journey. _____, there have been reports of animals escaping from the compartment and getting out onto the track, which compromises everyone's safety.

Due to the disruption caused by the selfishness of others, the number of passenger complaints has risen and the number of train tickets sold has fallen significantly, especially on market days.

_____, train travel is likely to become even more expensive in future _____ the train companies cannot afford to operate trains at low capacity.

8 Spelling and pronunciation: The letter *g*

The letter *g* is a hard sound in words like *glass*, *great* and *peg*. The phonetic symbol is /g/.

gu in words like *guard* and *guest* is also pronounced /g/. (In a few words, like *extinguish*, *gu* is pronounced /gw/.)

Notice how *g* is pronounced in *Egypt*, *giant* and *generous*. This is sometimes called 'soft g' and the phonetic symbol is /dʒ/. What other words do you know that have this sound?

Recognition 🔊

Many of the words in the following list are taken from the information you have read. Listen to the words on the recording. Mark them *g* if you think the *g* sound is hard, pronounced /g/. Mark them *s* if the *g* sound is soft, pronounced /dʒ/.

1	engineer	**5**	passengers	**9**	regulations
2	rigorously	**6**	guarantee	**10**	registered
3	challenge	**7**	oxygen	**11**	significant
4	figure	**8**	apology	**12**	ageing

Practice

/g/ and /dʒ/ are voiced sounds. If you place your fingers on the spot where your vocal cords are and say the sounds, you will feel your vocal cords vibrate. Practise saying the words in the list clearly to your partner. Does he/she think you are pronouncing the words correctly?

63

9 Spelling patterns

Did you notice how all the /dʒ/ sounds in exercise 8 were followed by the letters *e*, *i* or *y*? Look back at the word list and circle this spelling pattern for each soft-**g** word.

But hard **g** sounds are also sometimes followed by *e* or *i*, as in the words *get*, *tiger* and *girl*.

10 Vocabulary

Choose a word from the list in exercise 8 to match each of the following sentences.

1 She should offer one for breaking your vase.
2 We breathe this gas.
3 He or she is trained to repair machines.
4 The people who pay to travel on a plane, train or boat.
5 It's worthwhile but sometimes difficult too.
6 To promise that something will happen.
7 A word with a similar meaning to 'rules'.
8 Another word for 'number'.
9 The aircraft should be checked in this way if a fault is suspected.

What do you notice about the sounds of the words in 1–5 and 6–9?

11 Odd word out

Circle the odd word out in each list. Can you say why it is different?

A hygienic general vegetable gymnasium surgeon privilege changeable regard manager encourage

B grateful vague magazine guard Portuguese pigeon dialogue angry catalogue guilt guess

12 Look, say, cover, write, check

The following words can be problematic to spell. Read them first and check that you understand the meaning of each one. Then use the 'look, say, cover, write, check' method to learn to spell them correctly. (See 1. 1 What is happiness? exercise 6)

When you feel you have learned them properly, ask your partner to test you. All the words are taken from previous exercises.

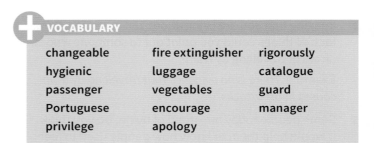

VOCABULARY		
changeable	fire extinguisher	rigorously
hygienic	luggage	catalogue
passenger	vegetables	guard
Portuguese	encourage	manager
privilege	apology	

Choose six of the words and put each one into a sentence to show its meaning.

13 Before you listen

What form of transport, if any, do you use to

- get to school or college?
- go shopping?
- visit friends?
- go to places of entertainment?

How satisfied do you feel with the forms of transport you use? Is there any form of transport you would prefer? Try to explain your views.

Vocabulary check

Before you listen, make sure you know the meaning of these words and expressions.

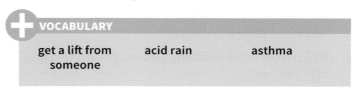

VOCABULARY		
get a lift from someone	acid rain	asthma

14 Listening for gist 🔊

You are going to listen to a discussion between two friends, Paolo and Linda, on the results of a survey. The survey was carried out to determine patterns of car usage by pupils in their school. Listen to the discussion first for general meaning.

15 Listening and note taking 🔊

Now listen again and try to complete these notes.

1 Average weekly number of car journeys: _____.

2 5% make more than _____.

3 _____ admitted using a car when it was not necessary.

4 The school:

   a _____.

   b has a train station only 5 minutes away.

5 Coming to school by train or bus is:

   a too expensive.

   b _____ (homes aren't near a bus stop or train station).

6 Parents' opinions of roads for walking or cycling: _____.

7 Reasons for not wanting own car in future:

   a effect on the environment.

   b _____.

8 When _____ they try to persuade them to get a small, fuel-efficient type.

16 Post-listening discussion

How do the results of the survey compare with your personal usage of the car?

Do you agree with Paolo and Linda that we should restrict car usage and use other forms of transport? How feasible would that be for you and your family? Share your ideas with your group.

17 Euphemisms

Paolo says pupils prefer to get lifts instead of walking. He comments that the reason is 'just laziness'. This is a very direct statement. If he were telling the school the results of the survey, he would probably avoid this remark because he could cause offence. He might prefer to use a euphemism like 'pupils prefer to take a relaxed approach to transport'.

Matching

Match the common euphemisms in italics with their meanings.

1 Her cardigan *had seen better days*.

2 I need the *bathroom*.

3 Discounts for *senior citizens*.

4 When is *the happy event*?

5 He's *careful* with his money.

6 The house *is in need of some modernisation*.

7 She's *looking the worse for wear*.

8 My grandfather has *passed away*.

A requires repairs and decoration

B toilet

C died

D very tired, dishevelled

E old people

F the birth

G mean, not generous

H was shabby, perhaps had holes in it

18 Vocabulary: Ways of walking

There are different ways of walking and different words for describing them. With a partner, match the styles of walking with the definitions.

1 limp   A to walk in a relaxed way, for pleasure

2 stumble   B to walk slowly with heavy steps, as if tired

3 stagger   C to walk as if your foot or leg hurts

65

4	stroll	**D**	to hit your foot against something and nearly fall
5	stride	**E**	to walk in an unbalanced way, as if you are going to fall
6	plod	**F**	to walk quite fast with long steps

19 Asking for a favour

Study this dialogue.

Joe: Dad, could you do me a favour? Would you mind giving me a lift to the sports hall? I've got a basketball game.
Dad: When do you want to go?
Joe: In about half an hour.
Dad: Oh, all right.
Joe: Thanks, Dad. Are you sure it's not too much trouble?
Dad: No, I need to go out anyway.
Joe: Well, thanks a lot. That's nice of you.

Asking for a favour

Could you do me a favour?
Can I ask you something?
Would you mind giving me a lift?
Could you please …?

Checking

Are you sure it's not too much trouble?
Are you sure it's all right with you?
Are you sure it's not too inconvenient?
Are you certain it's not too much bother?
I hope it doesn't put you out.
Are you sure it's OK? I don't want to be a nuisance.

Expressing thanks

Thanks, that's nice of you.
Thanks a lot. That really helps me out.
Thanks very much. I really appreciate it.

Practice

Take turns asking for a favour in the following situations. Work in pairs. Try to sound a little tentative.

1 You need a lift to the cinema.
2 You need to be picked up from a party.
3 You need someone to post a letter for you.
4 You need someone to take a parcel round to a friend's house.
5 You need to borrow a tennis racket.
6 You need someone to pick up your jacket from the dry cleaner's.

4.2 Nature under threat

20 Pre-reading discussion

Do you own a bicycle? How often do you cycle and where do you usually go to? If you do not own a bicycle, would you like one?

In pairs, work out the advantages and disadvantages of cycling as a form of transport. When you have finished, compare your ideas with those of other pairs and add any new points to your list.

Advantages

It doesn't pollute the environment.

_____

_____

_____

_____

_____

_____

Disadvantages

You can get knocked off and hurt.

_____

_____

_____

_____

_____

21 Predicting content

You are going to read a leaflet asking people to join a sponsored cycle ride. ('Sponsored' means that the people taking part will have asked 'sponsors' to donate money to charity.)

Look at the title of the leaflet and the pictures. What kind of people do you think will join the ride? What do you think the cycle route will be like?

22 Reading for gist

Skim-read the leaflet quickly to get a general idea of the content. There are three reasons the cycle ride is being held. What are they?

1 _____

_____

2 _____

_____

3 _____

_____

Bike to the Future

Registration is now open for Bike to the Future – Friends of the Earth's annual sponsored cycle ride. So shake off those winter blues and sign up early 5 for what promises to be another great May day out in the countryside!

Bike to the Future is the most popular event in Friends of the Earth's calendar. Year after year, people have 10 written in to tell us how much they've enjoyed the route, the warm and friendly atmosphere, and the high spirits of their fellow cyclists!

This year, Bike to the Future will 15 start near Hampton Court and take its riders through beautiful countryside to Eton. As ever, its gentle and undemanding 30 miles will be lined with refreshment stops, entertainment 20 and lots of surprises. Bike to the Future is first and foremost a fun day out, but there's a serious message too. The route will highlight the threats to the surrounding area from new road schemes – passing through Chobham Common, which is affected by plans to widen the M3, and areas close to where sections of the M25 and M4 are also currently marked out for widening.

These are just a few reminders of the continuing threats to our health and environment from increased traffic and pollution due to unnecessary road schemes. The funds raised from Bike to the Future will help sustain our campaign to halt unnecessary road schemes in favour of transport options which encourage less, rather than more, travel by road.

So help us get there! Register now for Bike to the Future to give yourself time to sign up as many sponsors as you can.

All you need is a bike

The route and all the practical details are taken care of by experts. It will be easy to get to the start and home again – British Rail is laying on special trains to take you and your bike to the start, and get you back to London from the finish. Marshals will guide you on the route, and first aid will be available for you and your bike if needed.

Good reasons to get sponsored

Once you've sent us your entry form and fee, we'll send you an official sponsorship form so you can start signing up your friends and workmates. Whether you cycle on your own or in a team, there are loads of prizes for reaching fundraising targets, including Bike to the Future badges and T-shirts, cycle accessories and even mountain bikes!

There are also prizes for your sponsors. Anyone who sponsors you for £5.00 or more will automatically be entered in a prize draw.

The more the merrier

You're welcome to register on your own. However, it can be more fun in a group – and if you get together a team of ten or more, we'll give you a free Bike to the Future T-shirt. Your team-mates will also be able to order T-shirts at half price.

The ride ends within sight of Windsor Castle in the village of Eton.

23 True/false comprehension

Are these statements about the cycle ride true or false? Try to spot answers in the text.

1 This is the first time the sponsored cycle ride has been held.
2 The route will be strenuous.
3 The day is primarily for enjoyment.
4 The cycle ride celebrates the victory over plans to develop Chobham Common.
5 Participants will help plan the route.
6 Extra trains to and from London will be provided.
7 Medical help will be available.
8 Prizes are only available to the teams.
9 Participants in teams of ten or more get a discount on the T-shirts.
10 The ride finishes at Chobham Common.

24 Post-reading discussion

Have you ever taken part in a sponsored charity event, e.g. a swim, a dance or a walk? Tell your partner what it was like.

25 Reordering an article

The following article in a school magazine puts forward the pros and cons of cycling.

Try to reorder it so that it is in a logical sequence. How do the words and phrases in italics link the text together?

The pros and cons of cycling

a Cycling at night is *particularly dangerous*, especially along dark country roads as a motorist may not see you until it is too late.
b *Above all*, cycling is very cheap.
c Second-hand bikes are *not expensive* and you can learn to carry out simple repairs yourself.

d *Although* cycling has many advantages, there are some *drawbacks* too.

e *In the first place,* owning a bike frees you from dependence on your parents to take you to places.

f Cycling is an enjoyable, efficient and liberating mode of transport.

g Cycling can be *dangerous* on busy roads and you can be seriously hurt if you are knocked off your bike by a motorist.

h *In addition,* attending a cycling proficiency training scheme enables you to cycle more safely and prepares you for tricky cycling conditions.

i *On balance, however,* I feel that the personal enjoyment and freedom you get from cycling outweigh the disadvantages.

j Many of the dangers of cycling *can be eliminated* if you take sensible precautions such as using lights at night and wearing reflector strips.

k *Furthermore,* many roads are polluted by traffic fumes which makes cycling unpleasant and perhaps even unhealthy.

l It *also* removes the frustrations of hanging around waiting for a bus to turn up.

26 What makes a good argument essay?

A When you have reordered the article correctly, read it through or write it out in full to get a feeling of how the text flows.

B The text above could be described as 'even-handed'. Why, do you think?

C The last paragraph shows the writer's point of view 'on balance'. Is this a good way of rounding off an argument? Why/Why not?

D A good argument essay needs to be convincing. This means it should help the reader understand the issues. It should present strong, believable arguments. (Whether or not the reader changes his/her mind about the topic in the end is irrelevant.) Do you think the article 'The pros and cons of cycling' achieves this? Try to explain how you feel to your group.

27 Presenting contrasting ideas in the same paragraph

'The pros and cons of cycling' devotes separate paragraphs to the advantages and disadvantages of cycling. It then sums up at the end. An alternative to this approach is to consider contrasting ideas in the same paragraph.

The following extract comes from a composition about whether cycle helmets should be made compulsory. Circle the word that contrasts one idea with its opposite.

I recognise that a feeling of freedom is part of the pleasure of cycling. Nevertheless, in my opinion, it is essential that cyclists are made aware of the dangers of not wearing a helmet.

Now rewrite the extract using a different linking word or phrase. Choose from: *although, however, but, yet, in spite of*. Make changes to the extract if you think it is necessary.

28 Presenting more contrasting ideas

Study these incomplete sentences from argument essays. Notice the use of a contrast word in each one. Then try to complete each sentence in an appropriate way.

1 Car accidents continue to increase *despite*

2 The government has launched a big safety campaign to encourage cyclists to take a cycling test. *Nevertheless,*

3 A new airport is planned for our area *in spite of*

4 I have always been a keen supporter of the private car. *However,*

5 It seems unfair to stop cars going into the town centre, *yet*

6 A good train service would help to reduce our carbon footprint. *On the other hand,*

7 Cycling is not encouraged in the town *although*

8 People are frightened of travelling by plane *even though*

9 The railway companies tell us train journeys are quick and comfortable *but*

10 I would always travel by sea rather than by air *despite*

29 Language study: Linking words

Linking words have a variety of functions in an argument essay. They can be used to express opinion, show contrast, express consequence, give reasons, etc.

Working in pairs, try to add words or expressions under each of the following headings. Then compare your ideas with the rest of the group.

Listing	Addition
First of all	*also*
_____	_____
_____	_____

Contrast	Reasoning
but	*because*
_____	_____
_____	_____
Opinion	Emphasis
We think	*Above all*
_____	_____
_____	_____
Consequence	Summing up
so	*On balance*
_____	_____
_____	_____

30 Brainstorming

Brainstorming is a group work activity you'll be using regularly to help spark off ideas on a topic. It's important because you can't write a convincing argument unless you have strong ideas to work with. Work in small groups to brainstorm ideas about the following topic.

Imagine that the local council is considering cutting down a small wood near a shopping centre to make a car park for the convenience of shoppers. Write down points for and against the idea. Take five minutes to do this.

Should Eaves Wood be cut down to provide a car park for shoppers?

POINTS FOR   POINTS AGAINST

_____   _____

_____   _____

31 Text completion

A local student, Roland Chang, heard about the proposal to cut down the wood. He felt very strongly about it so he wrote to his local newspaper. Study his letter carefully with a partner. Then try to complete each gap with appropriate linking words from the choices given.

1 However / On the other hand / In my opinion / Although / Because

2 In addition / In the first place / Nevertheless / Yet / But

3 on the contrary / without doubt / also / in my view / nevertheless

4 On the other hand / At the beginning / Furthermore / Also / Finally

5 secondly / not at all / because / however / such as

6 for example / yet / thirdly / even though / so

7 In addition / Despite / Therefore / Consequently / However

8 also / but / thirdly / last but not least / on the other hand

9 In the end / In my opinion / On the contrary / For instance / Furthermore

10 Alternatively / For example / After all / In fact / On the other hand

---

Dear Editor,

I was dismayed when I heard of the proposals to cut down Eaves Wood to make a car park for shoppers. **(1)** _____ I agree that the town is short of car parks, this solution would be insensitive and improper.

(2) _____, the wood is an area of natural beauty. There are many ancient trees of an unusual kind. I often go there for a picnic or just to relax at weekends. The wood is **(3)** _____ a vital habitat for birds, animals and insects. If the trees were cut down, many species would be lost.

(4) _____, the wood is right in the centre of a heavily polluted part of town. The trees help to make the air cleaner **(5)** _____ they trap dust, smoke and fume particles in their branches and leaves. The council says it is worried about global warming, **(6)** _____ trees help reduce the build-up of gases that contribute to global warming because they feed on carbon dioxide emissions.
(7) _____, that area **(8)** _____ suffers from high noise levels from passing lorries and the railway line. The trees help reduce the noise levels and have a beneficial effect on the whole environment.

(9) _____, cutting down the wood would be stupid, greedy and pointless. A car park may well attract shoppers to the town and increase the shopkeepers' trade. **(10)** _____, a unique and beautiful part of our heritage would be destroyed. I would be very interested in hearing what your other readers think.

Yours faithfully,

Roland Chang

32 Discussion

Do you think the letter is too formal, too informal or about right? Try to explain why.

How does Roland show an awareness of his audience in the letter?

Obviously, Roland is opposed to the council's plans. How convincing do you think his argument is? Try to mention particular examples to justify your opinion.

33 Words often confused

These words, some of which are taken from Roland's letter, are often confused. Complete each sentence with the correct alternative.

1 council/counsel

a The _____ meets once a month.

b The doctor may also _____ you about your personal problems.

2 affect/effect

a The medicine didn't have any _____ on my cold.

b The new rules _____ all aircraft over 30 years old.

3 there/they're/their

a _____ are plenty of pegs for the children's coats and lockers for _____ shoes.

b They said if _____ going to be late they will let us know.

4 lose/loose

a You must be careful not to _____ your passport.

b Since I lost weight, my trousers have been too _____.

5 alternate/alternative

a I have to work on _____ weekends.

b The last bus had gone so walking home was the only _____.

6 lightning/lightening

a The house was struck by _____.

b The sun came up, gradually _____ the sky.

7 practice/practise

a He tries to _____ the guitar once a day.

b We have music _____ on Tuesdays.

8 past/passed

a Have you seen Henryk in the _____ few days? Yes, I _____ him in the street on Saturday.

b Luckily, we all _____ our maths test.

4.3 A new motorway for Rosville?

34 Pre-reading discussion

Study the photographs and try to describe them. How do you think the people in the cars are feeling? What causes traffic jams to build up on main roads and motorways? Is there any way of preventing them?

Brainstorming

Divide into two groups. Group A should try to list all the advantages of motorways. Group B should aim to list all the disadvantages.

When you have finished compare your ideas. Can you add any new ideas between you?

Motorways – for and against

Advantages   Disadvantages

_____   _____

_____   _____

_____   _____

71

35 Reading an example text

Rosville's council is supporting government plans to build a new motorway. This will link Rosville to the capital and to some other large cities. Do you think this will be a good development for Rosville? Who is likely to benefit? Who might be against the idea? Try to think of reasons for your opinions.

Now scan the text quickly. Are any of the points you thought of in the discussion noted here?

Dear Editor,

We are delighted that a new motorway is being planned for Rosville because it will bring so many benefits to the town.

In the first place, Rosville has suffered from the recession and many young people are unemployed after leaving school. The motorway will bring a much-needed boost to business, as communications will be faster, cheaper and more efficient. Consequently, the businesses we already have will find life easier, new companies will be attracted to Rosville and there will be more jobs for everyone.

Furthermore, we know a large number of people commute daily to the city. The present winding road is tiring, time-wasting and, above all, dangerous. The new scheme will not only mean a big reduction in time spent commuting, it will also provide a much safer and more relaxing journey. We don't think anyone ever feels nostalgic about traffic jams!

Many readers might be worried about pollution from increased traffic. On the contrary, pollution will actually decrease as so many new trees, especially chosen for their ability to absorb car fumes, will be planted.

Finally, the new motorway will also serve as a bypass for the large lorries that now go through Rosville town centre.

There is no doubt that the motorway will really put Rosville on the map. If we want a bright future for ourselves and our children, we should all support it.

Yours faithfully,
The Rosville Business Group

36 Comprehension check

1   Where does the text in exercise 35 come from?
2   What are the writer's main points in favour of a new motorway?
3   How convincing do you find the argument? Give some reasons.

Vocabulary

Here are some definitions of words in the letter. Try to find the words and underline them.

a   a bad period in the country's economy
b   something which helps and encourages
c   routes linking one place to another
d   to travel between home and work every day
e   wishing something in the past would return
f   a main road built to avoid a town

37 Analysing the text

Work in pairs to answer these questions. They will help you analyse the way the model argument is structured.

1   Underline the word in the opening paragraph which expresses emotion. Which word introduces a reason for the feeling? Underline it. An opening paragraph should grab attention. Does this paragraph do that?
2   Which words are used in paragraph 3 for emphasis?
3   Paragraph 4 considers an opposing point of view. What is it? Which phrase is used to introduce a contrasting opinion?
4   *Finally* is used at the start of paragraph 5. Why?
5   The last paragraph of an argument essay should not 'tail off', leaving the reader wondering what you really think. It should be firm and decisive. How does the final paragraph of this letter sound?

38 Putting forward an opposing viewpoint

The Rosville Nature Society held a meeting to discuss the letter from the Rosville Business Group that appeared in the local newspaper. Look at the draft letter they wrote in reply. Read the points carefully and make sure you understand each one.

Are any of the points similar to the list of disadvantages of motorways you made earlier?

DRAFT LETTER

Dear Editor, We were horrified to hear of the plans for a new motorway for Rosville and we are sure our feelings are shared by many of your readers. We believe the scheme would destroy the environment and cause untold damage to wildlife. The motorway itself will cost a great deal of money to build. It would be better to use this money to help local businesses by improving the rail network. Commuters to the city would benefit from a better train service. The idea that the motorway will be more efficient is completely unfounded. The new road will soon attract extra traffic and eventually become heavily congested. The suggestion that planting trees alongside the motorway will eliminate pollution is ludicrous. Trees can help. They cannot make up for the destruction of wildflowers and wildlife. Many of us cycle or walk across the present road to get to school or work. The new motorway which replaces the old road will split the area into two, making it impossible to get to the other side on foot or by bicycle. Please, people of Rosville, don't stand by and watch your environment being destroyed. We urge you to support the Rosville Nature Society campaign by writing to your local councillor.

Yours faithfully,
The Rosville Nature Society

39 Redrafting

Redraft the letter so that it flows more smoothly. Remember, you will need linking words to show connection or contrast between ideas. Add words to express personal opinion or emphasis where you think it is appropriate. Finally, make sure you use paragraphs.

When you have finished, show your work to a partner. Does he/she agree that your letter now flows more smoothly, has an appropriately formal tone and sounds more persuasive?

40 Relating to your target audience

Your letter or article should reflect the interest of those who are going to read it. These people are called your 'target audience'.

Study the extracts A–E below. Decide with a partner whether each extract comes from:

- a school magazine
- a letter to a local newspaper
- a letter to a magazine
- a personal letter
- a formal letter.

Decide whether the target audience in each case is:

- school pupils
- elderly people
- the general public
- an individual the writer has not met
- a friend.

A

I think that's all for now about the good time we had at the party. Don't feel too left out! See you soon.

Love,

Tom

B

Most of us already have problems getting to school on time. The proposed cuts to the bus service will make things even worse. I suggest we have an urgent meeting to discuss a plan of action in the Common Room next Wednesday lunchtime.

C

> *I am writing to express my concern about your suggestion printed in yesterday's* **Evening News** *that the greenhouse effect has no scientific basis. Like many of the readers of this newspaper, I have no doubt that the greenhouse effect is a reality that is becoming steadily worse.*

D

> *Most people of our age will welcome the news, reported in your article 'Fair Dues At Last', that senior citizens will be able to travel free of charge at weekends.*

E

> *I would be grateful if you could contact me to discuss a mutually convenient time to meet.*

41 Writing a letter from outline notes

In your neighbourhood, there is a large open area called Antalya Place which is used by young people for ball games. Your council are proposing to dig up the area and plant a flower garden with benches for elderly people. Trees will be planted too. No ball games will be allowed.

Write a letter to the local newspaper giving your views. You should try to be even-handed in your discussion of the issues. However, your final paragraph should show clearly whether or not you are in favour of the proposal. Use the following outline to guide you.

Paragraph one: introduction

Points in favour

1 Flower garden attractive. Would brighten up area. Flowers and plants provide a habitat for a wide variety of insect life.

2 Old people lonely. Have no meeting place. Garden would provide focal point for meeting each other.

3 Trees welcome. Provide shade. Reduce pollution and noise levels. Provide protection against wind.

Points against

1 Young people need opportunity to practise ball games. Most live in flats – no gardens or other space nearby.

2 Local football and netball teams are winning matches. Will be less successful if cannot practise. Morale and team confidence will sink.

3 Young people meet friends, have picnics, watch matches, enjoy themselves here. Without this area, boredom and resentment might set in. Vandalism might be a problem.

Final paragraph

Sum up and state opinions firmly.

42 Understanding a typical exam-style stimulus

An argument essay question will often provide a stimulus will in the form of comments. Study this example. What does the question ask you to do?

There are proposals to develop a river near your home. A marina would be built, and tourists would be encouraged to come and use the river for boating and fishing. Write an article for the school magazine saying what you think of this idea.

Here are some comments from local people. You can use these for ideas, or use ideas of your own.

'The development will create jobs which we need.'

'Engine oil and litter from boats will pollute the water.'

'The plants which grow in the water help to absorb pollution. Many of them will die if the river becomes developed.'

'The river is in a beautiful, relaxing setting. It's only right to encourage more people to benefit from the tranquillity of the area.'

'Local people use the plants in the river for raw material for making things, such as reeds for making baskets. We will lose a source of raw material if the river is developed.'

'If too much fishing goes on, the river will become over-fished and many species will die out, disrupting the sensitive ecology of the river.'

'Our area needs to become more modern and to progress. Developing the river will help us achieve this aim.'

43 Redrafting an exam-style answer

With a partner, study the answer below to the exam-style question in exercise 42. What do you think are the strengths of the answer? What do you feel are the weaknesses? Write them down.

I think it is a good idea to develop the river because it will create jobs which we need in our area. Moreover, the river is set in a beautiful, relaxing part of the countryside. It is only right to encourage more people to benefit from the tranquillity of the area. Our area needs to become more modern and to progress. Developing the river will help us achieve this aim. On the other hand, engine oil and litter from boats will pollute the water. The plants which grow in the water help to absorb pollution. Many of them will die if the river becomes developed. Local people use the plants in the river for raw material. We will lose a source of raw material if the river is developed. If too much fishing goes on, the river will become over-fished and many species will die out, disrupting the ecological cycle. In my opinion, the river should be developed because there are more advantages than disadvantages in doing so.

Strengths

_____

_____

_____

Weaknesses

_____

_____

_____

Try to redraft the composition. Aim to develop a few points more fully, with more reasons and examples of your own. Remember to set out your writing clearly with paragraphing and logical connectors. The target audience is the readers of the school magazine, so try to link your answer in some way with their interests.

When you've finished, compare your version with a partner's. What are the main differences? Does he/she feel you have improved the original draft? How convincing is your argument and how well does it relate to the target audience?

4.4 Global warming

44 Vocabulary check

Complete the gaps in the paragraph with the following expressions. There is one more than you need. Do not use any expression more than once.

➕ VOCABULARY

climate change	greenhouse gases
carbon emissions	environmental pollution
global warming	carbon footprint

_____ means a continuing rise in the earth's average temperature. Many scientists think that this is the result of our production of _____, such as carbon dioxide, which become trapped and warm the earth's atmosphere.

A _____ measures the total greenhouse gas emissions caused by the activities of a person, group or country. Richer countries have a bigger carbon footprint per person.

There are fears that global warming is causing _____ and so many governments are aiming to reduce their _____.

45 Pre-reading discussion

A Read the following statements about climate change. One of them is incorrect. Discuss the ideas with a partner and cross out the incorrect statement.

1 Burning fossil fuels such as oil, coal and gas produces greenhouse gases, which may contribute to climate change.

2 Wind, waves and sunlight are all renewable sources of energy. These can help reduce climate change.

3 Nuclear energy is radioactive and produces greenhouse gases which cause climate change.

4 Climate change has caused unpredictable global weather patterns including floods, severe winters, drought and desertification.

INTERNATIONAL OVERVIEW

The pie chart shows the carbon footprint of a typical individual living in a More Economically Developed Country (MEDC).

1 Which activity has the greatest carbon footprint and which has the smallest?

2 Which of the following statements about the chart are true? Give those a tick.

a Activities at home which use electricity contribute almost one-eighth to the carbon footprint.

b Private transport contributes 7 per cent more than public transport to the carbon footprint.

c Recreation and leisure activities contribute less to the carbon footprint than holiday flights.

d House furnishings and buildings contribute just under 10% to the carbon footprint.

As a country develops, its carbon footprint increases. Can you find out the size of the carbon footprint of your country?

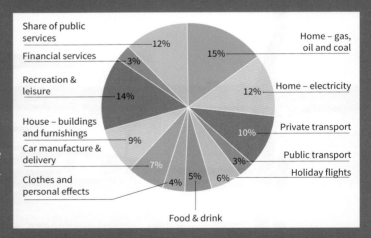

B How might the way of life in your country change if the climate became much warmer and drier, or much wetter and colder? Discuss the possible benefits and disadvantages.

C Here are some things students are doing to help reduce climate change. Which one idea is not sensible? Cross it out.

1 If it is cold, I put on a jumper rather than turn up the heating.

2 We insulate our hot water pipes to keep them warm and more efficient.

3 We're installing air conditioning in more rooms in our house, to keep it at an even temperature.

4 We changed our light bulbs to the energy-efficient type.

5 We are going to put solar panels on our roof so we can use the sun's energy for light and heating.

Have you or your family made any similar changes to help the environment? Share your ideas in your groups.

46 Reading for gist

Deepak has written an article for his school magazine on climate change. Before you read, make sure you know the meaning of these words.

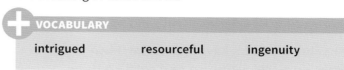

VOCABULARY

intrigued	resourceful	ingenuity

Now read the text on the following page for general understanding.

47 Comprehension check

1 What has Deepak learned about his lifestyle choices?

2 How have farmers in the Andes survived, despite more severe winters? Give **two** details.

3 Why are Bangladeshi farmers using wooden rafts?

4 Why is the future of the rice growers more secure?

5 What have the club members decided to do to help the environment?

6 What does Deepak invite the magazine readers to do?

48 Tone and register

The tone and register of this article are more informal than in the articles about the new motorway for Rosville (exercises 35 and 38). Underline any aspects of Deepak's writing which help create this impression. Do you think the tone and register he uses are appropriate for his audience? Why/Why not?

Although I don't usually write to the school magazine, I have recently joined a school club, Friends of the Planet. I thought you might be intrigued to know more about what we do.

The club members have been researching facts on global warming and putting them on our school blog. Do you know that by flying in a plane for an hour we produce the same carbon emissions as a Bangladeshi citizen produces in a whole year? Earlier this year, my whole family flew to America for a wedding so we definitely increased our carbon footprint. Being in the club has made me think more about the environmental impact of our lifestyle choices.

We have found out lots of other important things at the club too, such as ways people in different parts of the world are coping with climate change.

In the Andes in Peru, for example, farmers have had to cope with much more severe winters. The bitterly cold weather had been killing the alpaca, a domesticated animal which provides milk, cheese, meat and wool. The farmers could have given up, but they learned how to build strong shelters for the animals and developed veterinary skills. As a result, the communities are surviving and are even more resourceful than before.

In another part of the world, Bangladeshi farmers have found their own ways to overcome a problem of a different sort: widespread flooding. Using wooden rafts, the farmers developed vegetable gardens which float on water. Isn't that an amazing idea? And it works!

Finally, I want to tell you about Sri Lanka. Sea levels around the coast are rising due to climate change and, consequently, the rice paddies were being contaminated by salt. It was extremely worrying because rice is the farmers' main crop. However, they

experimented with different types of rice and found a strain of rice which can flourish in salty water! How is that for ingenuity!

In the club, we decided that, if other people can make changes, so can we. Therefore we are going to make one small change every day to our carbon footprint. We will be doing things like using our bikes, recycling rubbish and turning off electrical appliances when we leave the room. It might not sound like much, but we think it will eventually make a real difference.

Would you like to reduce your carbon footprint? Then join us at the club to find out how! We meet on Thursday lunchtime in Room 12. See you there!

✴ GRAMMAR SPOTLIGHT

The future

A We use **will** + the infinitive of a verb (without 'to') to talk about events in the future:

*Bike to the Future **will start** near Hampton Court.*

*The route **will highlight** the threats to the surrounding area.*

Can you find another example of *will* + verb in the fourth paragraph of the text in exercise 22?

B We use **will** + **be** in passive future sentences:

*Anyone who sponsors you for $5.00 or more **will** automatically **be entered** in a prize draw.*

C The short forms **I'll** and **we'll** are common in informal English:

***We'll send** you an official sponsorship form.*

Can you find another example in the penultimate paragraph of the text in exercise 22?

D We use **going to** + verb to talk about things we intend to do:

*We are **going to put** solar panels on our roof.*

Can you find another example of *going to* + verb in paragraph 7 of the letter in exercise 46?

EXAM-STYLE QUESTIONS

Speaking

1 Climate change

Many experts believe climate change may cause serious problems such as unpredictable weather patterns leading to storms, drought or flooding. Discuss this topic with the assessor.

You may wish to use the following ideas to help develop the conversation:

- what you like or dislike about the climate where you live
- the challenges and problems your country might face if the climate became much hotter, colder or wetter
- what people themselves can do to reduce climate change
- what governments can do to reduce problems such as drought or flooding
- whether there may be political conflicts in future over access to fresh water, rather than resources such as oil.

You are free to consider any other related ideas of your own. You are not allowed to make any written notes.

2 City living

We now know more about how carbon dioxide emissions can damage our planet. This has an implication for the way we live in cities. Discuss this topic with the assessor.

You may wish to use the following ideas to help develop the conversation:

- the idea that cities should be planned so that people can avoid motor transport and cycle or walk to most places
- whether electric cars, water taxis and free cycle hire should be encouraged
- the suggestion that car drivers should be banned from cities on certain days or pay a charge for entering the city
- the idea that one day each week people should not attend school or work, but use modern technology to work or study from home
- the view that large numbers of people moving to live in cities leads to more problems than benefits.

Writing

1   There are plans to build an airport near your town. Here are some comments from local newspaper readers on the topic.

'There will be many benefits for our economy.'
'A new airport will be disastrous for the environment.'

Write an email to your local newspaper outlining your views on the proposal. The comments above may give you some ideas but you should try to use some ideas of your own. You should write 150–200 words (or 100–150 words for Core level).

2   An article on the following topic appeared in your school magazine recently.

> Why should teenagers try to reduce their carbon footprint when new buildings, factories and roads cause so much pollution?

Here are some comments from the magazine readers on the topic.

'Making a few personal changes in lifestyle now will make a big change in the long term.'
'The future of our country depends on new developments.'

Write an article for your school magazine outlining your views. The comments above may give you some ideas but you should try to use some ideas of your own. Your article should be 150–200 words long (or 100–150 words for Core level).

3   There is a proposal in your country to raise the legal age for learning to drive a car by three years. Here are some comments from your friends on the idea.

'Most car accidents are caused by young people.'
'Learning to drive early is essential for independence.'

Write an article for the school magazine giving your views. The comments above may give you some ideas but you should try to use some ideas of your own. Your article should be 150–200 words long (or 100–150 words for Core level).

Form-filling

Abdul Latif is 16 years old and lives at 125 Arandene Road, Glasgow G2 7AW, Scotland. Abdul has been saving money for some time and has managed to buy a second-hand mountain bike. His parents had been reluctant to let him buy a bicycle and cycle to school as the roads are busy, and at the moment they take him by car. Matters are made worse because the school day starts and ends at the same time as the working day in a large block of offices nearby, so the traffic is particularly heavy at those times. This is unlikely to get better in future, as the offices are being extended. Abdul and his parents are not looking forward to the pollution and congestion this development is likely to bring.

Abdul's parents eventually agreed that he could buy a bicycle as long as he took part in his school's Advanced Cycling Training Scheme. He enjoyed the training scheme overall and passed the Advanced Cycling Test. The best part, in Abdul's view, was learning mountain biking techniques on local hillsides. His main worry currently is that there is nowhere safe at school to store bicycles, which means he is unlikely to cycle to school on a regular basis.

Abdul has decided to take part in his school's annual cycling mini-marathon on March 3rd to raise money for charity. His friend, Fergus MacSorley, who attends a different school but has passed his Advanced Cycling Test, would also like to take part. They have asked local factories and restaurants to sponsor them and have been very pleased by the amount of money they may be able to raise. Abdul and Fergus plan to leave home at 9.30 a.m. on March 3rd and join the route at the junction of Sandy Avenue and Canberra Road 20 minutes later.

Students have been asked to put forward their ideas about which charity to support. They have supported Sports Aid and Prem Baby Unit on previous occasions, and this time they would like to choose a different charity. Both Abdul and his friend are concerned about pollution, acid rain and the ozone layer. They would like to see the money given to a charity which campaigns on these issues.

Imagine you are Abdul and complete the form.

LOCH NEVIS HIGH SCHOOL CYCLING MINI-MARATHON
ENTRY FORM

SECTION A *(Please use block capitals for name and address.)*

Name: _____

Address: _____

_____

Have you passed the Advanced Cycling Test? *(Delete as necessary.)*
Yes / No

The cycling mini-marathon is open to anyone who holds the Advanced Cycling Certificate. If you have a friend or relative who would like to take part, please give their name in capitals.

_____

Please circle whichever is appropriate:
I can raise sponsorship from individuals / companies.

I / We will be joining the route at (*Please add time and place*):

_____

Below is a list of charities the school has supported in previous years. Please tick one charity you would like to support this year:

- [ ] **The Fellowship Foundation** for musically gifted children
- [ ] **Sports Aid** for the promotion of sport in deprived areas
- [ ] **Age Care** for elderly people in need
- [ ] **Mother Earth** for the conservation of the environment
- [ ] **Wildlife Concern** for endangered species
- [ ] **Prem Baby Unit** for premature babies
- [ ] **National Heritage Trust** for the preservation of ancient buildings
- [ ] **Allover Sanctuary** for aged horses and donkeys
- [ ] **Regeneration** for developing facilities in urban areas

---

SECTION B
Please write **one** sentence saying how the school could improve facilities for cyclists.

_____

_____

The school is proposing to change the times of the school day. We hope to begin at 8.15 a.m. instead of 8.45 a.m., and end at 3.45 p.m. instead of 4.15 p.m. Write **one** sentence saying whether you approve of this idea, giving your reasons.

_____

_____

_____

KEY ADVICE

1 **Writing an argument essay** requires the ability to think of relevant points in the first place. You can improve your understanding of controversial subjects by listening to or watching a current affairs programme once a week. Discuss matters of concern with your family or friends.

2 Take an active part in class discussions and school debates to practise thinking logically and giving your opinions orally. Even if you don't do this in English, it is still good practice. Offer to research a mini topic for your class and present your findings to everyone.

3 Improve your ability to write about controversial topics by reading newspaper and magazine articles which are opinion-based. Examine them carefully to see how the ideas are linked and expanded.

4 Have patience with your writing skills and be prepared to practise them. Show your written work to someone you trust and listen to their comments.

Exam techniques

5 Use a composition stimulus wisely. It is there to help you understand the rubric and to stimulate your own thoughts. Choose a few points and expand them; don't just copy them out. Give reasons of your own to support your views.

6 Express your ideas clearly and link them coherently with appropriate linking words. Remember to show some audience awareness if you can.

7 **Form-filling** exercises may not be difficult but still require careful attention to detail. Students are sometimes tempted to rush form-filling exercises, but it's important to be patient and careful as this is where many marks can be gained or lost.

- Read the scenario carefully and then take time to read through the entire form before starting to fill it in.

- Be careful that any information is copied out correctly from the text. Take special care with spelling names, addresses and any other factual terms of information. Details such as telephone numbers need to be exact.

- Take note of the instructions on the form. If CAPITAL LETTERS are required, for example, it is important that you use them.

- When you have completed the form, check it through quickly to make sure you have completed all the parts and have not misunderstood any of the questions.

UNIT FOCUS

In this unit you have learned to write a **formal argument composition**. You have learned to structure it so you write in favour, or against, or present both sides of a controversial topic.

You have listened to a discussion and taken notes on specific items of information.

You have read a detailed text and an advertising leaflet, and answered comprehension questions and made notes.

You have completed a **form based on a scenario.**

Unit 5:
Entertainment

5.1 Talking about entertainment

1 Introduction and discussion

A What kinds of entertainment do you like?
Using the list below, tell your partner about the
kinds of entertainment you most enjoy
and why.

- Listening to music – pop, jazz, classical, etc.
- Going to the cinema
- Accessing video-sharing sites, such as YouTube,
  on the internet
- Reading a novel for pleasure
- Playing computer games
- Going to a concert, gig or other live
  performance
- Going to the theatre
- Listening to the radio
- Watching TV or a film at home

B Have you ever been involved in entertaining people? For
example, have you ever performed on stage or helped
produce a play? Explain how you felt about it. If you've
never done this, would you like to? Why/Why not?

C Have you ever uploaded a video to a video-sharing
site such as YouTube? Tell your partner about it. If you
have never done this, would you like to?

D Would you like a job in the 'entertainment business'?
Explain what sort of work, if any, you would like. Why
would you like to do that kind of work?

2 Film vocabulary

As some exercises in this unit will require a working
knowledge of film vocabulary, this exercise will help you
be better prepared.

Complete the film review on the following page by choosing
from the words and phrases in the box to fill each space.

Gravity

Sandra Bullock deserves a(n) _____ for her superb _____ as Ryan Stone, the brave and intriguing _____ who undertakes her first mission on board the space shuttle *Explorer*. Still grieving for the loss of her young daughter, Ryan needs to prove to herself that life has a meaning and purpose. Her partner in outer space is Matt Kowalski, _____ George Clooney, who is entirely convincing in the _____ of the experienced veteran astronaut. The tense _____ becomes more frightening when Matt disappears and Ryan is left to cope entirely alone in a dark and mysterious universe.

The final _____, however, leaves no one doubting Ryan's courage or will to live. The other members of the _____ include Ed Harris as the voice of Mission Control, and Amy Warren as the voice of the captain of *Explorer*. They are both perfect as the calm but rather cold _____ typical of space missions. The film

is _____ Alfonso Cuarón, who may be remembered for other _____ hits such as 'Harry Potter and the Prisoner of Azkaban'. The _____ is a welcome addition to the growing science fiction fantasy _____ .

 **VOCABULARY**

box office	scene	performance
cast	plot	genre
played by	characters	film
heroine	directed by	
Oscar	role	

Make a note of unfamiliar words in your vocabulary book, with a translation if necessary.

3 Film quiz

What we look for when we watch a film is very personal. To help you understand more about your preferences and attitudes to films, complete this quiz.

What I want from a film

1 How do you choose a film you enjoy?
   a Recommendation from friends.
   b By looking at film reviews.
   c Turning up at the cinema and making a choice on the spot.
   d I've got my favourite actors – I'm prepared to see any film if they are acting in it.

2 The following comments are often made about films. How far do you agree with them? Mark each comment like this:

Agree strongly ✓✓   Agree ✓   Don't agree ✗

   a A lot of suspense should be an important ingredient.
   b Fast-moving action is essential.
   c The plot should contain many surprising twists.

d   It should be acted by big Hollywood stars.

e   It should have been made recently.

f   It should contain many emotional scenes.

g   It should make a serious point.

h   It should make you laugh.

i   It should contain many special effects.

3   Tick the statements you agree with.

a   There is too much violence in films today.

b   I prefer films which seem realistic and true to life rather than science fiction, horror or ghost movies.

c   My favourite films are based on true stories.

d   Seeing the film after you've read the book is usually disappointing.

e   Too many films come from Hollywood. We should be watching films that are made in our own country.

f   I'm sick of hearing about films in which evil people commit terrible crimes.

4   Pairwork: Asking for information

When you've finished the quiz, swap answers with a partner. Read your partner's answers carefully and pick out a few responses that interest you. Ask for more information in a friendly way, to show you're genuinely interested.

Examples:
May I ask why you think fast-moving action is essential / the plot should contain many surprising twists?

Would you mind telling me about your favourite actors / films that have made you laugh / films you've seen which are based on true stories?

What I'd like to know is why you prefer films that seem realistic and true to life / you don't like films about evil people.

Could you explain in more detail why you think suspense is an important ingredient / films should contain emotional scenes / films should make a serious point / more films should be made in your country?

Here are some more useful phrases for following up your partner's answers:

Something else I'd like to know is …

Can you give me an example?

What exactly do you mean by …?

Sorry, I don't quite understand why …

5   Following a model discussion about films 🔊

You are going to hear a model conversation in which two students tell their teacher about two films they have enjoyed.

You can follow the conversation while you listen. You will find the audioscript towards the end of the book, after Unit 10. Notice how the teacher asks for information and follows up the students' answers.

Later, when you want to write or talk about a film, you can look again at the conversation for examples of what you can say about a film.

6   Aspects of films

Which of these aspects of the films were mentioned by Carol and Sam? Check back in the conversation if you're not sure.

☐ characters
☐ genre
☐ hero
☐ message of the film
☐ plot
☐ reasons for recommending
☐ setting
☐ special effects
☐ suspense

You will need to include some or all of these aspects of films when speaking or writing about films later in the unit.

7   Tenses

Two main tenses are used by Sam and Carol: the present simple and the past simple.

Examples:
I was on the edge of my seat!
Dundee confronts an angry bull in the bush.

Why are these two different tenses used, do you think?

8 Comprehension

Read the following statements. Tick the points which reflect Sam's view of 'Crocodile Dundee'.

a He thought it was very realistic and believable.

b It contained some spectacular stunts.

c It was interesting but told him nothing memorable about life.

d He preferred the Australian location to the American location.

Tick the points which reflect Carol's view of 'The Hand that Rocks the Cradle'.

e She identified with the family in the film.

f She was on the edge of her seat from tension.

g She thought the ending was very emotional.

h It showed how we are exposed to evil, even in our everyday life.

i It made her realise how much power a nanny can have.

Do you feel that Sam and Carol's appraisals give you an understanding of the background to each film? Why do their reasons and examples manage to convey the qualities of each film?

9 Language study: *So … that* and *such … that*

These forms are often used to give emphasis when we say how we feel.

So … that … can be used with an adjective without a noun.

Example: *The film was so scary that I was on the edge of my seat.*

Such … that … is used with an adjective and a noun.

Example: *It's such an escapist film that I forgot all about my exams.*

In both cases you can leave out *that* if you wish to.

Practice

Join these pairs of sentences using *so … (that).*

1 I was keen to see the concert. I was prepared to pay a lot for a ticket.

2 She was disappointed not to get the role of princess. She cried all day.

Join these pairs of sentences with *such … (that).*

3 The film took a long time to make. The director ran out of money.

4 The story was fascinating. The film company wanted to make a film about it. (Begin: *It was …*)

10 Involving your listener

People can read film reviews for themselves, but when you talk about a film your listener is interested in **your** particular responses to a film.

Sentences like those below make your responses sound more personal and will engage your listener more effectively. Working with a partner, discuss how each of the sentences could end. Complete them appropriately, using a past tense.

Example: *The scene where the monster appears is so frightening that I jumped off my seat.*

1 The scene where the heroine dies is so sad that _____

2 It's such an intriguing plot that _____

3 The scene was so comical that _____

4 The scene where we find out the true identity of the murderer is so compelling that _____

5 The hero gives such a convincing performance as a blind man that _____

6 The gangster scenes are so violent that _____

5.2 Recommendations and reviews

11 Discussion

Using electronic devices and the internet to provide entertainment is such a normal part of many people's lives that it seems strange to remember that at one time all entertainment was live.

As technology progresses, it becomes less and less necessary for people to go out to places of entertainment and enjoy entertainment in the company of others. We can create playlists of our favourite music and listen at any time. Streaming means that films and music concerts can be enjoyed whenever we wish. As a result, cinema, theatre and concert audiences in some countries have fallen.

It has been claimed that these developments in entertainment have 'gone too far'. Some people think, for instance, that streaming is a poor substitute for the excitement of going out to the cinema or concert with friends and having fun together. They say we are creating a lonely and passive society. What do you think?

With a partner, try to think of the advantages, disadvantages and dangers of accessing entertainment through personal electronic devices and the internet. Add your ideas to those below.

Advantages
It's convenient.

_____

_____

Disadvantages
Films are less powerful watched on tablet computers.

_____

_____

Dangers
People can become more cut off and isolated.

_____

_____

12 Choosing a film

In pairs, read aloud this short dialogue between two friends, Astrid and Carmel. Astrid wants information which will help her decide which film she should watch with her little sister.

Astrid: I'd like to watch a film with Marta tonight. Have you seen any good ones lately?

Carmel: What about a historical romance like 'Jane Eyre'? It's set in nice English countryside. It's got a really nice heroine and the historical costumes are really good.

Astrid: Mmm, maybe ... What else is worth watching at the moment?

Carmel: 'How to Train Your Dragon' is a nice children's movie. The animation is very good.

Astrid: Uh huh. Can you recommend a thriller?

Carmel: '3 Days to Kill' is good. The acting is good too.

Astrid: I'm not sure. It might be too frightening for Marta. Maybe a comedy might be more fun.

Carmel: 'Airplane!' is a good comedy. It's got some good dialogue.

Astrid: Well ... Marta and I like science fiction films because of the special effects. Any ideas?

Carmel: 'Rise of the Guardians' is a good science fiction film with good special effects.

Astrid: Well, I'll think it over. Thanks for the help.

13 A wider vocabulary

You may not know all the films mentioned above, but try to replace *nice* and *good* with more precise, revealing adjectives from the box. Make an intelligent guess about the most likely adjective for that kind of plot, character, etc. There are more adjectives than you need, so think carefully before making a choice, consulting a dictionary if necessary.

Can you think of any adjectives to add to the groups in the box?

+ VOCABULARY

impressive	amusing	intriguing
striking	hilarious	absorbing
magnificent	witty	thought-provoking
stunning	sophisticated	engaging
superb	stylish	mesmerising
sumptuous	sparkling	convincing
dazzling	quirky	
glorious		
enjoyable	sad	appealing
satisfying	poignant	likeable
well made	heart-rending	attractive
skilful	memorable	
tough	dramatic	
ruthless	gripping	
embittered	breathtaking	
revengeful	mysterious	
violent	spine-chilling	
bloodthirsty	atmospheric	

14 Collocations

A character can be described as *amusing* or *convincing*. The plot of a film or an actor's performance can also be described in this way. However, some adjectives do not go with certain nouns. *Ruthless*, for example, can be used to describe a character but not a plot or performance.

Collocations, or word combinations, are based on conventional usage, not strict rules. Look again at the adjectives in the box. Working in small groups, decide which adjectives can be used with each of the nouns below. Some adjectives can go with more than one noun. When you've finished, compare your lists with those of another group.

PLOT   CHARACTERS   COSTUMES   SETTING
SPECIAL EFFECTS   PERFORMANCE

Make a note in your vocabulary book of the collocations that appeal to you … and make a promise to yourself to use them!

15 Understanding the style of short reviews

Short reviews are written to be scanned quickly by people in a hurry. They aim to outline the plot and give us a 'taste' of the atmosphere of a film, play or concert. To do this, reviews have developed a style and techniques of their own.

Scan-read these eight short reviews and match them with descriptions 1–7. There is one more review than you need.

A

Man of Tai Chi

Tiger Chen is the sole student of his elderly Tai Chi master. Whilst Tiger excels in the physical aspects of his training, Master Yang struggles to instill in Tiger the philosophical aspects of the discipline, and fears for his character. Tiger, however, is very ambitious, and is determined to prove the effectiveness of his personal style. He is a champion fighter, but he ignores the wise words of his master at his peril. He is soon trapped by an evil underworld where he is compelled to fight to the death. 'Man of Tai Chi' is a multilingual narrative and is partly inspired by the life story of well-known stuntman, Tiger Chen.

B

Maleficent

Maleficent is a beautiful young creature with stunning black wings. She has an idyllic life growing up in a forest kingdom, until the day when an invading army of humans threatens the harmony of the land. Maleficent rises to be the country's fiercest protector, but she ultimately suffers a ruthless betrayal. Bent on revenge, Maleficent faces an epic battle with the king of the humans and, as a result, places a curse upon the newborn infant daughter Aurora of the king's successor. As the child grows, Maleficent realises that Aurora holds the key to peace in the kingdom – and to her true happiness as well.

C

Never Let Me Go

In the remote countryside, innocent children enjoy a seemingly idyllic education at a traditional boarding school, but there is a dark secret: when the children grow up they will all be forced to donate their organs until they die or 'complete'. Inspired by Kazuo Ishiguro's award-winning novel of the same name, the film 'Never Let Me Go' is not only a thriller but also a philosophical work about mortality and the choice we face between challenging our destinies or accepting them.

D

Keeping Rosy

Steve Reeves's low-budget thriller is taut and well crafted, with Maxine Peake in fine form as Charlotte, a bright girl from an ordinary background who makes good in a London media agency. But a bad day gets immeasurably worse as an extraordinary chain of events leads to her losing her job and taking care of a baby girl, whom she names Rosy.

E

Ghosts

It is the eve of the 10th anniversary of her distinguished husband's death, and Helene Alving is about to open an orphanage as a memorial to his life and work. To mark this occasion, her son Oswald has returned from Paris. Helene plans to take the opportunity to reveal the truth to Oswald about his father. Richard Eyre's production of Henrik Ibsen's masterpiece is acclaimed by the critics. The play is running for a strictly limited season at Trafalgar Studios. It has also been nominated for five Olivier Awards.

F

Beyond the Edge

In 1953 Edmund Hillary and Tenzing Norgay conquered Mount Everest. This 3D documentary tells one of the world's greatest adventure stories of all time. Colour footage and photographs taken during the climb are woven into dramatic recreations to recount the historic triumph of the modest mountaineer from New Zealand and his expert Nepalese Sherpa. This account conveys both the climbers' heroic trials and the ambition and hope the wider world invested in their mission, at a time when it was starting to believe in a brighter new age.

G

22 Jump Street

Two police cop buddies enrol at college thinking that they will be hunting down real criminals. Much to their disappointment, they are given a dull task at an online university, looking for key words spoken during lectures that might suggest illegal activities. The comic duo persevere, however, and uncover information about a criminal gang in the docklands underworld. Following on from the box office hit '21 Jump Street', this new comedy is a lot more fun and a lot less dumb than you might have expected.

H

Police Story 4: First Strike

In the fourth instalment of the popular 'Police Story' series, Jackie Chan portrays a Hong Kong police officer who is contracted by the CIA and a Russian intelligence organisation to retrieve a stolen nuclear warhead. From the snow-capped mountains of eastern Europe to a shark-infested water park in Australia, Chan pursues a rogue CIA agent. Along the way he is attacked, assaulted, framed for murder and forced to defend himself any way he can. Everything within arm's reach becomes a weapon: ladders, brooms, tables, cars, stilts – even sharks!

1   This review indicates that the film includes original material from true life events.

2   This review tells the reader this is a live performance.

3   This review says that the film was inexpensively made.

4   This review suggests the film will make you think about the meaning of life and death.

5   This review says that the film has many different settings.

6   This review explains that several languages are spoken in the film.

7   This review indicates that this film is the sequel to an earlier film.

16   Signalling information in reviews

In film reviews, key words signal important information about setting, character and plot. The result is a compressed style in which maximum information is conveyed in the most concise form.

1   Examine the opening sentence of the review of 'Never Let Me Go' and identify the use of key words.

In the remote countryside, innocent children enjoy a seemingly idyllic education at a traditional boarding school, but there is a dark secret: when the children grow up, they will all be forced to donate their organs until they die or 'complete'.

Tick the adjective which indicates that the school is cut off from the outside world. Circle the adjective which suggests the children are sweet and appealing. Underline the adverb and adjective that suggest the boarding school only appears to be a happy place. Underline the adjective and noun that suggest the film's atmosphere is frightening. Circle the verb which indicates the children will have no choice. Why is the word 'complete' in inverted commas?

2   Examine this extract from 'First Strike'.

From the snow-capped mountains of eastern Europe to a shark-infested water park in Australia, Chan pursues a rogue CIA agent. Along the way he is attacked, assaulted, framed for murder and forced to defend himself any way he can.

Tick, circle or underline the key signals which tell us:

a   that the film has very different settings.

b   that the film has a fast-paced, dramatic plot.

c   that the CIA agent is not to be trusted.

d   that Chan himself doesn't initiate the violence in the film.

3   Examine the use of key words in an extract of your own choice.

17   Presenting a film or play to the class

Choose a film or play you found particularly powerful and give a short talk about it to your class.

Remember your classmates will be interested in your personal reactions and opinions, so think carefully about why the film or play was memorable. It is essential that your reasons are clear and that you provide examples of scenes. Refer back to exercises 5 and 6 to help structure your talk.

Before you begin, make a plan.

Introduction

Mention the title and genre (and the director and stars if you wish to).

Say why you have chosen to talk about this film or play. These reasons will be personal to you and will reveal something of your personality and attitudes. Looking back at your answers to the quiz in exercise 3 may remind you of what you look for in a film or play.

Plot, characters and setting

Your audience will expect a brief outline of what happens, who takes part in the action and where it takes place.

Try to arouse the interest of your audience by describing the plot, characters and setting in a fresh and lively way. Re-reading some of the short reviews may provide interesting ways of opening your description.

Tenses

Remember that the plot and characters should be described in the present tense.

Clarity

Plots can be complicated, so keep your description short, giving most attention to the beginning of the plot.

Conveying the quality of the film or play

Say why you thought the film or play was powerful. Try to use vivid adjectives. Aim to involve your listeners when you describe your reactions (exercise 10). Remember the importance of key words in signalling information (exercise 16).

Some points you may want to consider are:

■   the performance of the actors and their suitability for the roles they play

■   the use of humour, suspense or special effects (provide examples of scenes)

■   the underlying 'message' of the film or play.

89

Recommending the film or play

Say why you recommend the film or play. Link your recommendations to your knowledge of your audience. Do they need to relax and laugh? Are they very interested in a particular genre such as science fiction, horror or romance? Does the film or play raise topics that you have discussed in class (jobs, social problems, life in the future)?

Active listening

In good communication, listening is as important as talking. Listen attentively to the speaker. After he or she has finished, make one positive comment about what you have heard and then ask at least one question seeking further information.

Recording your talks

You may like to give your talks in small groups, record them and analyse the results. Check the clarity and vividness of the talk. Does the audience feel involved? Why? Listen for accuracy in the language – tenses, articles, collocations, etc. How would you correct any mistakes?

5.3 Working in the film industry or theatre

18 Pre-reading discussion

A Would you like to work in the film industry or theatre? What sort of work would you find most attractive: acting, designing sets or costumes, writing scripts or directing? Why?

B You are going to read about a young man who has built up a successful career as an animator. Looking at the pictures, what would you expect the films to be like? Would you like to watch one? Or have you already watched one?

C What do you think are the challenges presented in making an animated film using puppets or models?

D What kind of personal attributes do you think an animator needs? Tick from the list below.

- [ ] good at making things
- [ ] imagination
- [ ] ability to pay attention to detail
- [ ] single-mindedness
- [ ] a sense of humour
- [ ] enjoys working with technical equipment

Does the job of an animator appeal to you? Why/Why not?

19 Vocabulary check

Before you read, make sure you know the meaning of these words.

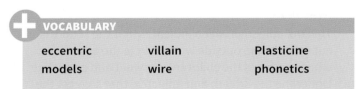

VOCABULARY

eccentric	villain	Plasticine
models	wire	phonetics

20 Reading for gist

Now read the article for general meaning. What did Nick study at the National Film and Television School? How many of the possible attributes listed in D above are mentioned or suggested by the text?

21 True/false comprehension

Decide whether the following statements are true or false.

1. Nick's father played a large part in helping him develop film-making skills.

2. Nick decided early on in his school career that he would take a degree in film-making.

3. A teacher at school gave him the confidence to aim for professional film-making.

4. The animated film 'A Grand Day Out' took a year to make.

An Interview with Nick Park

Philip Gray talks to Oscar-winning film-maker and animator, Nick Park, about his career and his amazing animations: Wallace, a slightly
5 eccentric inventor, and Gromit, his ever-faithful companion.

'Your work is seen by audiences around the world, but what was it that first started off your interest in
10 **film-making?'**

'It all started when my parents bought a simple home movie camera, and I discovered that it had an animation button to build up films one frame at a
15 *time. As a keen photographer, my father was able to help me with the technical side of camera work, and I worked with Plasticine models right from the start.'*

'At what stage did you realise
20 **that your hobby would turn into a full-time career?'**

'I don't remember a great deal of formal careers advice about the film industry while I was at school. There
25 *seemed to be very little information available, and the fact that I didn't tell people about my interest in animation probably explains why I didn't have much advice. I certainly didn't find out*
30 *that it was possible to take a degree in film-making until much later.*

'But one of my teachers did find out about my films – my English teacher, Mr Kelly. By watching my films, and
35 *encouraging me to show them to the school, he was one of the important*
65 *influences on my early career. By the time I was 17, one of my earliest films, "Archie's Concrete Nightmare", had*
40 *been shown on the BBC.*

'After completing a BA degree in
70 *communication arts at Sheffield Art School, I went on to study animation at the National Film and Television*
45 *School, where I started work on the first Wallace and Gromit adventure,*
75 *"A Grand Day Out". Then I joined the Bristol-based Aardman Animations studio. After four years, "A Grand*
50 *Day Out" was completed, followed by "Creature Comforts" and "The Wrong*
80 *Trousers".'*

Nick Park's art of animation

Nick's characters have been described as having too-close-together eyeballs
85 *and* mouths as wide as coathangers.
55 and mouths as wide as coathangers. Created from a recipe of ordinary Plasticine plus American modelling clay, beeswax and dental wax, they are then formed around a wire frame to
90 give them flexibility.
60 give them flexibility.

The characters are actors and they perform in accurately modelled sets that have been researched on location. Remarkable attention to detail extends down to the repeated bone pattern of
65 the wallpaper in Gromit's room.

The speech patterns of each character have to be broken down into phonetics, with each frame matched to a portion of a particular word and
70 animated with appropriate body, face and lip movements. No wonder one 30-minute film takes so long to make.

'With an Aardman Animations production team of nearly 30 people involved in "'The Wrong Trousers'",
75 **the list of credits reads like that of any other feature film. Can you give any clues about your next production?'**

'At the moment, we are hard at work on another Wallace and Gromit film. I can't give too much of the plot away, but I can tell you that it will be another fast-moving thriller. There will be a new villain
85 *on the scene, and I can promise some love interest for Wallace. I have plenty of exciting projects planned for the future, including a full-length feature film. As I have spent nearly ten years working with*
90 *Wallace and Gromit, there may well be some new characters in the film.'*

91

'What advice can you offer to our next generation of film-makers as they prepare for their college courses
95 and careers?'

'Firstly, I think commitment is essential in this work. Any film-maker must learn to be single-minded for those times when it is all too tempting
100 to do other things. Setting up with expensive equipment doesn't need to be

a major problem. I started with a cheap 8 mm cine-camera and one problem to overcome –the price of film.
105 'Secondly, without good powers 115 of observation, it is difficult to find sufficient inspiration. Study examples of animation to see exactly how they have been created. Many video players
110 will operate frame by frame to show 120 how the animator has worked.'

'Working hours must be very long during production. Can you find time to relax?'

'It's all too easy to spend very long hours on this type of work, as it certainly isn't a nine-to-five job. Filming sessions can be hectic, but I do find the time to relax occasionally, and have even managed to keep a few weekends clear just to get out into the countryside.'

5   'The Wrong Trousers' was his first film.

6   Matching his characters' speech to their body language takes less time than you would expect.

7   Nick is happy to talk freely about the story line of his next Wallace and Gromit film.

8   In his next production, he intends to stay with the successful formula he has worked out rather than risk new developments.

9   If you want to learn this work, you have to be prepared to invest in an expensive camera.

10   He has no difficulty limiting the length of his working week.

22 Guessing meaning from context

Try to guess the meanings of these words and phrases from the article.

1   frame (line 14)

2   influences (line 37)

3   wire frame (line 59)

4   on location (line 63)

5   list of credits (line 77)

6   powers of observation (line 105–6)

7   a nine-to-five job (line 117)

8   hectic (line 118)

Find two other places in the article where the word *frame* is used. Which of the above meanings (1 or 3) does the word have each time?

23 Spelling and pronunciation: The letter *c*

A   Have you noticed that **c** is pronounced in different ways? Say these words from the text aloud to show the different ways **c** can be pronounced.

camera   advice   sufficient

Can you think of the reason for these differences?

B   Study the following rules, underlining the letter(s) according to the rule.

c is pronounced /k/ before the vowels *a*, *o*, and *u*. This is called 'hard c'.

Examples: *camera   discovered   difficult   account*

c is also pronounced /k/ before most consonants.

Examples: *actors   crackers   clues*

c is pronounced /s/ before the vowels *e, i,* or *y*. This is called 'soft c'.

Examples: *receive* *cinema* *exciting* *icy*

> Before the letters *ea, ia, ie, ien* or *iou*, *c* is usually pronounced 'sh'. The phonetic symbol is /ʃ/.

Examples: *ocean* *conscious*

> When double *c* comes before *e* or *i*, the first *c* is hard and the second is soft; so the pronunciation is /ks/.

Examples: *accept* *accident*

Practice

Put each of the following words into the correct group, according to its sound. Most of the words come from the text.

Hard c /k/ (as in camera) Double c pronounced /ks/ (as in accent)	Soft c /s/ (as in cinema) 'Sh' sound pronounced /ʃ/ (as in ocean)
1 Oscar	13 certainly
2 career	14 influence
3 eccentric	15 communication
4 Wallace	16 recipe
5 scene	17 accurately
6 centimetre	18 accident
7 Plasticine	19 particular
8 action	20 face
9 comedy	21 credits
10 discovered	22 delicious
11 efficient	23 cine
12 advice	24 sufficient

With a partner, listen to each other saying the words aloud. Do you both agree that your pronunciation is correct?

24 Using words in context

Make up five sentences using words from the list above. Write them down and check your spelling. Then swap sentences with a partner. Read your partner's sentences aloud.

Examples:
Yasmin built up a successful career as a make-up artist.
English shows the influence of other languages.
The telephone is an efficient means of communication.

25 Spelling and pronunciation: The letters *ch*

Ch has three main sounds.

> In some words, *ch* is pronounced /k/.

Examples: *chemist* *technical* *school* *Christmas*

> In some words, *ch* is pronounced /tʃ/.

Examples: *cheese* *check* *teacher* *rich*

> In a few words, *ch* is pronounced /ʃ/.

Examples: *chef* *machine*

Practice: odd word out

Listen to the three groups of words and cross out the odd one out in each group, according to the pronunciation of *ch*. Rewrite the word in the correct sound group.

Group A	Group B	Group C
chemist	church	chauffeur
architect	watch	chute
mechanic	search	champagne
headache	scheme	sachet
chef	match	chocolate
technology	butcher	brochure

With a partner, practise saying each group of words. Do you know the meaning of each word?

26 More practice of *c* and *ch* sounds

Read this dialogue with a partner. Check each other's pronunciation.

93

Marc: Our drama club is putting on a production of 'Charlie and the Chocolate Factory' for the end of term.

Clare: That sounds exciting.

Marc: It is! The club is in charge of everything. We've chosen the actors, written the script, created the costumes, painted the scenery and even designed the brochure advertising it. The teachers weren't involved at all.

Clare: Sounds like a recipe for chaos to me!

Marc: Well, we've had one or two headaches but we've concentrated very hard on getting it right. There was one little slip, though. I play an eccentric character and I have to wear a big moustache. In our dress rehearsal the moustache fell off just as I was about to speak!

Clare: Never mind. I'm certain the audience will appreciate all the effort you've put in. How much do the tickets cost?

Marc: Actually, it's free but there's a collection at the end. Half the proceeds will go to the school fund and the other half will go to Children in Crisis, the school's charity.

Clare: Well, I really hope it's a big success.

27 Look, say, cover, write, check

Here are some words which often present spelling problems. Do you know what they mean? Can you say them properly? Use the 'look, say, cover, write, check' method to learn them.

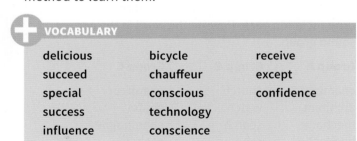

VOCABULARY

delicious	bicycle	receive
succeed	chauffeur	except
special	conscious	confidence
success	technology	
influence	conscience	

5.4 Reading for pleasure

28 Pre-listening discussion

It is sometimes claimed that reading for pleasure is now taking second place to entertainment that is presented in a visual form. What do you think? Would you rather watch a film than read a novel? What can you get out of reading novels that films can't provide?

In small groups, make notes of the unique pleasures that reading offers.

Special things about reading for pleasure
Examples:
You can take it at your own pace.
You can do it almost anywhere.

_____

_____

_____

_____

_____

_____

29 Listening for gist

You are going to listen to a radio interview. Jonathan, a librarian, is concerned that young people are giving up reading because of television and videos.

A Listen first for the general meaning and try to decide why Jonathan thinks videos are intellectually less stimulating than reading.

B Strategies for interrupting

The interviewer has some difficulty interrupting Jonathan. Tick the phrases he uses to try to interrupt.

☐ Just a minute …

☐ With respect …

☐ If I could just butt in here, …

☐ Excuse me, I'd like to say that …

☐ Hang on!

☐ But surely …

☐ If you don't mind my interrupting …

☐ If I could get a word in here …

94

30 Detailed listening 🔊

Listen again and answer the questions.

1 What are children not getting when they watch TV and films rather than read? Give two examples.

2 What is the difference, according to Jonathan, between reading a novel and watching a film?

3 How, according to Jonathan, are children affected by watching violence on screen?

4 How can parents help their children to understand what they read? Give two examples.

31 Post-listening discussion

A Do you feel reading quality fiction helps intellectual development more than watching films?

B Do you agree with Jonathan that violence in films and on TV influences behaviour more than violence in respected novels? Try to explain your point of view to your group.

32 Dialogue: Interrupting each other

Lee and Michelle are having a discussion about violence on television. They keep interrupting each other.

Read the dialogue aloud with a partner. Use a suitable phrase for interrupting each time you see the word *interrupting*. Choose from the list above.

Michelle: I agree with Jonathan that people are copying the violence they see on TV and it's time something was done about it. TV programmes are much more violent than they used to be. The crime rate is getting worse too. Children are being influenced to think that violence is all right and …

Lee: (interrupting) … Children are very sensible. They can tell the difference between what happens on TV and what goes on in real life. It's rubbish to suggest that people watch a programme and suddenly become more violent. I don't think violent scenes in books are better or worse than violence on TV. There isn't that much violence on TV anyway.

Michelle: (interrupting) … Some of the cartoons they are putting on even for very young children are very violent. They don't help children understand the terrible effects real violence has. How it can destroy lives. TV makes violence seem exciting and …

Lee: (interrupting) … Violent behaviour comes from your background and the way you're brought up. It has nothing to do with the television set. TV doesn't make people behave violently. If you see violence in your home or around you in your real life, that's the example you copy.

Michelle: (interrupting) … Violent TV programmes will make children who are growing up in bad homes even worse. They're even more likely to commit aggressive acts. Jonathan said parents should help children read more, and

INTERNATIONAL OVERVIEW

Internet use, TV and cinema across the world

A In which one of these countries do more than 90 per cent of people use the internet?

Australia   Brazil   China

Norway   Japan   USA

B People in these five countries watch, on average, more TV than anywhere else in the world (more than 4 hours per day). In which one of the five do you think people watch the least?

Italy   Poland   Spain

UK   USA

C Which country has the most cinema attendances per head of population per year? Choose from this list.

Iceland   Singapore   USA

New Zealand   Ireland   Australia

D These are the three countries which produce the most films per year. Can you put them in order?

USA   India   Nigeria

I think they should say what their children are allowed to watch too. They'll know if their children will be affected.

Lee: (interrupting) … That would be a complete waste of time. In the first place, children don't want their parents interfering. Surely kids have the right to some privacy about what they choose to read or watch on TV?

Michelle: (interrupting) … It's not only children who are influenced. Mentally unstable people, for instance, might not be able to discriminate about what they watch. They might think violence is fun, or even learn how to commit a crime. They find TV incredibly powerful and …

Lee: (interrupting) … Most TV programmes are really boring! I lose interest after five minutes. Not that I want to start reading so-called good books instead. I get enough mental stimulation at school. What I want is more exciting TV and less boring programmes!

5.5 Book and film reviews

33 Pre-reading tasks

A Do you enjoy reading novels? Do you prefer murder mysteries, romances, historical fiction or some other genre? Do you have a favourite author? What do you like about his/her books? Discuss your ideas with a partner.

B Write down the title of a novel you've enjoyed. Imagine you've been asked to write a review of it for your school magazine. You've already learned a lot about the skills of reviewing from your work on films earlier in the unit. You now need to build on those skills and extend them into book reviewing.

C The following questions may help you work out what made the novel memorable. Note down your answers.

Plot
Was the plot unusual at all? Was it gripping? Was it interesting but less important than the characters?

Setting
What did you like about the setting – historical details, fascinating details of fast-paced city life? How was the atmosphere conveyed through the setting?

Character(s)
Did the characters feel 'real'? Did they change during the book and cope with new challenges? Did you identify with any of them? Why? Think of one or more examples in the novel which show this.

Style
Did you like the style of the novel? Why? Was it punchy and direct or leisurely and gentle?

Audience
Remember to think about your target audience. Why would these people enjoy reading the novel?

Keep your notes safely as you will use them later.

34 Reading a book review

The following book review, and the film review in exercise 35, were written by students for the school magazine. Notice how the writers try to slant the reviews to their audience.

Great Expectations

Reviewed by Gilang Cheung

Have you ever liked the hero in a novel so much that you wanted everything to turn out all right for him? I felt like this when I read 'Great Expectations' by Charles Dickens. I'd like to recommend it for the school library because I'm sure other students will identify with the main character too.

Set in bleak 19th-century England, the novel tells the story of a poor orphan called Pip, who secretly helps an escaped prisoner. His good turn has unexpected consequences and he becomes rich beyond his wildest dreams. I won't spoil the story by telling you how the plot twists and turns, but I can guarantee surprises in store!

In a style I found painfully direct, Pip shares his innermost thoughts and aspirations – even ideas he later becomes ashamed of. During the course of the novel, Pip changes a lot. He becomes more

25 aware of his shortcomings and more compassionate. He pays a high price for self-knowledge and, like me, I think you'll be moved to tears at the end.

30   One of the things I learned from reading the novel is how corrupting money is. Pip, for example, no longer cares about keeping promises 35 he made when he was poor. The novel made me think about how the values of loyalty and integrity are more worthwhile than any amount of material wealth.

The novel provides a vivid and 40 rewarding insight into 19th-century Britain. Students of English language and literature will find it particularly fascinating.

Vocabulary

aspirations: hopes

shortcomings: personal failings

compassionate: feeling pity for others

corrupting: causing to become dishonest or immoral

integrity: honesty

Comprehension check

1   What is the title of the novel and who is the author?

2   When and where is the story set?

3   Why does Pip become rich?

4   How does Pip change during the novel?

5   Why does Gilang think money is corrupting?

35 Reading a film review

As you read this film review, try to work out the meaning of any unfamiliar words from the context.

How to Train Your Dragon

Reviewed by Lotta Svein

Do you love laughing so much you almost fall off your seat? If so, then I suggest you put 'How to Train Your Dragon' at the top of your must-see list.

5   This quirky animation is set on the Viking island of Berk and centres around a misfit teenager called Hiccup. Dragons regularly try to attack the island and everyone in the clan has 10 to fight them to survive. Hiccup feels ridiculed by others as he is timid and hopeless at fighting, but he wants to be valued by his community and to help. He decides to astonish everyone with 15 his talent for overcoming the worst beast of all, Night Fury. However, instead of killing Night Fury, he feels sorry for the dragon and a gentle friendship begins between Hiccup and 20 the beast.

The film combines lots of suspense with fun and humour, and the opening

scene of the attack by the dragons is truly exhilarating. The friendship 25 scenes between Hiccup and Night Fury are so touching that I didn't know whether to laugh or cry!

The film has a serious message too. It showed me how, by bonding with 30 the dragon instead of fighting, Hiccup finds happiness and peace of mind. His actions demonstrate that real peace lies not in fighting and killing, but in

finding a way to live with the things we 35 used to fear.

Try not to miss 'How to Train Your Dragon'. It's one of the funniest films I've ever seen, and it really makes you think. It is suitable for the 40 whole family too. Younger brothers and sisters will enjoy the hilarious twists and turns, whilst more mature viewers will be fascinated by the film's deeper themes.

Comprehension check

1 Why is the environment Hiccup is growing up in violent?
2 Why is Hiccup unhappy?
3 How does Hiccup hope to impress the people of Berk?
4 What does Hiccup learn from befriending Night Fury?
5 Why is the film recommended for everyone?

36 Analysing example reviews

A The opening of each review begins with a question. Do you find this effective?

B Compare the way the story of the book/film is described in the second paragraph of each review. Underline the phrases which are used to introduce the description. How does Gilang skate over a complicated plot?

C The third paragraph of each review gives reasons why the book or film was found to be enjoyable. Quite different kinds of things were found rewarding. What are they?

D The fourth paragraphs explain what Gilang and Lotta gained from reading the book/watching the film. Underline the phrases they use. Contrast what each student learned.

E Gilang and Lotta recommend 'Great Expectations' and 'How to Train Your Dragon' for different reasons. What are they? How do we know they are aware of their audience?

F Which review interested you more? Why?

37 Useful language for book reviews

Here is some typical language used by reviewers of novels. Which expressions would also be suitable for film reviewing? Tick those you'd like to use in your own reviews.

Style

It's beautifully written.

It's got a style of its own.

A subtle, poetic style that …

An elegant style which …

It flows beautifully.

Its light, chatty style …

Its crisp, punchy style …

Its leisurely style …

Setting

It's set in …

It's set against the powerful background of …

The historical details are superb.

It's a wonderful re-creation of …

Set in the midst of …

It has a marvellous sense of time and place.

Recommending

It's worth reading because …

You'll be delighted/enthralled/intrigued/ riveted by …

It's hard to put down.

It's a real page turner.

It's a winner from the first sentence.

It's well worth the paperback price of …

It's a masterpiece.

It's the best book I've (ever) read.

It's compelling …

It's not to be missed.

It's a classic.

You'll be moved to tears.

38 Criticising a film or a book

If you are writing a review under exam conditions, try to choose a film or book you found powerful. You'll remember it better and find more to say. However, you might still want to add a comment or two about what you didn't like.

Examples:
The performances were excellent, but the ending was very depressing.

The main character looked too old/young for the part.

The slapstick comedy delighted me but it wouldn't be to everyone's taste.

The characters were engaging but the plot was too far-fetched at times.

The photography was sumptuous although the special effects were surprisingly bland.

Although I enjoyed the 19th-century setting, the story was too sentimental for my taste.

The violent and bloodthirsty ending spoiled the story for me.

The plot was intriguing but the characters were not really believable.

39 Effective openings for book reviews

When writing an opening paragraph, remember that you should:

- immediately involve the reader
- make the reader want to read on
- convey the novel's special qualities
- use a concise style.

In small groups, read the following opening paragraphs A–F of book reviews written by students. Try to rank them from most to least effective, using the points above. Correct any structural errors as you work. Discuss the reasons for your choices.

A *I want to try to explain to you about a very good novel I recently read called 'In Our Stars'. Extremely, the writer did his best for this book and I couldn't leave any single moment in the book without reading it.*

B *I cannot always write to the school magazine but as I have been the one in my class that my teacher has asked me to do this as I have not done it before, I decided to write you about a book I read on holiday in France last week and I think you will really get surprised. I was I nearly fainted. I read a very long book called something like 'Twisters' by Harry and whose other name I forget. It is about a band but then the band gets famous and it is going on for a very long time.*

C *Last week I read one of the most gripping and moving books ever, 'The Bellmaker' by Brian Jacques. In the novel, animals are given human personalities and motives. However hard-hearted you are, this compelling tale of how a courageous group of animals band together to defend their kingdom against the evil schemer, Foxwolf, will bring a tear to your eye.*

D *If you've been recently bored and willing to read a book that I read about in a magazine I got from my older brother, I thought it was a true story but when I nearly finished it, I knew it was all made up and it was not true and I was disappointed. I recommend you read 'Anna is Missing'. It's a book*

about how a girl who lives in Alaska runs away from her boarding school into a worst place that she had never thought of before and she is trying not to stay there longer. But it is not a true story.

E *Have you ever wanted to be the hero in a novel? No matter how you reply you'll love reading 'Dark Eye'. The hero is a likeable but naive trainee police cop who is on a hunt for a gang of ruthless criminals in the underworld of New York. The suspense is great and the writing is just perfect.*

F *The book I thought was very long and want to explain you for my school magazine is 'Staying Alive' by Li Chang. I could read it more times too if I had time. I think the book has already sold a billion of them which is very scarce. I want to tell you about Jon (the detective in the book) and the strange and unusual things that happened to him after escaping from catching gangsters when he gets lost in a cellar that was not far from his house.*

40 Writing an opening paragraph

Write the opening paragraph for your own review of a novel you have enjoyed. You may find it helpful to refer to the notes you made for exercise 33.

Remember: Aim to convey the 'flavour' of the novel and to make the reader want to find out more. Try to be concise, choose revealing adjectives and avoid unnecessary words.

41 Writing a review of a thriller from prompts

Do you enjoy reading novels in which the plot is tense and unexpected and you can identify with the hero or heroine? If so, then you might enjoy 'The Kidnapping of Suzy Q' by Catherine Sefton.

Try to build up a complete review of it from the following prompts.

The Kidnapping of Suzy Q

'The Kidnapping of Suzy Q' / Catherine Sefton / be / most thought-provoking / atmospheric novel / have read. It be / set / modern urban Britain / it tell / story / through eyes / courageous heroine Suzy. One day / she be making / ordinary trip / supermarket / buy groceries / when supermarket be / raided. In the confusion / bungling criminals / kidnap Suzy / she be standing in / checkout queue.

The criminals / keep Suzy / captivity. Suzy recount / ordeal / graphic / painful detail. I be / impress / Suzy's courage / determination / refusal / panic / give up. Several incidents / novel / reveal Suzy's ability / cope / when she be threatened / them.

The story make / think / ordinary life / be dramatically changed / a fluke incident. It be also / inspiring / make me realise / inner strength / ordinary people can have / cope with / disaster.

The novel be / skilfully written. Catherine Sefton's style be / crisp / witty / characters be / strong / convincing. The plot be / intriguing / never predictable. If you like / spine-chilling / tense novels / you find this hard / put down.

42 Writing a film review based on a dialogue

Here is a conversation between two friends about the film 'The Net' which is based on the internet. Why not read it aloud with a partner? Then try to write a review of the film for your school magazine. Before you begin writing, make a plan of the points you want to include and their order.

Fatima: I saw 'The Net' last night and I would definitely recommend it.

Joanne: Is that the one about crime and the internet?

Fatima: Yes. It's very exciting. It's about a computer analyst called Angela who spends her days ironing out bugs in computer games and her nights chatting with other cyber-jockeys on the 'net'.

Joanne: Sandra Bullock plays Angela, doesn't she? I thought her performance in 'Speed' was really powerful.

Fatima: She gives a very convincing performance in this too. She plays an intelligent but lonely person whose main contact with people comes through computerised communication. She's rather cut off and isolated from real people. Her life changes dramatically when her fun and games on the 'net' at night lead to her being embroiled in a different kind of net: murder, corruption and conspiracy on an international business scale.

Joanne: Sounds like the sort of tense, action-packed thriller I like.

Fatima: Yes, and it makes you realise that the internet can mean trouble for ordinary people. There's a chance your confidential records can be seen by the wrong people. In the film, for instance, the criminals delete Angela's real identity and give her a false one. Then she discovers that it's impossible to convince the authorities who she really is.

Joanne: So she has to fight against the odds to clear her name? I think I'd like to see that. I admire gutsy heroines.

Fatima: Maybe your social studies teacher would agree to show it in class. It's interesting to discuss how face-to-face contact with people gets less necessary as we can communicate more and more through computers. It's inevitable that some people are going to end up cut off and isolated from real people.

Joanne: That's a good idea. I might be able to persuade him!

☀ GRAMMAR SPOTLIGHT

Will for prediction

We use ***will* + the infinitive of a verb (without 'to')** to predict responses. This is a useful structure to use in a review:

> *This compelling tale **will bring** a tear to your eye. (exercise 39)*

> *Younger brothers and sisters **will enjoy** the hilarious twists and turns. (exercise 35)*

Can you find another example like this in the final paragraph of the text in exercise 34?

Passive forms with *will* are also useful in reviews:

> *You'll be delighted/enthralled/intrigued/riveted by …*

> *More mature viewers **will be fascinated by** the film's deeper themes. (exercise 35)*

Can you find another example like this in the third paragraph of the text in exercise 34?

The superlative

The superlative + present perfect is often used in recommendations and reviews:

> *It's the best book I've ever read.*

Can you find another example in the final paragraph of the text in exercise 35?

EXAM-STYLE QUESTIONS

Speaking

1 A film or play I have enjoyed

Tell the assessor about any film or play you have enjoyed recently. Explain what it was about and say why you particularly enjoyed it.

Points to consider are:

- the influence and importance of the main character(s)
- the setting and atmosphere
- why you enjoyed it (e.g. special effects, performance of characters)
- what you learned from watching the film or play (its 'message').

You are, of course, free to consider any other related ideas of your own. You are not allowed to make any written notes.

2 Live performances

Buying a CD or accessing music on the internet may be cheaper than paying to hear a concert performance. However, many people think going to a live performance is money well spent. Do you agree? Discuss this topic with the assessor.

In your discussion, you could consider such things as:

- the fact that live performances enable you to see a famous performer 'in person'
- the unique atmosphere of some live performances
- the opportunity to see the details of a performance (costumes, setting, etc.) exactly as they really are
- the fact that you can listen to a CD many times but a live performance is a one-off event
- the fact that some live performances can be disappointing.

You are free to consider any other related ideas of your own. You are not allowed to make any written notes.

3 Entertainment through the internet

Enjoying entertainment through the internet is now widespread, but some people are concerned about the lack of regulation controlling the use of the internet.

Discuss this topic with the assessor.

You may wish to use the following ideas to help develop the conversation:

- whether you use the internet for entertainment
- the benefits and drawbacks of video-sharing sites such as YouTube

- the suggestion that creative artists are exploited if their work is accessed on the internet without their permission
- the idea that some people get addicted to internet entertainment and become cut off from others as a result
- whether you think governments should have stronger controls over access to the internet.

You are free to consider any other related ideas of your own. You are not allowed to make any written notes.

Writing

1 Write a review of a film you have enjoyed and wish to recommend for the new film club mentioned below. Your article should be suitable for publication in the school magazine. Write about 150–200 words (or 100–150 words for Core level).

Competition!

Calling all students! Form Six is starting a film club for all students. We want to choose films which we can show to students on Tuesdays after school. The headteacher is inviting you all to submit reviews based on films you want to recommend for the club. All entries will be published in the school magazine. The panel judging the entries will be made up of the headteacher, the head of English and two student representatives.

We are looking for well-expressed, thoughtful reviews and clear recommendations.

Closing date for entries: 10th March

---

2 Write a short article for a teenage magazine describing a novel you have recently read and enjoyed. In your article you should:

- outline the plot
- say why you enjoyed the novel (e.g. style, setting, development of characters)
- say why you think other people would enjoy reading it too.

Your article should be about 150–200 words long (or 100–150 words for Core level).

3 You recently attended a concert or other live performance. Write a review of it for a teenage magazine. You should write about 150–200 words (or 100–150 words for Core level).

4   You and a friend recently made a video and uploaded it to a video-sharing site on the internet.

Write an email to your cousin in which you:

- explain what the video was about
- describe why you decided to upload it
- say how you felt about the experience.

The email should be 150–200 words long (or 100–150 words for Core level).

Listening 🔊

You will hear six people talking about film making. For each of Speakers 1–6, choose from the list A–G which idea each speaker expresses. Write the letter in the box. Use each letter only once. There is one extra letter which you do not need to use.

You will hear the full recording twice.

☐ Speaker 1

☐ Speaker 2

☐ Speaker 3

☐ Speaker 4

☐ Speaker 5

☐ Speaker 6

A   I sometimes change my views during the film's development.

B   Disagreements make the atmosphere during filming unpleasant.

C   Things have to be returned to normal after filming.

D   I like to seem confident.

E   I protect my public image.

F   Lack of time for the job puts pressure on me.

G   The audience should believe in the character.

Form-filling

Bella Diallo attends Mallon School, and belongs to the Castle Arts Youth Club in her town, Rina, in Slovakia. The club, whose members are all aged between 15 and 18, enjoy a variety of activities: writing poetry, drawing and painting, and reading and discussing new novels. They have recently enjoyed 'The Silent Touch', a thriller, and 'Never Look Back', an adventure novel based on a true story.

Bella has heard about a local drama competition and suggests that members of the youth club would enjoy entering. At first, the club feel that they are not talented enough to enter competitions and have no suitable experience. Bella is so enthusiastic, however, that she finally persuades them to agree. She points out that one of the prizes is a set of free tickets to see the wonderful film 'Danger' which everyone has been longing to see. She also promises to be responsible for organising the entry.

After lots of discussion about whether to write their own play or not, the group decide to base their performance on a novel they read at the club some months previously. This was 'The Lily Pond' by Anna Franckel. As they all enjoy singing and dancing, they have decided to adapt a few scenes from the novel and perform them as a short musical, with the same title. Bella is persuaded to write the script. This is quite challenging, as she has to write interesting and credible-sounding dialogue.

The club have held auditions for the main parts. In the end, it was decided that Lauren Binichi should play Natalia, the romantic heroine. Paolo Ilpress has a beautiful singing voice and his talent makes him suitable to play Julius Swan, the leading male role, which involves singing a solo and playing the guitar. Mario Galliano's mature appearance and deep voice made him the favourite choice to play the part of Claudio, Natalia's father. The other significant character in the play is that of rich factory owner Francisco Chavez. It was decided that Pavel Ansell should take this role. Pavel has a gift for bringing out the humorous aspects of the part. The other members of the club, Anita Ronnay, Rosina Dilip, Nicolae Barrna and Christophe Lidel, will take supporting roles as factory staff.

Yi Tong has offered to be wardrobe mistress and to take care of the costumes – she is very good at sewing. Scenery and props are going to be kept very simple. A dark green curtain will be used to suggest the forest scenes, and a simple armchair and lamp will suggest interiors. Tom Andrews will be in charge of these. Annabelle Misty will use her artistic skills to good effect as make-up artist.

There will be no choir, but everyone involved in the musical will appear on stage at the end (the performance will last 15 minutes) to sing 'I Have A Dream'. As this is a very traditional song, the audience will be encouraged to join in at this point.

The group plan to get to the competition by bus, which should arrive at the theatre at about 3.30 p.m. Bella Diallo's address for correspondence is 11 Dimitri Castille, Rina, Slovakia. Her email address is diallo.b3@mymail.com.

Imagine you are Bella and complete the form.

RINA DISTRICT ANNUAL DRAMA COMPETITION
ENTRY FORM

SECTION 1 (*Please write your name and address in block capitals.*)

Name of organiser: _____

Title: Mr   Mrs   Miss   Ms   Dr   (*Please circle*)

Address: _____

_____

_____

Email: _____

Name of group or organisation:

_____

Is this the group's first drama competition entry?

Yes / No (*Please circle*)

How would you describe the genre of your performance?
(*Please tick*)

☐ Historical drama   ☐ Tragedy

☐ Comedy   ☐ Musical

☐ Adventure   ☐ Thriller

☐ Romance

Other (*Please specify*): _____

Title of performance: _____

Approximate length: _____

Please list up to four names of those acting the lead parts:

1 _____

2 _____

3 _____

4 _____

How many members of your group will perform a supporting acting role?

_____

The competition is scheduled to start at 5 p.m. All competitors are advised to arrive at the theatre one hour before the first entry. Will this be possible for you?

Yes / No (*Please circle*)

For lucky winners there is a choice of prizes. Please tick the prize your group would prefer:

☐ Sports vouchers

☐ Restaurant meal

☐ Book tokens

☐ Cinema tickets for a film of your choice

☐ Theatre tickets for a performance of your choice

☐ Zoo trip

SECTION 2
Please give the names of those responsible for the following:

Script _____

Costumes _____

Scenery _____

Make-up _____

SECTION 3
Write one sentence of 12–20 words explaining what your group has most enjoyed about rehearsing for this competition entry.

_____

_____

103

KEY ADVICE

1 Practise your **reviewing skills** by exchanging views about TV programmes, books and films with your friends. Try to use some of the language you have been learning in this unit and avoid the adjectives *nice* and *good*.

2 Read book and film reviews in your own language and English to become more familiar with the language of reviewing.

3 Try to **read for pleasure** in English. Make time for reading – remember you can do it anywhere! Keep a book in your bag or pocket to fill a few spare minutes profitably. Allow a couple of hours occasionally to really get into a book.

Find authors you enjoy. Book reviews are a useful source of information, and so is exchanging views with friends. Browsing in a library or a bookshop which sells English books can give inspiration too.

4 Look for magazines in English that reflect your own hobbies and interests.

5 Try to **enlarge your range of interest**. Read about different themes or dip into information books (astronomy, transport, inventions) which you usually pass over. Some libraries carry a wide range of journals and newspapers. Pick up one or two about topics which are new for you.

Try some poetry if you usually ignore it.

6 Watch again a film you have really enjoyed. Analyse why and how it appeals to you. Do this with books too.

Exam techniques

7 If you write a **review** in an exam, choose a novel or film you know well and enjoyed. Don't write about books or films you found generally disappointing, as it is more difficult to write in enough detail about something which did not engage your interest in the first place. This doesn't mean the book or film has to be perfect. You can pick out its weak points as well as highlighting what was powerful.

8 Use a broad vocabulary and appropriate structures to express your reactions to a book or film. Give specific details about characters, performance, special effects, etc. Avoid writing very generally: it is much better to use specific examples.

9 Don't get too caught up with **describing the plot**. Plots can be very complicated and it is not necessary to retell the story. Just give an idea of what it is about. Describing the beginning can be enough.

10 If you have to review a **live performance**, e.g. a play, dance or music concert, use the skills you have learned in this unit to:

  ▪ describe the costumes, special effects, etc. if appropriate
  ▪ convey the quality of the performance
  ▪ describe your reactions to the performance
  ▪ describe the atmosphere in the audience
  ▪ say why you would recommend the performance to other people.

UNIT FOCUS

In this unit you have learned to present a talk about a film, play or live performance and answer questions. You have discussed the way the internet is changing our access to entertainment.

You have developed skills for **writing a review** of a novel, film or live performance.

You have listened to a radio interview and answered comprehension questions.

You have answered comprehension questions on a detailed reading text.

You have completed a **form based on a scenario**.

Unit 6:
Travel and the Outdoor Life

6.1 Holiday time

1 Holiday quiz

What do you really like doing on holiday? With a partner, rate the following points on a scale of 1 (unimportant) to 4 (very important). Add anything else you or your partner like doing.

		MYSELF	MY PARTNER
1	Staying in a comfortable, well-equipped hotel / holiday home, etc.	☐	☐
2	Seeing beautiful scenery and new places	☐	☐
3	Making new friends	☐	☐
4	Doing outdoor activities, e.g. hiking, climbing, swimming	☐	☐
5	Learning a new skill, e.g. sailing, fencing, windsurfing	☐	☐
6	Having an exciting nightlife	☐	☐
7	Having time for reading and quiet thought	☐	☐
8	Exploring city attractions, e.g. art galleries, museums	☐	☐
9	Learning more about local culture and customs	☐	☐
10	Lazing on a sunny beach with a bottle of suntan lotion	☐	☐

Share your ideas in your group. What are the most popular things to do on holiday? What are the least popular?

2 Pre-reading discussion

The brochure describes summer camps aimed at students who want to learn English.

Look carefully at the pictures without reading the text. Who can you see? Where are they? What are they doing? How do you think they are feeling? What is the atmosphere like, do you think?

English in Action

Kingswood Camps has a superb reputation for leading the way in integrated language and activity camps. Set in holiday locations that UK youngsters love to visit, all our camps combine quality English teaching with an action-packed programme of sports and activities.

Through mini projects using research and thinking skills, we focus on building confidence and developing the language skills needed in real-life situations.

The programme is filled with fun, excitement and activities galore. You never have time to be bored at Kingswood Camps!
Our range of daytime and evening activities is a terrific opportunity for international students to make new friends from Britain and around the world. You can speak English all day while you swim, surf, go climbing or horse riding, try archery, enjoy discos and campfires, and much more …

Our teachers are hand-picked for their teaching ability and friendly, outgoing personalities. They always take the time to explain things carefully and to bring the language to life. Whether you are at beginner level or already quite fluent, the daily English lessons help you to understand the kind of practical language that is used in everyday situations.

Upgrade your stay and experience even more

Experience even more by upgrading your stay with a Specialist Holiday. Pick a favourite hobby or try something completely new and, for a supplement cost, spend a minimum of 15 hours a week focusing on your chosen activity, sharing your passion with like-minded friends. Choose from Stable Club, Surf School, Watersports, Football Academy, Bushcraft and Dance.

Excursions

From scenic river cruises, trips to historic cities and the bright lights of London, to theme park rollercoasters, famous museums and a spot of shopping, we have exciting excursions covered. One full day and one half day excursion are included in your programme.

All our residential centres offer excellent accommodation and three hot meals per day, including vegetarian options.
Whether you are travelling alone or in a group, you can choose to be met on arrival in the UK. Our special transfer service will then transport you safely to your camp.

Contact

Visit our website at www.kingswood.co.uk/international to download our brochure and to find out more.
Call us on +44 (0)1273 648212 to speak to our team or make a booking.

Parents and legal guardians

IT IS IMPORTANT to complete and return the Pre-visit Pack as soon as a booking has been made.
A booking is NOT confirmed until a completed form is received. If any information changes prior to arrival, please notify us immediately.

Brainstorming

What do you think might be the good points and bad points in general of this kind of holiday? In pairs, jot down any ideas at all that you can think of. Try to add at least another two or three good and bad points.

Good points

Trying new skills

Sampling independence away from home

_____

_____

Bad points

Not enough time to learn a new skill properly

A pressurised schedule which leaves little time for yourself

_____

_____

When you've finished, share your ideas in your group. Add to your list any new ideas mentioned by your classmates.

3 Reading for gist

Read the brochure quickly for general meaning. Don't worry about understanding every word. As you read, underline anything which is factual about Kingswood Camps and circle anything which is opinion.

4 Comprehension: Scanning the text

Scan the text to find answers to these questions.

1   Apart from international campers, who else goes on Kingswood Camps holidays?

2   How often can campers attend English lessons?

3   What can you suggest to a camper who likes horse riding?

4   What opportunities are there for visiting other places in the UK?

5   How is the safe transfer of campers ensured when they arrive in the UK?

6   What should you do if you would like Kingswood Camps a brochure?

7   What do parents need to do to get a confirmed place for their child?

5 An eye-catching advert?

Who are the two main target groups this brochure is aimed at? What persuasive techniques are used to influence the target groups?

Consider:

- opinion language
- the choice of photographs (who is in them and what they are doing)
- the layout.

6 The best way to learn?

Do you think learning English through the medium of other activities is a good idea? If you are learning a new skill, e.g. water skiing or horse riding, what language would you expect to acquire?

Has this advert convinced you that learning English at a holiday camp is worth doing? Why/Why not?

7 *Quite*

The brochure says that all levels of English are catered for, whether students are *'absolute beginners or already* **quite** *fluent'.*

Quite is a modifier often used before adjectives. It usually means 'moderately' (more than 'a little' but less than 'very'). But it can also mean 'completely', when used with certain adjectives. Which do you think it means in the following sentence?

'Don't worry, Mrs Chavez. Your daughter will be **quite safe** *at Kingswood Camps.'*

8 Shifting stress

The pattern of stress in some words alters when they are used as different parts of speech. For example, the words 'progress' and 'escort' found in the text can have different stress depending on whether they are used as nouns or verbs:

You'll make good **pro***gress on the course.* (noun)

*You can pro****gress*** *to a higher level.* (verb)

An **es***cort will meet you at the airport.* (noun)

*We es****cort*** *students to the camp.* (verb)

Marking the stress

Mark the stress in the words in italics in the following sentences as you listen.

1 The farmers sell their *produce* in the market.
2 The factories *produce* spare parts for cars.
3 Please *record* all accidents in the accident book.
4 His ambition is to break the world *record* for athletics.
5 I *object* to people smoking on public transport.
6 She brought many strange *objects* back from her travels.
7 Black and red make a striking *contrast*.
8 If you *contrast* his early work with his later work, you will see how much it has changed.
9 I can't get a work *permit*.
10 The teacher does not *permit* talking in class.
11 I bought Dad a birthday *present* yesterday.
12 The artist will *present* his work at the next exhibition.

Now practise saying the sentences aloud to a partner. Do you both agree about the stress?

Where does the stress fall when the word is a noun and when it is a verb? Can you work out the rule?

6.2 Outdoor activities

9 Pairwork

What is your favourite outdoor activity? Work in pairs to ask and answer these questions. If you prefer, one of your group can go to the front of the class to reply to the questions.

What / you like / do / your free time?

Where / you do it?

What / you feel like / when you do it?

What special equipment / you use?

How good / you be / at it?

How / you feel / after / activity?

Why / you recommend it?

10 Reading: Identifying free-time activities

Read the following descriptions. What free-time activities are being described? What key phrases help you to decide? Find at least four in each extract.

Match the photographs with three of the descriptions.

A

B

C

1   *I like going to quiet places which are uncrowded. Last week, I chose a route where the rough path made it hard to keep the frame straight. I got stuck in a lot of muddy holes which were almost impossible to pedal my way out of. The descent was exhilarating, though. I felt like I was flying. I reached the foot of the*

mountain in about half an hour. I was exhausted but delighted that I had done it. To enjoy this activity, you need a good, all-round level of fitness before you start.

2 *Each time I set myself a goal, which might be to get to the railway station or all around the park without stopping once. All the equipment you need is a good pair of trainers. While I'm doing it, my mind's blank. I don't think about anything. On the way home, I slow down gradually. I feel satisfied because I've achieved what I set out to do. This is a good activity for someone who enjoys being alone.*

3 *I often practise in a large sports field near my home. I fit an arrow to the bow, pull the bowstring back with all my strength and wait for the 'thunk'! I get another arrow from the quiver without pausing to check the target. My fingers and upper body have become very strong since I started playing. If you don't have the speed for ball games, this could be an ideal sport for you.*

4 *We've got a large outdoor court where you can hire a racket. I sometimes play friendly games with a partner who, like me, is not very competitive. I enjoy concentrating on the ball and I like running, so I usually get to most of the shots. I don't feel I am very skilled but I can perform the basic strokes adequately. If you want a sociable sport you would enjoy this.*

5 *I always go early in the morning when everything is peaceful. I love listening to the birds and breathing the fresh, clear air. I put on the saddle and bridle and mount by putting my left foot in the stirrup. When I trot, I rise up and down in the stirrups to avoid the 'bumps'. It's an ideal activity if you prefer something non-competitive.*

6 *I've never felt scared or worried doing this. Even at the age of two or three, I loved submerging my face and never used artificial buoyancy aids. I also like floating on my back. I feel as though I'm weightless. It's very soothing and pleasant, and it's cheap. Everyone can enjoy this, however unfit or badly coordinated they think they are.*

11 Writing in a more mature style

Most IGCSE students can write a simple description of an outdoor activity they enjoy. However, writing in a way which engages your listener as well as giving facts demands more skill.

Certain language structures can help you.

The **-ing form (gerund)** is often used when describing how much you like something. Remember that *love, like, enjoy, prefer, hate,* etc. are followed by *-ing* forms.

Examples: *I like being in the open air.*

I enjoy testing my own limits.

Clauses (beginning *which, where,* etc.) can link two ideas and provide extra information.

Example: *There's a large outdoor court where you can hire rackets.*

Since can be used to indicate the point in time something began.

Example: *I have been skiing since I was tiny.*

Like, as, as though, as if are used to compare one thing to another.

Examples: *After waterskiing my legs feel like jelly.*

I felt as if I was flying.

Using **precise adjectives and adverbs** gives your writing more clarity.

Examples: *I felt scared.*

The descent was exhilarating.

I can perform the basic strokes adequately.

12 Analysing language structures

Study the extracts in exercise 10. Underline any structures or expressions you would like to use in writing about your own favourite outdoor activity.

13 Describing a favourite activity

Write a description of an outdoor activity you enjoy. Aim for a mature style using a wide vocabulary and a range of structures.

You need to mention:

- why you like the activity
- the skills and equipment you need (check any technical words)
- when and where you can do it
- any other personal responses to it
- why other people might enjoy it too.

Write at least 100 words.

14 Reading aloud

When you've finished, read out your description to your group. If you like, you can substitute the word *'blank'* instead of naming the activity. Let them guess what you are describing.

15 Pre-listening discussion

A Have you ever been camping? Talk to your partner about what it was like. If you have never been, look at the picture and tell your partner what you think it would be like.

B What qualities do you need to be a good camper? Do you think you have them?

C Camping holidays are good fun but can sometimes be stressful too. What might people find stressful or argue with each other about on a camping trip?

16 Listening for gist 🔊

Paul and Marcus have just come back from their first camping holiday with the youth club. What did they find difficult about the holiday? Note three things.

Overall, do you think they enjoyed the trip despite the difficulties?

17 Listening for detail

Now listen for detail and choose the best ending for each statement.

1 The boys had difficulty getting the tent up because
   a it started to rain when the tent was halfway up.
   b they were in a hurry to go swimming.
   c the instruction leaflet had been forgotten.

2 As a result of going on the walk, the boys
   a missed the chance of visiting an aircraft museum.
   b missed the chance of visiting a war museum.
   c missed the chance of visiting a historic village.

3 The boys think Mr Barker was funny because
   a he was at least 40 years old.
   b he wore a woollen hat and specs.
   c he didn't listen to what they wanted to do.

4 The boys blame the girls for
   a not buying bread for breakfast.
   b not putting food into airtight containers.
   c not taking their turn to put food away.

5 The boys' attitude to going on a camping trip in future is
   a dismissive – there are too many discomforts and problems.
   b cautious – OK, but there are risks involved in this kind of trip.
   c enthusiastic – they would look forward to going camping again.

18 Post-listening discussion

A Paul and Marcus mention the uncomfortable aspects of camping, like *stone-cold showers*. What do you think they might have enjoyed about their trip which they did not mention? Try to think of three things.

B If you went camping, where would you prefer to go? In your own country or abroad? Try to explain why.

19 Blame

Paul blames himself for forgetting the instruction leaflet. Paul and Marcus blame the girls for some of the things they didn't enjoy on holiday.

Here are some expressions people use to blame each other, admit guilt or absolve each other from blame. Tick the ones the boys use. Which expressions sound most critical? When would it be acceptable to use them? When would it be inappropriate? Think about this carefully – it's easy to give offence!

Blaming

It's your fault.

You're responsible.

I blame you for it.

It was down to you.

Admitting guilt/responsibility

It's my fault.

I do feel guilty.

I feel bad about it.

I'm responsible.

I should have been more careful.

Absolving someone from blame

Don't blame yourself.

It wasn't your fault.

It was just one of those things.

You shouldn't feel bad about it.

20 Comparing cultures

What do you say in your language when you want to blame someone, admit guilt or absolve someone from blame? How does it compare with what is acceptable in English?

21 Functional language: Writing a dialogue

Try to think of a situation where the question of blame might arise. For example, imagine you have gone on a picnic and find that one of you didn't pack the cold drinks. You don't want to cause ill feeling. What would you say to each other?

Write out this or a similar dialogue. Remember to refer back to exercise 19 for suitable expressions. Practise the dialogue in pairs. Finally, exchange dialogues with another pair in your group.

22 Colloquial expressions: Adjective collocations

On the recording you heard showers described as *'stone cold'*, bread described as *'rock hard'*, the night as *'pitch dark'* and boots as *'brand new'*.

In colloquial language, the meaning of an adjective is often emphasised by the addition of a noun or another adjective before it.

Examples: *stone cold (noun + adjective)*

icy cold (adjective + adjective)

Combinations like these give extra impact to descriptions.

Complete the gaps in the following sentences with an adjective or noun from the box. You will need to use one word twice.

VOCABULARY

bone	freezing	wafer
crystal	plain	wide
dirt	sky	
fast	stiff	

1   It was _____ stupid of him to leave his bicycle unlocked in a busy street.

2   Wasn't Jeremy's talk fascinating?
    I'm afraid I don't agree. In fact, I was bored _____.

3   The resort was idyllic – a beautiful sandy beach and _____ clear water.

4   I was scared _____ when the plane began to shake.

5   No wonder it's _____ cold in here. You've left the window _____ open.

6   Chantal looked so pretty in her _____-blue outfit.

7   I was exhausted after our long trek back to the campsite. As soon as my head hit the pillow, I was _____ asleep.

8   Why did you buy so many bananas?
    I couldn't resist it. They were _____ cheap.

9   These _____-thin sandwiches are no good for hungry hikers.

10   The rain was lashing down, but his feet were _____ dry inside his new boots.

23 More colloquial expressions

Instead of 'getting up very early', you heard Marcus talk about *'getting up at the crack of dawn'*. Like the collocations, colloquial expressions like this make what you say more emphatic.

Complete the sentences below with these colloquial phrases.

VOCABULARY

a penny to his name	in the nick of time
a speck of dirt	a hair out of place
a bite to eat	a drop of rain
a stroke of work	hear a pin drop

1   We stopped at a café on the way home as we hadn't had _____ all day.

2   The farmers are very worried about their crops. There hasn't been _____ for months.

3 The library was so quiet that you could

_____.

4 The hotel kitchen is spotlessly clean. You never see _____ anywhere.

5 Her appearance is immaculate. She never has

_____.

6 We were delayed on the way to the airport and only arrived for our flight _____.

7 Hassan used to be a millionaire but now he doesn't have _____.

8 The workmen they employed didn't do _____ all day.

Now work in pairs to create some sentences of your own with these expressions. You need to use the whole expression – you can't use just part of it.

24 Word building: Adjective suffixes

Many adjectives are formed by adding suffixes to nouns, etc. Below are some examples from the recording. Notice the way the spelling changes in some words.

waterproof (water + proof)

fortyish (forty + ish)

quaint-sounding (quaint + sounding)

picturesque (pictur\e\ + esque)

historic (histor\y\ + ic)

In groups of two or three, discuss how you could form adjectives from the following words by adding suitable suffixes. In some cases, more than one suffix is possible. Check your ideas in a dictionary. Then try to create sentences of your own.

+ VOCABULARY

bullet	statue	panorama
odd	Arab	scene
twenty	Islam	sound
child	boy	pink
irony	pleasant	

25 Punctuating direct speech

In written English, inverted commas (also called quotation marks) must be put around all the words someone actually says. You open inverted commas at the beginning of the speech and close them at the end.

Study the examples below of the way direct speech is punctuated. Focus in particular on:

■ the use of capital letters

■ the position of other punctuation marks (commas, question marks, etc.)

■ the correct way to punctuate quoted words within direct speech.

1 Melissa said, 'I don't have any money, do you?'

2 Gran paused and reached into her bag. 'Do you want to see our holiday photographs? We've just had them printed,' she said.

3 'Have another piece of cake,' urged Mum. 'I baked it specially.'

4 Costas shouted, 'You tell me, "Don't worry about it," but I can't help worrying.'

5 'Look out!' screamed Uju. 'Can't you see that lorry?!'

Practice

Complete the punctuation in the following conversation. You need to add inverted commas and commas.

What was the best part of your holiday in America? Naomi asked when she saw Kevin again.

Going along Highway One from Los Angeles to San Francisco said Kevin without hesitation. I wouldn't have missed it for the world.

What's so special about Highway One? Naomi asked wrinkling her nose. Isn't it just another dead straight American highway?

Well replied Kevin. The road runs between a range of mountains on one side and the shores of the Pacific on the other. The views are incredibly beautiful. Seagulls fly over crashing waves. There are great cliffs studded with redwoods. Yes he paused for a moment it's truly magnificent.

What was the weather like? Naomi asked thoughtfully. Every time I checked the international weather forecast there was one word hot.

In fact Kevin laughed we had stormy weather but when the sun broke through it created fantastic rainbows. We visited a jade cove where you can hunt for jade. Anything you find is yours and I'd almost given up looking when I found this. He reached into his pocket and pulled out a tiny green fragment. Here he said it's for you.

6.3 Tourism: The pros and cons

26 Brainstorming

Tourism is now probably the world's biggest single industry.

Work in groups of three or four and jot down anything you can think of under the following headings. Don't worry if it doesn't seem relevant. Pool your ideas with other groups and add any new ones. Keep your notes carefully as you are going to need them later.

A What are some of the pleasures and drawbacks of being a tourist?

Pleasures

You can see a different way of life.

_____

_____

_____

Drawbacks

Your holiday is too short to get a real understanding of the country.

_____

_____

_____

B What are the advantages and disadvantages to the host country of a rise in tourism?

Advantages

It creates jobs.

_____

_____

_____

_____

Disadvantages

Pollution increases.

Foreign companies take the profits from tourism back to their own countries.

_____

_____

_____

_____

C How can tourists behave responsibly when they go abroad?

They can buy from local traders.

_____

_____

_____

_____

27 Tourism with a difference

Tourism Concern is an agency which wants to develop 'sustainable tourism'. This means that tourists try to make sure that tourism benefits the local community. For example, they fly with a local airline and use local accommodation rather than international hotels. What do you think of this idea?

28 Pre-reading discussion

A You are going to read an article about tourism in Sicily and Sardinia, two islands off the Italian coast. First, describe what you can see in the pictures.

B What do you think a holiday on these islands would be like? What do you think you would enjoy? Would you find anything difficult to get used to? Would you like the opportunity to go? Why/Why not?

C What do you think foreign visitors expect your own country to be like? Are their perceptions correct, do you think? How do foreign visitors to your country usually behave? If you get a lot of visitors, does the atmosphere in your area change? How? Try to explain your views.

114

29 Vocabulary check

Can you match the following words from the article with their definitions?

1	whiff	A	to shine with a warm, bright light
2	gilded	B	growing thickly and strongly
3	glow incandescently	C	strong
4	pastures	D	to fly high
5	enigmatic	E	covered or decorated with gold
6	soar	F	grassy fields
7	gorges	G	steep, narrow valleys
8	lush	H	a brief smell
9	secluded	I	private, hidden away
10	robust	J	mysterious

30 Reading and underlining

Read the article carefully, underlining the descriptive language as you read.

31 Comprehension check

Now try to answer the following questions.

1 What, according to the writer, is the main reason that Sicily and Sardinia have remained unspoiled?

2 Why is the writer reminded of North Africa? Give two examples.

3 What has been the result of the combination of Arabic and Italian influences on the architecture?

4 What sort of activities is Sardinia well suited to? Give two examples.

5 What is a striking feature of the Sardinian landscape? Give one example.

Offshore Italy

UNSPOILED, EVEN WILD, THE ITALIAN ISLANDS OF SICILY AND SARDINIA GIVE AN UNEXPECTED FLAVOUR TO HOLIDAYS IN THE MEDITERRANEAN.

5   Holidays are often about nostalgia. What most of us want is to visit a 'real' country. We want unspoiled landscapes, markets, traditions, cuisine and distinctive
10 architecture. We want people who are welcoming yet different from us.
   Historically there are two ways in which local character is preserved.

The first is poverty; the second
15 is physical separation from the mainland – the key reason why Sicily and Sardinia have stayed unspoiled.

Sicily – mosaics, ruins and gleaming churches

I recently went to Taormina, Sicily's best-known seaside
20 resort. Perching high on Monte Tauro, a funicular ride from its two sweeping bays below, its location is so charming that D H

Lawrence made it his home for a
25 while. Now, although the maze of traffic-free medieval streets is crowded in high summer, and pools are stacked up in blue terraces overlooking the sea, nothing has
30 diminished the town's magic. After all, what other major holiday resort has a backdrop that includes a world-class Graeco-Roman amphitheatre, ravishing hills and a
35 3,323-metre volcano, Mount Etna?
   Here, in the east of Sicily, there's a link with southern Italy, but move further west and the influence is decidedly more Arab. By the time you
40 enter the Sicilian capital, Palermo, with its souk-ish Vucciria street market and couscous cafés, there's an exciting whiff of North Africa.
   In Palermo this fusion of the
45 two traditions has produced some of the most beautifully decorated buildings in this part of the world. There's the Cappella Reale, the chapel which King Roger II built for

50 himself in the 12th century. Entering
from the central courtyard, it takes
a while for your eyes to adjust to
the darkness. But gradually the
gilded mosaics which line the walls
55 come alive; while overhead, richly
carved ceiling paintings of exotic
gardens and hunting scenes glow
incandescently against a deep blue
sky. The chapel is the undisputed
60 jewel of the city, yet a few kilometres
away, on the hilltop at Monreale, is a
cathedral which rivals it for the sheer
unbroken beauty of its mosaics.
    Sicily may not have as much
65 mountain wildness as Sardinia, but
it is a lovely broad landscape with
rolling plains and corn-coloured hills.
Life is taken at a relatively slow pace
and sleepy hilltop towns come to life
70 only for a festival or wedding (both
astonishingly frequent events). In
some of this lovely country, farmers
are waking up to the possibilities
of *agriturismo*, boosting an income
75 by offering hospitality (converted
cottages and, sometimes, country
food) to enthusiastic tourists.
    Visiting Sicily now, it is easy
to forget that for nearly 3,000 years
80 it was the most fought-over island
in the Mediterranean. The ancient
Greeks loved it as one of their richest
colonies and left behind a marvellous
(and well-preserved) collection of
85 temples to prove it.

Sardinia – wild at heart, with glamorous resorts

Sardinia has some of the most
astonishing country in Europe. Much
of the population is concentrated in
its two main towns, Cagliari in the
90 south and Sassari in the north, so in
the centre of the island shepherds
still herd sheep and goats to remote
valleys, visiting pastures used in
Roman times. The land is dotted
95 with enigmatic *nuraghi*, mysterious
stone dwellings left behind by the
Sardinians' prehistoric ancestors.
    Eagles and black vultures soar
over the mountains, pink flamingos
100 flash their wings by the coast –
everywhere you look is a riot of
nature with gorges, caves, wild boar,

deer and flowers. All this makes
Sardinia a terrific destination for
105 fishing, cycling, walking and riding.
    Yet despite extensive areas of
wilderness, the island has very
sophisticated tourist villages and some
of the best resort hotels in all Italy.
110   One of the most successful of the
tourist developments is Forte Village.
Set in 55 acres of lush garden with a
wide range of sports on offer, there
are three hotels to choose from, plus
115 a selection of secluded cottages,
entertainment and childminding
services. It may not be the 'real'
Sardinia, but it's hard to find a better
quality holiday resort.

116

32 Post-reading discussion

The writer says that when tourists go on holiday they
want to visit a 'real' country. They want *'unspoiled
landscapes, traditions and people who are welcoming
yet different'*. However, she also mentions the
popularity of specially built 'tourist villages' which offer
entertainment and childminding services.

Do you think meeting the needs tourists have for
comfort can ever be in conflict with protecting a
beautiful landscape and ancient traditions? Do tourists
expect too much? What are your views?

33 Adverbs as intensifiers

We can use adverbs before adjectives to make the
adjective stronger. There are several examples in the text:
beautifully decorated (line 46)
richly carved (lines 55–6)
relatively slow (line 68)
astonishingly frequent (line 71)

Combining adverbs appropriately with adjectives is a
matter of practice. There are no hard and fast rules.
Choose adverbs from the box to complete the sentences

below. After you have finished, compare your answers with a partner's. Sometimes more than one answer is possible.

➕ **VOCABULARY**

alarmingly	faintly	strangely
appallingly	fully	strikingly
badly	painstakingly	surprisingly
dazzlingly	seriously	utterly

1   I found the standard of service in the hotel _____ bad.

2   He has _____ recovered from his accident.

3   The temple is a(n) _____ attractive building.

4   The buildings were _____ bombed in the war.

5   I was _____ ill in hospital.

6   The beggar was _____ destitute.

7   You'll need sunglasses as the midday sun is _____ bright.

8   They expected prices to be high on holiday but everything was _____ cheap.

9   The ancient relics in the museum had been _____ restored.

10   Even after washing, the coffee stain on that white tablecloth is still _____ visible.

11   We held our breath as the coach went _____ fast around steep mountain bends.

12   The disco, which was usually very noisy, was _____ quiet.

34 Imagery in descriptions

Striking images convey a lot of information in a few words.

The writer describes Sicily as *'a lovely, broad landscape with rolling plains and corn-coloured hills'.*

Does she describe everything about the Sicilian countryside or select a few key features? What kind of image does the phrase *'rolling plains and corn-coloured hills'* convey?

What kind of images of Sardinia come to your mind when you read that *'shepherds still herd sheep and goats to remote valleys, visiting pastures used in Roman times'*

or

'Eagles and black vultures soar over the mountains, pink flamingos flash their wings by the coast'?

Study the examples carefully and underline key adjectives or images that suggest the area is still wild and untouched by modern life.

35 Adjectives: Quality not quantity

Using numerous adjectives before a noun is unsophisticated. It's far better to be selective.

How many adjectives have been used before the nouns in the following examples? How successfully do they evoke a particular atmosphere?

traffic-free medieval streets (line 26)

exotic gardens (line 56-7)

sleepy hilltop towns (line 69)

Choose an example of descriptive writing from the text which you think contains pleasing images. Comment on it in the same way.

36 Comparing two styles

Compare the following two descriptions of the same place. In which extract is the style more mature? What techniques have been used to create a more sophisticated effect?

Style one

> *The village is very, very nice. Tourists like going there but there is not a lot of new development, crowds or traffic or things like that. There are stone houses near the harbour. The buildings are not painted in dark colours. They are painted white or cream. The buildings have blue, grey or brown shutters. There are hills around the village. There are many pine trees on the hills. The view from the top of the hills is very good. You can see the whole area.*

Style two

> *The village is strikingly pretty and unspoilt. The houses, rising up from the harbour, are pale-coloured with painted shutters and made of stone. The village is surrounded by pine-clad hills which provide panoramic views of the area.*

117

37 Developing a mature style

There are a number of ways you can make your writing more mature:

- Choose your adjectives with care and use them **precisely**. You don't need a great many – just a few fresh or powerful ones.
- Remember that you can create adjectives by adding **suffixes** to nouns or adjectives, e.g. *panoramic, colourful.* (See exercise 24.)
- You can make adjectives more emphatic by using adverbs as **intensifiers**, e.g. *staggeringly, exceptionally.* (See exercise 33.)
- Adjective **collocations**, such as *crystal clear,* are another way of adding impact to your descriptions. (See exercise 22.)
- Use **clauses** to link ideas beginning with *which, where, when,* etc., and **phrases** beginning with *made of, with,* etc.
- Use **comparisons**: *like, as, as though, as if.*
- All the above techniques will help you to write more **concisely** – using fewer words to greater effect.

Practice

Now rewrite this description in a more mature style.

> *The town developed around a marketplace. The marketplace is very, very old. It is in the shape of a rectangle. In the town the people live in the way that they used to live hundreds of years ago. They like visitors, they do not commit crimes. They will always help you. You do not need to be afraid of them. They wear clothes that are very simple. They wear long, loose, white cotton robes. The town has many very, very old buildings. The buildings were built in the 13th century. It also has many restaurants. There are many different kinds of restaurants. You can eat nice food. The food is from different cultures.*

38 Writing your own description

Think about your last holiday or day out. Try to recall what was distinctive about the experience. Was it the people's way of life? The landscape? The food? The places of interest? Where you stayed? Or a combination of all of these?

What particular images come to your mind? When you are ready, jot them down. Don't worry about trying to write neatly or accurately. Just let the words flow out onto the page.

Re-read what you have written and select the most outstanding images. Concentrate on those that convey the flavour of the experience. Don't try to describe everything.

Now try to write a sophisticated description. Remember, your writing will be more mature if you use the techniques you have learned in the unit so far. Write about 100 words.

INTERNATIONAL OVERVIEW

International tourism around the world is growing steadily.

1. From the countries on this list, try to guess the top three international tourist destinations in 2013, in order of popularity.

Australia	Brazil	China
Egypt	France	India
South Africa	Spain	UK
USA		

2. Which country on the list would you most like to visit?
3. Which country would you most like to visit if you could choose anywhere in the world? Why?
4. Which holiday destinations abroad are popular with people from your country?

Share your ideas with a partner.

39 Giving a short talk

'More tourists = more economic and social benefits'

Prepare a talk of about five minutes on the above topic for your group.

Planning the talk

Remember to plan your talk first, before you begin. Use the notes you made earlier to help you produce a list of key points under main headings.

Give your talk depth by adding examples of your own. Try to think of specific ways tourism affects your country. What have you noticed yourself about the behaviour of tourists, the effect they have on the environment / the local atmosphere, etc?

If you have travelled, you could compare tourism in your country with tourism abroad. What was your own experience of being a tourist in a foreign country like? How were you treated? What did you learn from that about the treatment of tourists in your own country?

Presentation

Use your notes to jog your memory, but don't read from a 'script'. It is artificial and boring. Try to interest your listeners. Make eye contact with them, speak clearly and be prepared to answer questions.

Being a good listener

Remember, it's kind and courteous to show an interest in the speaker. Listen attentively and have at least one question or comment ready to put to the speaker at the end.

40 Words from names

The island of Sardinia gave its name to *sardines.* Many words in English are derived from the names of people or places.

Try to match these names to the people in the sentences below. Check the meaning of any unfamiliar words.

> ➕ VOCABULARY
>
> | | | |
> |---|---|---|
> | Morse | Fahrenheit | Diesel |
> | Volta | Marx | Sandwich |
> | Cardigan | Pasteur | |

1 Lord _____ didn't have time for a proper meal so he devised a way of eating meat between two slices of bread.

2 Lord _____ was the first person to wear a long-sleeved jacket made of wool.

3 Louis _____ invented a method of making milk safe to drink.

4 Gabriel _____ developed a thermometer which showed boiling and freezing points.

5 Samuel _____ invented a secret code to be used for sending messages.

6 Alessandro _____ invented the electric battery.

7 Karl _____ developed the idea of communism.

8 Rudolf _____ devised a special type of oil-burning engine.

Can suffixes be added to any of the names? Which ones?

Are any words in your own language derived from these names? Compare ideas with your classmates.

41 More homophones

Problems with homophones are the root of many spelling errors. Remember that homophones have the same sound but different spellings. (Look back at exercises 19 and 20 in Unit 1.)

Work with a partner to try to find a homophone for each of these words. The words have come from the texts you have read in the unit so far.

> ➕ VOCABULARY
>
> | | | | |
> |---|---|---|---|
> | real | flower | soar | sail |
> | scene | sea | blue | herd |
> | boar | right | two | deer |

Finally, put each homophone into a sentence.

6.4 Personal challenges

42 Reading an example letter

Read the letter which describes an activity holiday. How good a description do you think it is?

Dear Lucia

Just a quick letter to let you know about my activity holiday in Tasmania. As you know, I was a bit scared about going away by myself, but I loved every minute of it. The group leaders were caring and thoughtful and I never felt alone.

We stayed in a strikingly scenic area in a converted boarding school. I shared my room with two other girls and we are now firm friends. I had heard the weather in that area is rather unpredictable but we were lucky. It was mostly fine, with only one heavy downpour.

Each day we chose an activity from an incredibly varied programme. I liked the canoeing sessions best. We had a very experienced instructor who made us laugh and forget our nervousness. First he taught us safety drills, which were quite easy to learn. Then we practised our technique on a placid river which stretched through a pleasant valley. It's amazing what you can accomplish in a week. I now feel quite confident. I was thrilled because I didn't capsize the canoe once!

I think you would really enjoy this kind of holiday too, Lucia. It's stimulating, you feel independent and you get the chance to learn new skills in a safe and friendly environment. As for me, I only wish it could begin again!

Write soon.

Love,
Kosi

43 Comprehension

1 Where did Kosi go on holiday?

2 How did she feel before she went? Were her feelings justified?

3 What was her favourite activity? Why?

4 Why does she think Lucia would like the same type of holiday?

5 How does she feel overall about the trip?

44 Analysing the letter

1 What is the main topic of each paragraph?

2 Analyse the language Kosi uses to describe:
   - the place
   - the activities
   - the instructor
   - her feelings.

3 How does she close the letter? Consider the last sentence of the final paragraph, and the closing phrase.

45 Vocabulary: The weather

The weather, particularly on holiday, is a popular topic of conversation among British people. Decide whether the following statements about the weather are likely to be true or false.

1 I was pleased to find a lot of slush when I went skiing.

2 The blizzard made driving home easy.

3 Early in the morning the grass is wet with dew.

4 People usually switch on the lights at dusk.

5 I put on my sunglasses because the sky was overcast.

6 The weather was so mild that we did not need coats.

7 It's not worth hanging out the washing as it has begun to drizzle.

8 The gale blew several trees over.

9 Constant low temperatures and hard frosts meant there was no chance of a thaw.

10 Farmers are very happy about the recent drought.

46 Spelling revision

Some adjectives are formed from nouns by adding -y. You need to remember the rules for adding suffixes.

> A final -e in a word is usually dropped when adding -y: *ice icy*
>
> The rule for one-syllable words is that we double the final consonant if the word ends in **one** vowel and **one** consonant.

Examples:
*sun   sun**n**y   BUT   cloud   cloudy*

47 Writing about the weather

Choose an appropriate noun from the box and change it into an adjective to fill each gap in the postcard. Take care with your spelling.

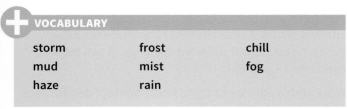

VOCABULARY		
storm	frost	chill
mud	mist	fog
haze	rain	

Dear All,

We're having a good time here but the weather isn't great. Every day starts _____ or even _____. This clears up by midday and we get a little _____ sunshine. We had a _____ day yesterday and the ground was too _____ for walking. It's generally _____ and I'm glad we brought warm clothes. Our boat trip was cancelled because it was _____. We're hoping for calmer weather tomorrow.

Love,
Ashwin

48 Discussion: Voluntary work abroad

Spending a year in a developing country as a volunteer in a school, hospital or a charity project is very popular with young people. However, it is sometimes claimed that young, inexperienced students from affluent nations have little to offer the world's poorer countries. They enter a difficult situation with little training or worldly knowledge. They might have ideas which are inappropriate for the country. In addition, they might be very homesick – almost an extra burden on the charity.

How far do you agree with these ideas? Is there any way problems like these could be overcome? Discuss your views with your partner.

49 Building a letter from notes

This letter was written by a student to her old school friends. She is working as a voluntary teacher in Cameroon. Use the notes to build up a complete letter.

Dear Everyone,

The first month / I be very lonely / but now I begin / enjoy myself here. The climate be warm / sunny / except for / last night / there be / big storm / which turn / paths / into rivers.

The family / I stay with / be very kind. The house be / three-bedroomed / and be quite comfortable. I be very close / my 'sisters' / who tell me off / if I do anything

wrong! Each morning I wake up / sound / exotic birds / dart / among trees.

Yesterday I take / bus / through breathtaking countryside / to local city. I go / bustling market. Everywhere / people sell things / but I be not sure / who buy!

I help / teach / young children / junior school. The children be delightful / and be very polite. The work be demanding / rewarding.

I miss everyone / home / but I feel / grow up quickly / and I be / more confident now.

Love to you all,
Eleni

50 Look, say, cover, write, check

The following words are problematic to spell. Most of them come from various exercises in the unit. Use the 'look, say, cover, write, check' method to help you learn them.

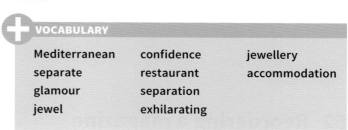

VOCABULARY

Mediterranean	confidence	jewellery
separate	restaurant	accommodation
glamour	separation	
jewel	exhilarating	

51 Discussion: Working as a tour guide

A   Talk to your partner about what you can see in the photograph.

B Study these comments made by tour guides working in the tourist industry. Discuss each of them with your partner and decide if this work attracts either of you.

1   *It's essential that you like travel and, above all, have a lot of patience with people.*

2   *Although the clients are on holiday, you've got to remember you're not on holiday and always be prepared to be responsible.*

3   *Touring a country with a group makes it hard to keep up friendships at home.*

4   *You have to be able to live for two weeks out of a suitcase or rucksack.*

5   *You're with the group 24 hours a day on a tour. There's not much privacy.*

6   *You've got to be well organised and methodical at all times. The arrangements you are in charge of can be very complicated.*

52 Reordering a magazine article

The following article was printed in a school magazine. Reorder the sentences logically and divide the article into three paragraphs. Underline the words and phrases which help you to link the text.

Life as a resort rep in Rhodes by a former pupil

a Initially, they relied a lot on me to explain about the banks and shops and to recommend local restaurants and the best sightseeing trips.

b Finally, I hope this has given you some idea of what life as a resort rep is all about.

c The work itself is very varied and I have the opportunity to meet new people and see interesting places.

d I have groups of all ages.

e In addition, there are many stunning, unspoilt beaches and peaceful villages.

f It is the first time they have been abroad.

g Although it gives you the chance to have lots of fun, it's not all glamour.

h Now, however, they are much more relaxed.

i However, if any of you are keen to get involved, I would definitely recommend it!

j It's got an impressive old town and a new town with graceful, modern buildings.

k In fact, they are more independent than many much younger tourists.

l First of all, let me give you an idea of what Rhodes is like.

m Next, I'd like to tell you a bit about my job.

n At the moment, for example, I'm looking after a group of elderly people.

✦ GRAMMAR SPOTLIGHT

Adverbs of frequency

A   The adverbs of frequency *always, usually, often, seldom, rarely, hardly ever* and *never* show how often something happens.

They usually go immediately **before the main verb**:

*I **always take** too many clothes on holiday.*

*You **never have** time to be bored at Kingswood Camps.*

So if the verb has two parts, the adverb goes **before the second verb**:

*She had **never enjoyed** camping.*

B   The word *sometimes*, another common adverb of frequency, is different because it can go in three positions:

***Sometimes** I eat toast for breakfast.*

*I **sometimes** eat toast for breakfast.*

*I eat toast for breakfast **sometimes**.*

C   With the verb '**be**', adverbs of frequency go **after** the verb:

*I **am usually** hungry after school.*

*Joel **was sometimes** late for class.*

*Students **are always** met and escorted by holiday camp staff.*

1   Look at extracts 3, 4, 5 and 6 in exercise 10. Notice the frequency adverbs and underline them.

2   Correct the mistakes in these sentences by putting the adverb in the correct position. **One** sentence is already correct!

a   I ride always my bike to school.

b   Angela often goes swimming with her friends.

c   He prefers usually the buffet-style breakfast.

d   Visitors to the Taj Mahal seldom are disappointed.

e   We play sometimes tennis after college.

f   Lewis hardly ever is on time – it's so annoying!

g   The children go rarely to the cinema.

h   She never has been on holiday abroad.

EXAM-STYLE QUESTIONS

Form-filling

Jonathan Kilby and his friend Alan Meakes, who are 18 and live in England, have recently left school and are planning to go to university next year. In the meantime, they are working as helpers in a building firm. It is heavy work, as they have to dig and lift heavy sacks of materials, but it pays well and they are pleased with the way their muscles are developing!

For achieving high exam grades, Alan was presented with a book at his school prize-giving day. The book is called 'Go For It!' and describes the work of organisations that arrange for students to participate in voluntary projects. Both boys are keen to get involved with one of these projects. The book was presented by the boys' former headteacher, Mr Harold Williams, who has offered to be a referee for both of them.

They have decided they would like to work together on a project outside the UK as Alan, who would love to travel, has never been abroad. He is interested in China, the Maldives, Brazil, Tibet and Nepal. Jonathan, who has visited the Seychelles, Italy and Mexico, thinks they should also consider projects in Sweden, Vietnam, Uganda and New Zealand.

Both boys have a wide range of hobbies and would be interested in projects which link to their interests. Jonathan is very enthusiastic about ancient cultures and artefacts and has worked as an assistant in a museum. Alan has decided that he would like to work helping people, in a hospital or school, for example. Both boys enjoy nature and the outdoors and are keen birdwatchers. They feel saddened when they hear of damage to wildlife or the environment and want stop it.

They have been told that people from all over the world work on the voluntary projects, so they are both trying to improve their knowledge of Spanish. They have also been attending a first aid course in the evenings to acquire a knowledge of first aid and have passed the examination.

The boys hoped to be free to start a project at the end of January, but Alan's parents have decided to hold a special celebration for his grandfather, who will be 80 on 27th February, and Alan does not want to miss it. Furthermore, Jonathan has some cousins visiting from America on 18th–28th of March and he would like to see them. So the boys have made up their minds to leave England on or around 1st April.

They hope to be able to work on a project until the end of September, as they have to do about two weeks' preparatory study before going to university. The university term starts on 19th October.

The friends hope to save up about £1,200 each from their jobs before leaving, and to raise about £100 each from selling their bicycles and sports equipment. In addition, their parents will give each of them £100 towards the cost of the trip. Alan, who lives at 234 Elm Tree Way, London W10 4SZ, England, will now contact Worldscape Adventure Projects to register their interest in voluntary projects and ask for further information.

Imagine you are Alan and fill in the form.

WORLDSCAPE ADVENTURE PROJECTS

GENERAL ENQUIRY FORM

SECTION A *(Please use block capitals for Section A.)*

Name of volunteer: _____

Address: _____

_____

_____

If you wish to work on one of our projects with a friend, please give his/her name:

_____

(Your friend should, however, complete his/her own enquiry form.)

SECTION B

Is this your first enquiry? Yes / No *(Delete as appropriate.)*

How did you find out about our organisation?

_____

Please say which overseas countries you would like information on. (Please note that we have no projects in the following places: North America, Central or South America, Scandinavia or Nepal.)

_____

England and Wales will soon be added to the list of countries in which we are developing projects.

Would you like us to send you information on these projects? Yes / No *(Delete as appropriate.)*

We have a wide range of projects. Please tick all projects you would like further information on:

☐ Health   ☐ Conservation   ☐ Hotel and Catering

☐ Information Technology   ☐ Education   ☐ Administration

☐ Water and Sanitation   ☐ Manufacturing   ☐ Archaeology

☐ Transportation   ☐ Wildlife Protection   ☐ Sales and Retail

Projects vary in length from one month to three years. What length of time are you able to commit to?

Years _____ Months _____

SECTION C

Volunteers must be prepared to do labouring tasks. Describe any previous experience in labouring work.

_____

_____

How would you describe your general level of fitness?

Good   Average   Below average   *(Please circle.)*

Do you hold a recent first aid qualification? Yes / No *(Delete as appropriate.)*

Volunteers are expected to pay their own travel and subsistence costs. The actual amount varies according to the nature of the project. Please underline the maximum amount per person that you would be able to pay.

£500   £1,000   £1,000–£1,500   £1,500–£2,000 £2,000–£2,500

Name of person willing to provide a reference:

_____

What is his/her relationship to you? _____

SECTION D

Please write one sentence of between 12 and 20 words, saying what you hope to gain from taking part in a voluntary project.

_____

_____

125

Writing

1   You have just returned from a week's activity holiday. Write an account of the holiday for your school newsletter in which you:

   - describe the place
   - say what activity/activities you enjoyed
   - explain why you think other people would enjoy such a holiday.

   Write 150–200 words (or 100–150 words for Core level).

2   A travel company 'Explore' awarded you first prize in a recent competition. You were given the chance to travel to any of the destinations mentioned in the advertisement below. You have just arrived home from your holiday. Write a letter to a friend in which you:

   - explain why you chose that particular holiday
   - tell your friend about special places of interest you visited
   - say why you would recommend this place to other people.

   Your letter should be 150–200 words long (or 100–150 words for Core level).

EXPLORE

TRAVEL TO NEW AND UNUSUAL DESTINATIONS!

Wildlife and Natural History
We visit many of the world's greatest game parks – tracking rare mountain gorillas in **Uganda** or bushwalking with guides in **Kenya**.

Wilderness Experience
Discover the haunting beauty of the living rainforest in **Borneo** or **Costa Rica**, or experience the powerful mystique of deserts like the Namib, Gobi or Sahara.

Raft and River Journeys
River journeys can last from a few hours to several days, and range from two-person inflatables on the Dordogne River in **France** to the excitement of an Amazon riverboat in **Brazil**.

3   A friend has written to you complaining that he/she is bored and asking you to recommend a new spare-time activity.

   Write an email to your friend in which you:

   - suggest an interesting spare-time activity
   - explain why you think he/she would enjoy it
   - say if any special equipment or training are required.

   You should write 150–200 words (or 100–150 words for Core level).

Speaking

1 Tourism

Imagine that an area near where you live is being developed in order to attract tourists. There may be benefits to the new developments, but some disadvantages too. Discuss this topic with the assessor.

You may wish to use the following ideas to help develop the conversation:

   - how tourists might behave and the expectations they might have
   - the kind of new jobs that might be created
   - other ways tourism could be good for the local economy
   - whether new buildings would be erected and the impact of these
   - ways to protect areas of special beauty or fragility.

You are free to consider any other related ideas of your own. Do not make any written notes.

2 Travel at home and abroad

Nowadays many people expect to travel, either for holidays, business or for some other reason. Discuss this topic with the assessor.

Here are some possible ideas for developing the conversation:

   - places you have particularly enjoyed visiting in your own country
   - the suggestion that foreign travel is better than travelling in one's own country
   - the idea that air travel enables family members living abroad to see each other easily
   - whether you would find the idea of studying abroad attractive
   - the advantages and possible drawbacks of working for a large international company.

You are not allowed to make any written notes.

3 Spare-time activities

Hobbies and spare-time activities are very important to some people, whereas others have few hobbies or none at all. Discuss this topic with the assessor.

You may wish to talk about:

   - the activities you enjoy in your spare time
   - a spare-time activity that you would like to learn, if you had the chance
   - the advantages and drawbacks of hobbies people enjoy outdoors
   - the idea that everyone should have a hobby of some kind
   - the view that modern teenagers do not persevere with hobbies.

You are, of course, free to use any other related ideas of your own. Do not make any written notes.

KEY ADVICE

1 Many students have difficulty concentrating on a topic for very long. We become skilled at taking in condensed information from different sources (TV, radio, computers, etc.) but find sustaining attention on a topic for a longer time quite hard.

Try to **strengthen your powers of concentration**. Time your ability to concentrate on a topic without getting distracted or having a break. Gradually try to extend the length of time you can do this. If distracting thoughts come, try to bring your mind back to what you are doing. Slowly, you will build up the length of time you can concentrate. This will empower you, not only for exams, but for the rest of your life.

Exam techniques

2 Read a composition question carefully and underline what you have to do. If you are given a detailed stimulus, such as a printed text from a magazine, be extra careful. Make sure you only write what is expected of you.

3 Make a very brief **plan** before you begin. Students sometimes panic at the thought of planning because they think it will use up valuable time. However, it is essential if you are to have a clear structure for your writing. If there is no time to write a complete essay, a clear plan should gain some marks.

4 Try to **draw on personal experience** in developing ideas for a description. This will make writing come more easily and convey more individuality.

Aim to produce a **mature style** by using some of the techniques you've developed in this unit. Avoid lots of bald, short sentences with the words 'nice' or 'good'. Use clauses, comparisons, unusual adjectives and images to make your descriptions interesting and distinctive.

5 Description alone is not enough. You will have to **explain your reasons** for liking something. You usually have to say why you think other people would enjoy whatever it is too. Try to give clear, interesting reasons that relate sensibly to your topic.

6 As always, check through your work for mistakes in spelling, grammar and punctuation.

Make sure you have written in paragraphs. If you did not, indicating where they should be is the next best thing. Aim to leave enough time to do this.

7 In an exam you may be required to scan-read an **advert, notice or page from a brochure** for factual detail. Look for clues to meaning from pictures, headings, etc. first. Then read the information quickly to get the sense before you try to answer the questions. It's usually possible to 'spot' the information in the text.

Sometimes information is given about prices, total amounts, etc. Careful reading is required, not adding or subtracting skills.

UNIT FOCUS

In this unit you have developed skills for **describing places and activities**.

You have read and analysed a persuasive **advertising brochure** and answered questions on **factual detail**.

You have read and answered detailed questions on a **complex travel article**.

You have completed a **form based on a scenario**.

You have listened to a conversation about a camping holiday and answered **multiple-choice questions**.

You have presented a short talk on a topical issue.

Unit 7:
Student Life

7.1 Challenges of student life

1 Completing a checklist

In Britain and some other countries it is traditional for students to leave home and attend a college or university in another town. This is usually an exciting and challenging time. If you left home to study, what do you think you would look forward to? What do you think you might find difficult?

Work by yourself. To help focus your thoughts, complete the checklist. Mark the ideas like this:

✓✓ *I'd really look forward to this.*

✓ *I wouldn't mind this.*

? *I'm not sure how I'd feel about this.*

✗ *This would definitely worry me. I don't know how I'd cope.*

☐ Having my own place

☐ Shopping for food and other essentials

☐ Making sure I eat regularly and sensibly

☐ Cooking for myself

☐ Finding new friends

☐ Organising myself and working alone

☐ Managing on a budget

☐ Being more responsible for my own studies

☐ Deciding how to spend my free time

☐ Doing my own laundry

☐ Keeping where I live clean and tidy

☐ Being more responsible for my own health

☐ Keeping in touch with my family and friends

If you have already left home to study, mark the checklist according to what you know about your ability to cope from your actual experience:

✓✓   *I've really enjoyed this.*

✓   *This has been demanding but I've managed.*

?   *I'm still learning to cope with this.*

✗   *This is a problem for me.*

2 Before you listen: Interactive skills

You are going to analyse the way two teenagers talking about starting university interact with each other.

Before you listen, answer these questions:

- What do you think makes a good listener?
- What makes a conversation lively and interesting?
- What makes it dull or boring?
- A good conversation may be likened to a game of table tennis. Why?

Improving communication

Here are some strategies people use to improve communication. Can you extend the list?

Using good body language

Looking and sounding interested. Making eye contact. Smiling and nodding.

Asking open questions

How/What do you feel/think about …?

Why …?

Where …?

Is there anything else …?

Spoken encouragement

That's interesting. Tell me more.

That surprises me. I've always thought you were a capable student / a confident cook, etc.

Paraphrasing

You mean …?

What you're trying to say is …?

In other words you feel …?

Asking for more information/clarification

Why do you feel like that? Can you explain a bit more?

I'm not sure I follow you. Can you give me an example?

Reflecting the speaker's feelings / state of mind

I can see you're excited/anxious at the thought of starting university / your new independence / developing a new social life.

Making suggestions / offering advice

Maybe you could …

If I were you I'd …

Your best idea would be to …

Have you considered …?

Why don't you …?

3 Reading and listening at the same time 🔊

Now follow the conversation. As you listen, underline examples of interactive techniques.

Dora:	I'm really looking forward to having my own room when I start college.
Peter:	Why do you feel like that?
Dora:	Well, I've always had to share with my younger sister and she keeps bursting in when I'm trying to have a few moments to myself. She's got another annoying habit too. She's always borrowing my clothes without asking.
Peter:	I can see you'll be glad to get some privacy. But won't it be a bore keeping your own place clean and tidy?
Dora:	No, because I like to keep things in order. How do *you* feel about going to college?
Peter:	Actually, I'm a bit nervous about leaving home and coping alone.
Dora:	That surprises me. You always seem so confident.
Peter:	People think I am, but I don't think I'll be very good at looking after myself. To be honest, I've never even made myself beans on toast. Mum always does the washing and ironing so I've no experience of that either.
Dora:	So what you're really saying is that it's the chores that are bothering you rather than your social life?
Peter:	Yes, you could say that.
Dora:	Well, how about learning now? Get your mum to teach you a few easy recipes. You could even have a go at ironing a shirt! Why not do it while you've still got someone around to show you?
Peter:	Now, that's a good idea. Perhaps I will. Is there anything else about leaving home that you're worried about?

129

Dora: Yes. I'm really hoping to have a good social life. I think I'm good at making friends, and I like parties and going to clubs. But I'm sure money will be a big issue.

Peter: I'm not sure I follow you. What do you mean?

Dora: I mean I'll have to be careful that I don't spend all my money at once. I'm really impulsive in shops. I don't know what I'm going to do about it.

Peter: Maybe you could work out a budget, so you know how much you'll need each week for things like rent and food. It's the opposite for me. My family can't afford to give me a lot of money, so I'll need a part-time job to get through college. There's no way I want to get into debt.

Dora: I've heard they need helpers in the college social centre. It might be a good idea to contact them. There are usually some part-time jobs in the restaurant or the office. You get paid and you can get into all the events for nothing. What do you think?

Peter: Thanks for the tip. I'll think it over.

4 Conversation study

Do you feel the conversation between Peter and Dora sounds friendly? With a partner, try to work out the tone of the conversation. To help you do this, circle an example in the dialogue which illustrates each of these points.

a The speaker shows a desire to understand.

b The speaker offers advice in an understated way.

c The speaker feels warm and positive towards the other person.

d The speaker is using a chatty, informal register.

5 Developing your own conversation

Look back at the list you marked in exercise 1 about the challenges of going to college. Think about the reasons you had for your answers. When you're ready, work in pairs to develop a conversation like the one above.

You can base the conversation on starting college or any other situation you find challenging, such as going away to stay with friends, starting a new school, or going on a group holiday without your family.

Remember:

- Explain your ideas clearly. Give reasons and examples.
- Say things which are true about yourself.
- Be good listeners to each other – interact well.
- Try to offer appropriate advice.
- Don't forget your body language.

6 Recording your conversation

Why not record your conversation and listen to it carefully? How well did you interact? Does it sound friendly and supportive? Have you helped each other explain your ideas?

7 Comparing languages

You might like to record an informal discussion in your first language and compare the similarities and differences in interactive patterns with those of English. How do these affect the tone of the conversation?

8 Reading and discussing a problem email

Read this extract from an email written by Sheryl, a young university student, to a friend. What does she enjoy about university? What is she finding difficult? Did you note any of these points yourself in your own discussion?

What advice would you give in reply? Share your ideas with your partner. Use suitable advice phrases, such as:

She should …

She could consider …

If I were her I'd …

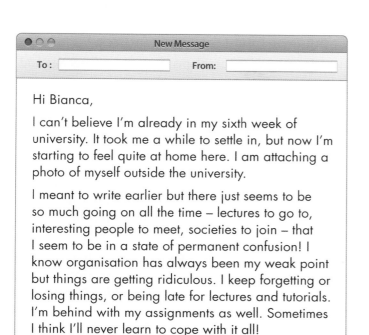

Hi Bianca,

I can't believe I'm already in my sixth week of university. It took me a while to settle in, but now I'm starting to feel quite at home here. I am attaching a photo of myself outside the university.

I meant to write earlier but there just seems to be so much going on all the time – lectures to go to, interesting people to meet, societies to join – that I seem to be in a state of permanent confusion! I know organisation has always been my weak point but things are getting ridiculous. I keep forgetting or losing things, or being late for lectures and tutorials. I'm behind with my assignments as well. Sometimes I think I'll never learn to cope with it all!

Is there any way I can get my act together? What do you think?

One thing you might find helpful is to make a list each morning of things you have to do that day. Try to include everything on your list, from attending a lecture to returning your books to the library. Keeping on top of the assignments is challenging too, but all you really have to do is draw up your own study timetable and stick to it. I know you're a 'morning' person, so why not schedule demanding intellectual tasks then? When you've got a minute during the day, don't forget to tick off things that have been completed.

The university social scene sounds brilliant. You seem to be having a cool time. I remember how popular and outgoing you were at school, so it must be tempting to say 'yes' to every social invitation. It's not a good idea to go out every night, though! You won't forget to pace yourself and save some time for recharging your batteries, * will you?

I'll definitely be able to make the weekend of the 22nd. I'm really looking forward to seeing the college and meeting some of your new friends. I'm sure by the time we meet you'll be super-organised and my advice will be irrelevant!

Love,

Bianca

*recharging your batteries: resting after effort

9 Reading an example email of reply

With a partner, read Bianca's email of reply. What do you think of the advice offered? How does it compare with your own ideas? Underline the advice phrases as you read.

Hi Sheryl,

It was great to hear from you. We miss you here – you're such a special person. Thanks also for the photo – what an impressive building!

I'm not surprised you feel chaotic and a bit overwhelmed. After all, only a few weeks ago you were bound by your parents' routine and expectations and by a strict school timetable as well. Now you're suddenly expected to be completely responsible for yourself. When I started university I remember finding things a bit scary, but I found planning ahead was the key to getting organised.

131

10 Analysing the example email

A How does Bianca achieve an appropriate tone in the opening of the email? Which details are included to develop the opening more fully?

B Paragraph 2 shows that the writer understands why Sheryl feels confused. How does she define the problem for Sheryl? What link does she make with her own experience? How does this affect the tone?

C Paragraph 3 offers Sheryl advice on being organised. Bianca doesn't sound bossy or superior – how does she achieve this? How is the advice linked to the writer's knowledge of Sheryl? How does this affect the tone of the email?

D Paragraph 4 shows Bianca's attitude to Sheryl's social life. Her recognition of Sheryl's enthusiasm for parties is balanced by a note of caution. How is this expressed? Do you think Sheryl is going to be annoyed when she reads this, or is she likely to accept the advice?

E The last paragraph confirms an invitation. How? Does Bianca manage to round off the email appropriately? How?

F Circle the words and phrases in the email which create a warm and informal tone and register.

11 Advice phrases

Here are some typical advice phrases. Which phrases are stronger (**S**)? Which are more low-key (**LK**)? Tick the phrases which appeal to you.

You need to …

You'd better …

You really should …

If I were you I'd …

Why not …?

Remember …

You could always …

You could consider …

Maybe you could …

All you have to do is …

Try to …

You may like to try …

How about …?

You really ought to …

You absolutely must …

Have you ever thought of …?

Perhaps you need to …

You know best, but perhaps you could …

It's a good idea / not a good idea to …

One thing you might find helpful is …

12 Expressing problems

The way people express their problems or ask for advice in English varies according to the seriousness of the situation and the formality of the context. Discuss the following statements and questions with a partner and suggest a context in which you might use each one.

a *I'm frantic.*

b *I hope an acceptable solution can be found.*

c *I'm not sure what to do.*

d *I don't know where to turn.*

e *What do you think would be best?*

f *I'd like some advice about this, please.*

g *I'm out of my mind with worry.*

h *What on earth should I do?*

i *I would be grateful for any suggestions you can make.*

j *Do you have any ideas about this?*

Comparing languages and cultures

How do you express problems in your own language and culture? Do you use dramatic or low-key language?

13 Tone and register in students' emails

A Oliver has just moved to a new town and started going to college. Working in groups of three or four, select one of you to read aloud this extract from an email he wrote to a friend at his old school.

The tutors are very helpful at my new college but it's hard to make friends. I spend all my spare time watching TV. How can I meet some friendly people?

If you were in Oliver's shoes, how would you be feeling? What would you hope to hear in a reply? Share your ideas in the group.

B The following are openings to emails that students wrote in reply. Take turns in your group in reading them aloud. Decide whether the tone and register sound right or not, and why.

1 *I received your email of 1st December explaining that you are not satisfied with your new life. If people don't like you, you must face the situation and solve it. There are many suitable activities you should take up which would help you overcome this feeling.*

2 *It was great to hear from you – knowing you had problems really made my day. The way I see it is that you are glued to the TV. All I can say is you should join a sports club and get some of your weight off as well. It will be useful for your health and good exercise for your legs.*

3 *You might want to know why I haven't written. I have been working in my grandfather's shop. I get paid even though I'm working for my family. I meet lots of new people and the work is interesting too. What is your ideal career?*

4 *I hope you are now happy since writing me that awful email. Why do you feel lonely? Don't you have friends there? You said how boring you are at your new college. I think there are many places of entertainment obtaining in that area which you have not looked for. Don't always be sorry for yourself. You ought to adapt yourself to your new world.*

5 *I was sorry to hear that you are not enjoying your new college as much as you deserve to. I know how you must be feeling because we had* *to move a lot with Dad's job. However, have you considered joining the college drama club? You used to give some brilliant performances in the school theatre society. With your acting talent and sociable personality, I'm sure it won't be long before you are striking up new friendships.*

14 Rewriting a paragraph

Choose one of the paragraphs you didn't like and rewrite it. When you are ready, read out your new version to the group, explaining the reasons for any alterations you have made.

7.2 The pressure of exams

15 Pre-reading task

Studying for exams can be a stressful time. You are going to read interviews with three students, their mothers and an education expert, about exam tension.

Here are some of the problems students say they have with exams. Read them through in twos or threes. Can you or your partner(s) suggest any solutions? Finally, share your ideas with other groups.

A

> *Getting bad marks in the mocks* makes me nervous about the real exams.*

B

> *I don't have time to watch my favourite TV programmes.*

C

> *My parents still expect me to help in the house even though I've got to study.*

D

> *I'm worried about turning up late for exams or getting the day wrong.*

E

> *I hate having to give up sport and seeing my friends.*

F

> *I've fallen behind with my coursework* and I haven't got time to catch up.*

G

> *There are so many websites I could use for my research, I don't know where to begin.*

H

> *I hate listening to other students comparing answers after a test.*

**mocks:* tests which are set by teachers in preparation for the real exams.

**coursework:* work such as projects, assignments and classwork done during the school year. Coursework is marked by the teacher but the grades go towards the final exam mark.

16 Reading for gist

Skim-read the magazine article on the following page. Does the advice given include any of the ideas you thought of? Try to work out the meaning of any unfamiliar words from the context.

17 Comprehension check

1   Tick any statements which are true for Clare.

   a   She works best in her bedroom.

   b   She leaves the work she is doing for her exams in different rooms.

   c   Her mother has tried different approaches to encourage her to study.

   d   The expert thinks Clare has found the right balance between studies, her part-time job and her social life.

2   Tick any statements which are true for Khalid.

   a   He doesn't get anxious about exams.

   b   He likes listening to music while studying.

   c   His mother gave him practical help with his maths.

   d   The expert thinks it is wrong for Khalid to give up sport and a social life during his exams.

3   Tick any statements which are true for Luca.

   a   He finds it hard to do homework unless he is very interested in the subject.

   b   He was disappointed with his grades for his mocks.

   c   His mother was happy with his progress until a short time ago.

   d   The expert thinks Luca needs to be much more motivated, and to use his parents' help to plan his study programme.

EXAM TENSION: What can you do?

PUPILS OF EQUAL ABILITY CAN END UP WITH VASTLY DIFFERING GRADES. TO FIND OUT WHY, LINDA GRAY TALKED TO THREE TEENAGERS, AND ASKED BEHAVIOUR SPECIALIST JULIET NEILL-HALL HOW PARENTS CAN HELP.

Clare Parry, 16, is taking nine GCSEs.

What homework did you do last night?

'English and Geography coursework, though it should have been in three days ago. I was tired at first but I worked until 2 a.m., mostly on the computer. I can't work in my bedroom. I like to be with others, so I work in the dining room or on the floor.'

What do you give up during exams?

'I've been working in a newsagent's every day after school and on Saturdays, and going out every night. Now I've cut back on the work and I only see my friends at weekends and on Tuesdays, when I babysit.'

Are exams stressful?

'Yes! There's so much pressure to get coursework done and then there are exam nerves. It's stressful hearing other people saying what they've done when you haven't learned it.'

What's the most helpful/irritating thing your parents do?

'Mum says, "I must have the brainiest daughter in the school, because she never needs to do her homework." And it can be noisy because Dad goes out to work at nights. The most helpful thing is they don't moan about the paper all over the house.'

Is there anything you'd do differently?

'Although I didn't work for my mocks, I did all right. For GCSEs, I'll make a revision timetable and really stick to it.'

Ann Parry says: 'I've tried nagging and I've tried not. I warn her that unless she gets on with it, she's going to panic. I've put my foot down about her going out during the week – I'm not popular! But she has only one chance and if she doesn't get the right grades, she can't go to sixth-form college.'

Expert advice: *'It does sound as though Clare is trying to do too much. While her newsagent's job is bringing in money short-term, her long-term prospects for earning are more important. GCSEs require three to four hours' homework daily, and three nights out a week seems quite enough without a job after school (the best time for getting down to study). Rather than laying down the law, Ann should try to get Clare to see this for herself and take more responsibility for her own work patterns. Where Clare does need support and encouragement is in planning what needs to be done by when, and plenty of praise for 'getting on' and completing tasks. I felt that wanting to work in the middle of the family, rather than working in her bedroom, was Clare's way of asking for this kind of constructive daily input.'*

Khalid Helal, 17, has seven B- and C-grade GCSEs. He is taking Photography GCSE this summer and Photography, Design and Theatre Studies at A level next year.

What homework did you do last night?

'None – but I did loads the night before, finishing a design assignment. It took till 1 o'clock in the morning.'

What do you give up during exams?

'I gave up going out at weekends and stopped my sport – mountain-biking, circuit-training and rowing – so I put on weight. I did go to a concert the day before my Geography exam – a big mistake! I didn't get back until early next morning.'

Are exams stressful?

'There's pressure from other students as well as the school. If they say they've finished revising, and you haven't started, you don't show you're worried about it, but you are. Music helps – our teachers say it's okay to have it on while you work as long as it's not too loud.'

134

What's the most helpful/irritating thing your parents do?

90 'Maths was a problem. I'd got a really bad mark in the mocks, so my mum gave me extra work and marked it – she's a science graduate. She bought me loads of revision books too.'

Is there anything you'd do differently?

95 'I should have revised more. My mum didn't push me because she was worried about my dad. He was very ill in hospital the term before the exams and she moved to London to be with
100 him.'

Krysia Helal says: 'I had so much on my mind, the exam period just went by, but I did help with his maths. He gets exam nerves, which is a worry,
105 and always panics afterwards when they compare answers.'

Expert advice: *'Khalid did remarkably well in his GCSEs considering the emotional pressure he*
110 *must have been under with his father so ill. Krysia did an excellent job of supporting him with his maths by taking a positive interest and being prepared to be involved. She needs to*
115 *encourage Khalid to keep up with his sport – sport is an excellent way to calm nerves, and a balance of work, exercise and fun is essential. Khalid should be encouraged not to compare*
120 *himself with other people – he's obviously trying to do his best.'*

Luca Bonetti, 15, is taking nine GCSEs. He passed Italian with a starred A last year.

What homework did you do last night?

125 'None. I don't do much unless I'm interested in it, like Technology, which I do at lunchtime.'

What do you give up during exams?

'I'm out at weekends, either working in a hotel, or at football or enjoying myself.
130 Mum and Dad want me to give up my job and they say they'll make up the money.'

Are exams stressful?

'The coursework is worrying me. It should be in by now, but I've got lots to
135 do. Exams aren't so bad. I didn't revise for my mocks, but I got good grades. Listening to music and working out help.'

What's the most helpful/irritating thing your parents do?

'I hate it when they compare me with
140 my brother or discuss me with friends.'

Is there anything you'd do differently?

'I'd look at the exam timetable! I missed one of my mocks and had to do it later.'

145 **Gina Bonetti says:** 'Until recently Luca was okay, now I have to nag. I don't like him going to the gym so often – he's too tired to work.'

Expert advice: *'Luca is a bright boy*
150 *but he has lost his motivation. The job and the exercise have become ways of distracting himself. His parents need to sit down with Luca and his teachers to find out exactly where he is up to*
155 *with his coursework. Rather than comparing him with others, they should address his particular worries. Their offer of making up his money is generous but must be linked to Luca*
160 *using his time more constructively. As he loves music, maybe Gina could offer him a reward of a music voucher for every completed set of subject coursework.'*

135

---

18 Post-reading discussion

1 Who do you think is the most hard-working of the students? Try to say why.

2 Do you sympathise with Clare, Khalid and Luca in any way? Try to explain why or why not.

3 Do you agree with the expert's advice for each student? Do you think the expert was generally helpful or rather too critical?

4 What do you think, in general, of the attitudes of the mothers?

5 Are there any other ways Clare, Khalid and Luca could help themselves? What do you think?

6 What are the methods you feel work best for you when you are studying for exams? Share your thoughts in your group.

7 Clare says she is going to make a revision timetable. How useful are timetables? Some people claim 'time budgets' are better because they are more flexible. What do you think?

8 Students at Lake View School were asked where they preferred to do their homework. The results are shown in the pie chart below.

a Where do most students prefer to do their homework?

b Which is the least popular place?

c Which two places are equal in popularity?

d Where do you usually do your homework? Do you feel it is a good place for you to study and concentrate?

Preferred place to do homework

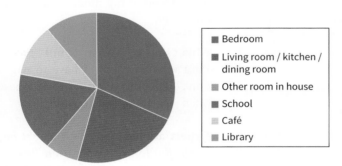

- ■ Bedroom
- ■ Living room / kitchen / dining room
- ■ Other room in house
- ■ School
- ■ Café
- ■ Library

19 Vocabulary: Colloquial words and phrases

A The following colloquial words and phrases were used in the text. Use them to replace the words in italics in the sentences below. There is one more than you need.

VOCABULARY

exam nerves	put your foot down about it	working out
moan		nagging
stick to	loads	

1 You *complain* about your daughter coming in late. It's time you *insisted it stopped*.

2 Luckily, we don't suffer from *worry and tension about exams.*

3 I have a study timetable and I am determined to *persevere with* it.

4 He enjoys *taking exercise in a gym.*

5 She does *a great deal* of work for her favourite charity.

B Do you know any other meanings of *moan, loads, working out* and *stick to?* Try to think of some examples.

20 Word building

Building nouns from verbs

Clare's mother was advised to give her 'support and *encouragement'.* The suffix *-ment* can be added to some verbs to make nouns.

Add *-ment* to each of the following verbs to make a noun. Then use each one in a sentence to show its meaning.

appoint	*advertise*
astonish	*improve*
arrange	*manage*
entertain	*disagree*

Building adjectives from nouns

Khalid was described as having been 'under *emotional* pressure'. The suffix *-al* can be added to some nouns to make adjectives.

Add *-al* to each of the following nouns to make an adjective. Then use each one in a sentence to show its meaning. Be careful, as the spelling sometimes changes too.

magic	*culture*
music	*function*
classic	*mathematics*
person	*nature*

21 Language study: Giving advice

Here are some expressions the expert used in the text to give advice.

a *Khalid should be encouraged not to compare himself with other people.*

b *Khalid's mother needs to encourage him to keep up with his sport.*

c *Luca's parents' offer of making up his money is generous but must be linked to Luca using his time more constructively.*

d *His parents need to sit down with Luca and his teachers to find out exactly where he is up to with his coursework.*

1 Which advice sounds most direct? Which least direct?

2 Which advice verb is followed by the infinitive with *to*? Which are followed by the infinitive without *to*?

3 How would you change statements **a**, **b** and **d** into questions?

4 How would you make **b**, **c** and **d** into negative statements?

5 Can you replace *should*, *need(s) to* and *must* with any other expressions of similar meaning? What are they?

22 *Should/shouldn't have*

Should/Shouldn't + *have* + past participle have a different meaning from giving advice. With a partner try to work out the meaning from these examples.

1 She should have taken an umbrella with her – I told her it was going to rain!

2 You shouldn't have bought her a box of chocolates when you knew she was trying to lose weight.

3 He should have checked the exam timetable before he took the day off to play football.

4 I shouldn't have lost my temper about something so unimportant.

5 You should have telephoned to cancel your appointment if you couldn't come.

Practice

Join each pair of sentences to make one sentence containing *should have* or *shouldn't have* and a suitable linking word.

1 Joseph took a part-time job. He had exams coming up.

2 Indira went to the concert. She had an exam the next day.

3 He didn't check his bank balance. He spent a lot of money.

4 I shouted at my brother. He was trying to be helpful.

5 I borrowed my sister's jacket. I didn't ask her first.

6 Why didn't you buy some extra bread? You knew we needed to make sandwiches.

23 Using a more informal tone

Rewrite these sentences to make them sound more informal. Use the verbs *should*, *ought*, *need*, *must* or *had better*.

1 It isn't necessary for me to cook. Bruno is taking us out for a meal.

2 It is necessary to do your homework at a regular time each evening.

3 It was unwise to make a promise you can't keep.

4 It was wrong to leave all my revision to the last minute.

5 It's vital that Abdul gets more rest or he will fail his exams.

6 I regret not having listened to her advice.

7 It was wrong of him to play computer games instead of revising for the exam.

24 Spelling and pronunciation: Silent letters

Many English words contain silent letters. They can be at the beginning of words as in:

wrinkle　　**k**nitting

psychology　　**h**onour

in the middle, as in:

sal**l**mon　　forei**g**ner

cu**p**board　　lis**t**ener

or at the end, as in:

com**b**　　autum**n**

Sometimes a pair of letters is silent, as in:

ri**gh**t　　dau**gh**ter

Practise saying the words above with a partner. Check each other's pronunciation.

25 Crossing out silent letters

These words, taken from the text 'Exam Tension', contain silent letters. Work with a partner to cross out the letters which are not pronounced.

137

1	design	7	should
2	answers	8	calm
3	what	9	circuit
4	law	10	assignment
5	night	11	weight
6	science	12	hours

Now practise saying the words correctly with your partner. Do you both agree your pronunciation is correct?

26 Adding silent letters

Complete these sentences with the missing silent letters. Choose from the letters in the box.

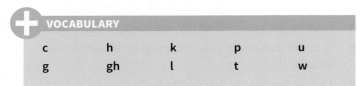

VOCABULARY

c	h	k	p	u
g	gh	l	t	w

1 The drou____t has ruined the crops.
2 Please ta____k to them about it.
3 Wou____d you like a bisc____it with your coffee?
4 W____ereabouts do you live?
5 Do you want a ha____f or a ____hole bag of sweets?
6 Can you ____rite your ans____ers here?
7 We turn on the li____ts when it gets dark.
8 He hurt his ____rist and his ____nee when he fell over.
9 Snow is always w____ite.
10 ____onesty is the best policy.
11 These flowers have a lovely s____ent.
12 The referee blows the w____is____le if something is ____rong.
13 She ____rote under a ____seudonym as she wanted to keep her identity secret.
14 Queen Victoria rei____ned for over 60 years.
15 She is ____sychic and can tell the future.

27 Detecting patterns

A Can you see a regular pattern for any of the silent letters? Discuss your ideas with a partner and note any patterns you can detect.

B Are there any silent letters in your own language? Share some examples in your group.

28 Idiomatic expressions

Can you work out the meaning of these idiomatic expressions from the context? (They each contain silent letters.)

1 I don't like the country and prefer the *hustle and bustle* of city life.
2 I thought the suitcase would be heavy, but when I picked it up it was *as light as a feather.*
3 He *risked life and limb* to save the baby from the burning car.

29 Look, say, cover, write, check

Silent letters often cause spelling mistakes. Students say they sometimes forget to include them in a word. Here is a list of words with silent letters which often cause spelling problems. First check the meaning and then try to identify the silent letter(s) in each word. Finally, use the 'look, say, cover, write, check' method to learn each word correctly.

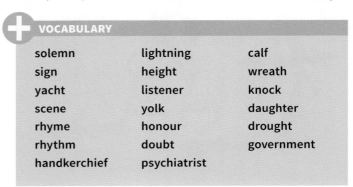

VOCABULARY

solemn	lightning	calf
sign	height	wreath
yacht	listener	knock
scene	yolk	daughter
rhyme	honour	drought
rhythm	doubt	government
handkerchief	psychiatrist	

7.3 Studying effectively

30 Punctuation reminders

Correct punctuation is important because it helps make meaning clear.

Full stops and capital letters

Remember, full stops are used to end a sentence. Capital letters are needed after a full stop. Capital letters are also used for proper names (*Ayesha, Pepe*), place names (*Cairo, the Amazon*) and acronyms (*BBC, DNA*).

Here is a description of how one student does homework. Punctuate it correctly. Remember to read it first to get the sense correct.

138

I need a few quiet moments to myself when i get in from school i have a drink and relax for a while then i get out my homework i work at a desk in the corner of the living room it is peaceful but not silent i like French and maths homework the best

Apostrophes

Remember, apostrophes are used to indicate possession (*Zina's pen, the girls' coats*) and to show that a letter is missing. (*It's hot.*)

Punctuate the next part of the description.

ive got a few reference books which i keep on a shelf above my desk i borrow my brothers paints for artwork and i use my mums laptop for igcse coursework ive used my dads tools for some technology projects too they dont mind me borrowing their things as long as i take care of them

Commas

Commas are used in the following ways.

a To separate things in a list:

I need pens, pencils, rulers and a rubber.

b To separate a non-defining clause or an extra phrase from the main sentence:

Mr Rivers, our geography teacher, comes from Nigeria.

c To separate a participle phrase from the main clause:

Having run all the way to the station, we were disappointed to find the train had just left.

d After certain linking words and phrases:

On the other hand, Nevertheless, However,

These are just some of the uses of commas. Remember – we generally put commas where we would pause in speech.

Now punctuate the rest of the extract correctly.

our school has a homework link on the school website this means that you can use the homework page to check the homework youve been set it also stops teachers setting too many subjects for homework at once about two years ago i had english history german physics biology maths and technology homework on the same night it was a nightmare the homework page prevents these problems however it also means teachers refuse to accept silly excuses for not handing in homework

31 Rewriting an email

Read the email below, which was written to a student who is not able to join his friends on holiday as he needs to retake an examination.

First read it carefully to get the sense. Then discuss it with a partner and rewrite it as necessary. Expect to make at least two drafts.

You should consider:

a **the paragraphing**

Remember – a new paragraph is usually needed for a change of topic.

b **the tone and register**

Are they right for this situation? If not, think of alternative expressions you could use.

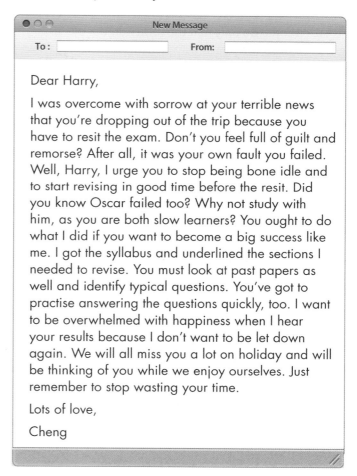

New Message

To: From:

Dear Harry,

I was overcome with sorrow at your terrible news that you're dropping out of the trip because you have to resit the exam. Don't you feel full of guilt and remorse? After all, it was your own fault you failed. Well, Harry, I urge you to stop being bone idle and to start revising in good time before the resit. Did you know Oscar failed too? Why not study with him, as you are both slow learners? You ought to do what I did if you want to become a big success like me. I got the syllabus and underlined the sections I needed to revise. You must look at past papers as well and identify typical questions. You've got to practise answering the questions quickly, too. I want to be overwhelmed with happiness when I hear your results because I don't want to be let down again. We will all miss you a lot on holiday and will be thinking of you while we enjoy ourselves. Just remember to stop wasting your time.

Lots of love,

Cheng

32 Reading aloud

Read your new version to your group. Do you all agree you have achieved a sympathetic email which sounds 'balanced'?

33 More idiomatic expressions

The idioms in italics in the following sentences express feelings and attitudes. Discuss each with a partner and choose the definition you feel is correct.

1 At the party the other students *gave her the cold shoulder.*

   a   They ignored her.

   b   They offered her cold meat.

   c   They told her they disliked her.

   d   They made her promise to keep a secret.

2 When I read the exam paper I *couldn't make head nor tail of it.*

   a   I realised I could not finish in the time.

   b   I could not understand any of the questions.

   c   I found the second part of the paper very difficult.

   d   I could do only half the total number of questions.

3 The tutor's warning that her work was below standard was *like water off a duck's back.*

   a   She was worried that she was going to fail.

   b   She made up her mind to do better.

   c   The advice made no difference to her attitude.

   d   She decided to leave the college.

4 He's *set his heart on* becoming a doctor.

   a   He's sure he'll be a successful doctor.

   b   He's very emotional about becoming a doctor.

   c   He's very realistic about his prospects.

   d   He really wants to qualify as a doctor.

5 I've never failed an exam, *touch wood.*

   a   It's due to my careful preparation.

   b   I really hope my good luck continues.

   c   I always expect to do well in exams.

   d   I believe I shall fail the next one.

6 When I told her she'd won the scholarship, she thought I was *pulling her leg.*

   a   She didn't like the way I explained it.

   b   She was convinced I was joking.

   c   She thought I wanted something from her.

   d   She was angry and walked away.

7 I thought this training programme would be right for me, but now I feel that I'm *out of my depth.*

   a   The programme is generally too difficult for me.

   b   The programme is working out more expensive than I expected.

   c   The other trainees dominate the discussions.

   d   The instructors misrepresented the course to me.

34 Increasing your stock of idioms

Select the idiomatic expressions you would like to remember from exercise 33. Use each in a sentence of your own to show its meaning.

35 Sentence correction

The following sentences from students' letters contain mistakes of grammar and vocabulary. Try to rewrite them correctly.

1 If you be wisdom one you follow your professor advice.

2 You should build up a correct concept of mind to your work.

3 The qualities of good friend is invisible but uncountable.

4 You should never take the drugs they give much trouble more than they bring the pleasure.

5 Your email talking ideas many people thinking too.

INTERNATIONAL OVERVIEW

Most popular countries for international students

Destination country	Total number of overseas students
1 USA	740,482
2 UK	427,686
3 France	271,399
4 Australia	249,588
5 Germany	206,986
6 Russia	173,627
7 Japan	150,617
8 Canada	120,960
9 China	88,979
10 Italy	77,732

Study the data which shows the most popular countries for students who wish to study abroad.

1 How many countries are being compared?

2 Which is the third most popular country for international students?

3 Which country has just under half the number of international students as Australia?

4 If you were choosing to study abroad, where would you like to go? Share your ideas with a partner, explaining why that country would appeal to you.

7.4 A range of advice

36 Pre-listening tasks

A More and more people are now said to be turning to professional counsellors if they have problems. The following points are sometimes made in favour of counsellors. In groups of three or four, discuss how far you agree with them.

1 Counselling is a real skill and the counsellors are properly trained and qualified.

2 Their advice is objective.

3 It's not embarrassing to see them because you won't have to deal with them in any other role, e.g. employer, friend.

B Can you see any disadvantages in going to a counsellor? Would you consult one? Why/Why not?

C You are going to listen to a college counsellor talking about her job. Her talk will cover the following topics:

- students' problems
- approaches to counselling
- her feelings about being a counsellor.

What would you like to find out about each of these? Write a question of your own on each topic. Compare your questions with those of a partner.

37 Listening for gist: A college counsellor 🔊

Listen to the interview. Which of the questions that you wrote are answered?

38 Detailed listening 🔊

Now listen again and complete the notes.

Typical student problem

Lacking sufficient money to get through college and getting (a) _____.

Possible solutions:

  Save money on travel and rent by moving to a cheaper flat near the college.

  Write to outside agencies for financial help.

  Apply to the (b) _____ fund at the college.

Dealing with exam stress

Apply study techniques.

Summarise notes into (c) _____.

Quality time spent studying is better than quantity time.

As well as studying, it is important to have time for (d) _____ and (e) _____.

Students also explore underlying worries that may be causing stress.

Personal and family problems

Ask family members to visit her too. Help students to express their feelings to their (f) _____.

She suggests ways that a student might get more space and privacy at home.

Approaches to counselling

Everything is confidential. Students' problems never discussed with others unless something (g) _____ is involved.

Good quality counselling needs (h) _____.

Counselling is mainly concerned with supporting people who are confused or (i) _____ to explore issues.

Problems being experienced now might be linked to back to bad (j) _____ experiences.

Counsellor's attitude to the job

She remembers she is not responsible for others' problems. Only they can make (k) _____ in their lives.

141

Inference

What can you infer from the interview about the benefits to the counsellor herself of the work she does? Try to think of one or two things. (Remember – inference means drawing reasonable conclusions from information given when the information is not explicitly stated.)

39 Rewriting a letter of advice

A You know that a friend of yours, Roberto, has difficulty getting on with his younger brother. He says that his brother scribbles on his posters, plays with his phone and starts arguments with him. What kind of advice would you give? Note your ideas.

B **Tone and register**
Now read the letter of advice that was written to Roberto by a fellow student. Do you think the tone and register sound right for the situation? Try to work out why or why not.

Rewrite the letter, making any changes you think are appropriate.

Dear Roberto,

I was devastated to hear of this tragic problem. It seems as if your brother has ruined your life. I know that you have always been untidy and careless. The result of this behaviour is that your little brother can find your things and spoil them. It seems as if you are bad-tempered and impatient with him too. Of course he will not like you if you are unkind to him. You must learn to put away your things and control your moods. I also have a younger brother so I am very careful to put my things away in a place where he cannot reach them. My younger brother and I have a close relationship. We play football together and I help him with his homework. We no longer quarrel because I am not selfish and have tried to understand him. We discussed the problem calmly with my parents. I did not shout or get angry which, as I see it, would be your reaction. It is a pity you cannot do the same.

Please write to me telling me that you have resolved your horrible problem. I hope to hear that you have achieved a pleasant atmosphere in your home.

All the best,

Daniel

40 Building a letter from a list of points

You read about this problem in your school newsletter.

'*I never seem to be in the right mood for homework or have the right stuff with me. I end up on websites that have nothing to do with anything! I am always getting distracted by my phone too. My parents are fed up with me. Any ideas?* Polly.'

Discuss this problem with a partner and jot down your thoughts about what could help Polly.

Now read the list of helpful homework tips below.

1 Have a treat to look forward to when you finish your homework.

2 Don't leave it too late in the evening to start.

3 Make sure you understand what homework you have to do before you leave school.

4 Put your phone on silent or put it away in a drawer.

5 Keep the equipment you need for your homework (pens, reference books, etc.) where you can find it at home.

6 On the internet, be selective and avoid clicking on links that are not relevant.

7 Plan your time: short, concentrated sessions are better than one long session.

8 Save useful website addresses for research topics in your 'favourites' list.

9 Use a clear surface to work on.

10 Keep a homework diary to help you keep a check on the homework you have done.

Add any ideas of your own to the list.

Writing

Write a reply to Polly which will be published in the newsletter. Offer her some advice about doing homework. Choose ideas from the list above. Develop the points into three coherent, interesting paragraphs. Use a friendly tone and register. Remember to add an opening and closing sentence.

41 Pre-writing discussion

Do you think bullying is a common problem? Why do you think some people become bullies? Why do some people become the victims of bullies, but others don't?

A younger friend of yours writes to you saying:

> *A boy in my class is bullying me. When I arrive at school he calls me names, and he threatens to push me off my bike and take it for himself. He says he will hurt me if I report him to a teacher.*

What advice would you give to help your friend? Jot down a few ideas.

42 Email completion

Now try to complete this email of advice about bullying.

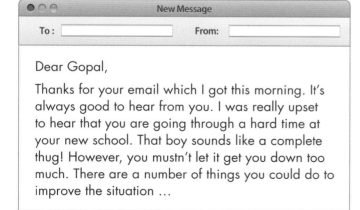

New Message

To : _____ From: _____

Dear Gopal,

Thanks for your email which I got this morning. It's always good to hear from you. I was really upset to hear that you are going through a hard time at your new school. That boy sounds like a complete thug! However, you mustn't let it get you down too much. There are a number of things you could do to improve the situation …

✴ GRAMMAR SPOTLIGHT

'Text speak'

A text message is a concise form of writing. It is usually very informal and written in 'text speak' instead of proper sentences. As you already know, 'text speak' is not appropriate for formal situations.

Typical features of text messages are:

a Missing pronouns, e.g. *Will try to call* = I will try to call.

b Missing articles, e.g. *Bus is late* = The bus is late.

c Missing capital letters, e.g. *saw maya at meeting in dubai* = I saw Maya at the meeting in Dubai.

d Missing prepositions, e.g. *Train arrives madrid 8 p.m.* = The train arrives in Madrid at 8 p.m.

e Very little or no punctuation, e.g. *cant talk now will call later* = I can't talk now. I'll call later.

f Special 'text speak' abbreviations & unusual spellings, e.g. *b4* = before, *2day* = today, *l8r* = later, *c u soon* = (I'll) see you soon, *yr* = your, *y'day* = yesterday, *2moro* = tomorrow.

All these features are used in order to save time when texting.

Some people use a lot of these features when they are texting, while others don't. You can, of course, make up your own 'text speak', if you think the other person will understand what you mean. There are no rules – it's up to you!

Study these extracts from text messages and then try to rewrite them in full sentences, with correct grammar, spelling and punctuation. You also need to make the style of one of them more appropriate to the situation.

1 hi libby! hope yr w/end in dublin went well

2 sorry but cant come 2nite. will fone u when i get home.

3 on way but gonna b 20 min late lotta traffic plse w8 4 me

4 hiya mr poulos! yeah gr8! i definitely want 2 take the job. thanks!

5 wl txt b4 i come round 2 make sure u r in

EXAM-STYLE QUESTIONS

Writing

1 You have a penfriend who was hoping to learn your language. However, in his last email he sounded discouraged about his progress and is thinking of giving up.

Write him an email in which you:

- say why he should continue to learn
- suggest some techniques which would help him to learn
- explain the future benefits to him of being able to speak your language fluently.

Your email should be 150–200 words long (or 100–150 words for Core level).

2 You have a friend who, although a competent student, becomes very nervous before exams and doesn't always do well in them. You know she has some important exams coming up and you would like to see her be successful.

Write her an email in which you:

- describe some ways she could revise effectively
- suggest some things which would help her relax
- explain the importance of following the examination rubric.

Your email should be 150–200 words long (or 100–150 words for Core level).

3 Your grandparents, who are both quite elderly, live in another town and would like to visit you at your school or college. They would like to stay in a modestly priced guest house. They can stay for only three days and are anxious to see as much as possible. Your grandfather has some difficulty walking long distances and uses a stick.

Write them a letter in which you:

- welcome them
- offer advice about accommodation and travel
- suggest ways to make the most of their trip.

Your letter should be 150–200 words long (or 100–150 words for Core level).

Speaking

1 Living more independently

Many young people look forward to the day when they can leave their parents' home and live a more independent life. What problems and challenges might leaving home bring? Discuss this topic with the assessor.

You may wish to use the following ideas to help develop the conversation:

- balancing a budget
- cooking, cleaning and generally looking after yourself
- coping with feeling lonely
- learning to be responsible for your own health
- coping with the possible dangers that you might meet.

You are free to consider any other related ideas of your own. You are not allowed to make any written notes.

2 The internet

The internet is popular with many students at school or college who believe it is a useful learning tool. Discuss this topic with the assessor. You may wish to use the following ideas to help develop the conversation:

- the extent to which you use the internet for your studies
- the idea that doing research on the internet can be frustrating and waste time
- the view that, in the future, the internet may make libraries unnecessary
- the problems that could arise if people copy material from the internet and pretend it is their original work
- whether 'virtual universities' should be encouraged by governments.

You are free to consider any other related ideas of your own. You are not allowed to make any written notes.

Form-filling

Shafiq Zader and Mohammed Bahry are from Jordan, and Primrose Urmaghi comes from Brunei. They have just started a university course at MacDonald University, Brisbane, Australia. After their first lecture, they meet for coffee in the cafeteria. Read their conversation.

Shafiq: I'm not used to listening to lectures in English. I was worried I wouldn't be able to understand the lecturer, but I didn't have to use my Arabic dictionary once!

Primrose: I was a bit worried too, but I understood nearly everything he said.

Mohammed: I think you can get English language support if you need it. I saw a poster about it in the corridor.

Shafiq: I think I'm going to be OK without it. I'm too busy. But I wouldn't mind having some help with study skills in general. I'm glad I chose to come here to do Aerospace Engineering, but it involves a lot of theoretical work.

Primrose: Well, I'd like to have some English support. In Psychology we're going to have to write essays every week!

Mohammed: I saw you taking lots of notes in the lecture, Primrose.

Primrose: That's how I like to learn – taking notes and drawing diagrams.

Mohammed: I don't mind taking notes but I really prefer being told and having the chance to talk things over.

Primrose: But if you take notes you can remember things better.

Shafiq: Our course tutor Mr Samsing is always advising us to read our notes over again and highlight key words if we want to remember things better. I haven't started doing that yet, though.

Mohammed: I think it's easier to remember things if you repeat them aloud to yourself.

Shafiq: I have to link new information with familiar things if I want to be sure of remembering it. The door where I live on campus has a security number you have to key in. It's S1814B. I remember it by thinking that S is my initial, 18 is my age, 14 is my sister's age, and B is the first initial of my middle name, Bilal.

Primrose: My student mentor lives in Bridgeway Hostel. Is that where you live, Shafiq?

Shafiq: No, my hostel's the one next to Bridgeway. It's called Lancaster. I haven't applied for a mentor yet, but I like the idea of having one, especially if it's someone on any kind of engineering course.

Primrose: I'd really recommend it. They can give you a lot of guidance. I usually meet my mentor in the students' canteen at dinner.

Shafiq: Do you? I'm cooking for myself – it's cheaper to make your own meals.

Primrose: I like to use the canteen. It's a good place to relax, too.

Shafiq: I do that in the sports centre. I've been playing basketball and lifting weights. I might learn to row and then join the rowing club. I've got some friends in the hostel who want me to join the football club, but I think I'm only going to have enough spare time for one thing.

Mohammed: I hope you're not going to be too busy for the International Students' Association. I'm definitely going to join.

Shafiq: Actually, I'm already a member. In fact, I've just volunteered to be treasurer! Nobody else wanted to do it. We've already sold 50 tickets for the barbecue next week.

Primrose: That's brave of you. And it will look good on your CV – having been treasurer, I mean.

Shafiq: I hope I won't need a CV! I'm going to work in my father's engineering firm when I graduate. Anyway, if you want tickets for the barbecue, just email me on s.zader3@oneworld.net. Or try my mobile – 2390765221.

New students are required to register with the Student Support Service. Imagine that you are Shafiq and complete the form.

STUDENT SUPPORT SERVICE
REGISTRATION FORM

SECTION A

Name: _____

Age: _____

Email: _____

Mobile phone: _____

If you are living on campus, please write the name of your student hostel: _____

Course of study: _____

Name of faculty coordinator or course tutor: _____

Please give details of any memberships of university clubs or societies, indicating if any positions of responsibility are held:

_____

_____

SECTION B

Country of usual residence: _____

What is your first language? _____

If English is not your first language, specialist English language support is available. Would you like us to contact you with details?
Yes / No   (*Please circle*.)

The Student Information Service holds study skills workshops at regular intervals. Would you be interested in receiving details?
Yes / No   (*Please circle*.)

We are currently gathering information about techniques students use to help them remember information. Please give us one example of a technique you use to help your memory.

_____

_____

If you would like us to arrange a Student Mentor for you, please tell us about any preferences you have, e.g. gender or nationality. If you have no preferences, write 'None'.

_____

_____

Do you regularly eat in the students' canteen?
Yes / No   (*Please circle*.)
If Yes, can you suggest any improvements?

_____

_____

SECTION C

In one sentence of about 12–20 words, please explain what you have liked about MacDonald University so far.

_____

_____

Thank you for completing this form! We look forward to being able to help you.

145

KEY ADVICE

1 Listening to English radio, watching TV and reading magazines, newspapers and books can help you understand more about the way people adapt their language to different occasions and for different target groups. For example, a magazine article for adults about ways of studying will be written in a different tone and register from an article on the same topic for 12-year-olds.

2 Speaking or writing on the same topic in a variety of tones and registers will also develop your ability.

3 Students often say they would like to improve their grammar. Here are some suggestions:

Study the errors you frequently make. Use your knowledge of regular grammar patterns and the exceptions to try to work out the differences between your version and the correct version.

- Use a good grammar book to check explanations of points you usually make mistakes with. You need a book which gives lots of examples, not just the rules and their exceptions.

- Work with a friend who speaks your first language. Work together to analyse your mistakes. As always, investigate the grammar pattern and think about exceptions too. See if you can work out a rule for that particular grammar point before looking it up in your grammar book.

- Apply your new knowledge of grammar in different situations. This will help you remember the point, and help you understand when it is correct and when grammar has to change to fit new situations.

- Exploring meaningful patterns and their exceptions will help your spelling and vocabulary work too. In fact, you can detect patterns in all the subjects you're learning (maths, science, art, etc.) if you look for them.

Exam techniques: speaking test

4 Usually the first part of a speaking test is an unmarked warm-up phase in which you will be asked a few questions about yourself.

5 In the test, you should aim to make the most of your ability with spoken English. Try to answer questions as fully as possible. Avoid 'Yes/No' replies or 'I don't know'. Don't be afraid to take a little extra time to think of replies which will be helpful in keeping an interesting conversation going.

Remember, communicating effectively in a natural and lively way is much more important than having perfect grammar or pronunciation.

6 Ask for clarification if necessary with questions such as 'Do you mean …?', 'Could you repeat that? I didn't quite understand.'

7 Aim to show that you are capable of abstract thought. Try to think around a topic from many different angles. Be prepared for a wide range of questions.

UNIT FOCUS

In this unit you have studied **tone and register** and developed skills for **giving advice** and encouragement.

You have learned to become more aware of **conversational techniques.**

You have read a detailed magazine article and answered comprehension questions.

You have listened to an informal discussion and completed a **set of notes.**

You have completed a **form based on a scenario.**

Unit 8:
Happy Endings

8.1 The call of the sea

1 Visualisation

Close your eyes and think of the sea. What sights and sounds come to your mind? What do you feel when you think about the sea? Now open your eyes and spend a few minutes writing down whatever came into your mind, in your own language or English.

2 Discussion

From the days of pirates and 'running away to sea', to modern-day beach holidays and scuba diving, the sea has drawn people like a magnet. Why do you think this is?

Discuss these remarks about the sea with a partner. Grade them as:

A *I identify strongly with this idea.*

B *This idea is interesting but I don't identify closely with it.*

C *I don't identify in any way with this idea.*

1 'The sea is a place of great adventure. When you set sail in a boat, you never know what you are going to find.'

2 'I love swimming. Being in water, especially the sea, brings great pleasure.'

3 'I live by the sea and love its changing atmospheres. On hot days the atmosphere is cool and restful. On bleak winter days, great storms bring drama and excitement.'

4 'When I go out in my boat, I feel free. All my worries are left behind on the shore.'

5 'Below its surface, the sea is full of life. I'd love to explore its depths and see the underwater world for myself.'

6 'I think the sea is mysterious. Huge ships have disappeared in it, never to be seen again.'

7 'I live in a dry area far away from the sea. My dream is to see the magnificence of the ocean and hear its wonderful sounds.'

8 'I admire anyone whose employment is connected with the sea. No other work requires such presence of mind.'

9 'Sailing presents a great spiritual challenge. In a storm or crisis, I discover unknown aspects of myself. After each trip I think I become a slightly different, more developed, person.'

3 Sea vocabulary: Odd word out

In pairs or small groups, circle the word which does not belong in each of the following groups. Use a dictionary to help you. You'll need many of the words later in the unit, so make a note in your vocabulary book of any that are unfamiliar.

Sea associations

Which word is not associated with the sea?

spray tides waves ocean cliffs bay shore
rocks hive current port horizon channel
shipwreck voyage cargo dock jetty surf

On the beach

Which item would you not expect to find on the beach?

shingle pebbles shells rocks starfish sand
spanner sand dunes flotsam and jetsam
seaweed driftwood turtle

Sea creatures

Which creature is not associated with the sea?

porpoise turtle lobster whale shark
seal dolphin puffin penguin crab squirrel

Words for boats

Which of the following is not a word for a kind of boat?

yacht dinghy raft tram tug speedboat liner
vessel canoe barge car ferry catamaran
oil tanker galleon trawler

Occupations connected with the sea

Which is the odd one out in this group of occupations?

captain   coastguard   helmsman   solicitor
sailor   pirate   fisherman   skipper   purser
lighthouse keeper   mariner   smuggler

Watersports

Which of these sports is not connected with water?

scuba diving   surfing   rowing   canoeing
swimming   diving   sailing   windsurfing
jet skiing   abseiling   snorkelling

Now match the four photographs on the previous page with four of the words above.

4 Sea vocabulary: Onomatopoeic words

A   Certain words are called *onomatopoeic* because the sound of the word is like its meaning.

Example:
*I love hearing the birds **twitter** on a sunny morning.*

Twitter is an onomatopoeic word because it sounds like the sound birds actually make.

Sea vocabulary is often onomatopoeic. Match these sounds to the things which make them.

Some sounds can be linked to more than one thing.

➕ VOCABULARY

lapping	hooting	howling
slapping	roaring	splashing
screeching	squelching	crashing

boats   waves   seagulls   wind   mud

B   What other onomatopoeic words do you know? Make a list with your partner.

C   What onomatopoeic words do you know in your own language? Share them with your group.

5 Writing a descriptive paragraph

Yesterday you made a trip to the coast. Write a paragraph describing what you saw, the sounds you heard and the way you felt.

Write about 75 words.

6 Reading aloud

In small groups, read your paragraphs aloud to each other. Be good listeners and make comments on what you hear.

7 Pre-reading discussion

A   For countries which have a coastline, the sea may be a means of defence in war, a source of riches from trade or fishing, and a way of maintaining separation from other countries. The sea is usually an important part of such nations' national identity. What part, if any, has the sea played in the history of your country?

B   There are many, many stories which centre around the excitement and drama of the sea. Do you have any favourites?

C   Daniel Defoe's novel 'Robinson Crusoe' is one of the most famous of these stories. What, if anything, do you know of it?

8 Reading and sequencing

Read the following version of the story of Robinson Crusoe. Try to guess the meaning of unfamiliar words.

As you read, number these events in the order in which they happened.

a   Crusoe is shipwrecked.

b   He meets Friday.

Never have any adventurer's misfortunes, I believe, begun earlier or continued longer than mine. I am Robinson Crusoe and this is my
5 story …

I was born in the year 1632 in the city of York. I had always wanted to go to sea but my father wanted me to enter the law. Against the wishes
10 of my parents, I joined a big trading ship when it was in dock at Hull. I knew I was breaking my father's heart but the call of the sea was too strong.
15 At first I was terribly seasick but I gradually learned to adapt and weather the great storms which blew up. On one occasion, to my misfortune, I was taken as a slave but
20 I escaped. For some time I even ran a plantation in Brazil but I could not resist returning to the sea. This time, however, the ship was wrecked and I was the only survivor.
25 The sea had washed me up onto a deserted tropical island. 'Am I all alone?' I called, and my despair knew no depths as I realised I was condemned to live in a silent world,
30 forever an outcast in this horrid place.

I knew I had to swim back to the ship before it sank completely and salvage everything of value. The task
35 was urgent as my survival depended on it. On the boat I found the ship's dog and two cats. These creatures, with a parrot I taught to speak, and a goat, were for many years my only
40 companions on the island.

For a home, I built a strong shelter close to fresh water. I explored the island and found fruit trees and a herd of goats. I sowed barley
45 I had taken from the ship, and made a calendar to mark the passing of the days. I resolved to look on the bright side rather than the dark side of my condition.
50 The doings of the greedy, material world and my own past wickedness became more and more remote. I spent many hours in hard labour, improvising baskets, pots, a boat
55 and other necessities, but I always made time for spiritual contemplation.

Each year the crops increased, my 'family' was contented and I learned
60 to love the beauty of the island. Yet I longed to see a human face and hear a human voice.

My solitude ended when, walking towards my boat, I stopped,
65 thunderstruck, at the sight of a strange footprint in the sand. This incident marked the beginning of my friendship with a man who lived on a distant island. He was escaping the
70 anger of his countrymen and I gave him refuge. 'Friday', as I called him, wanted to learn English and gradually we learned to understand one another and appreciate each other's way
75 of life.

My luck changed when an English ship appeared on the horizon. Friday and I observed a rowing boat coming ashore. My guess was right. The
80 crew of the ship had mutinied and the captain and some of his loyal followers had been taken prisoner. Friday and I worked out a way to capture the mutineers and set the
85 captain free.

The captain of the ship offered to take me back to England. Friday, who I had found as true and good a friend as a man could ever wish for,
90 was going to accompany me.

So, on 19th December 1686, after 28 years on the island, one of the strangest stories ever told ended as I, Robinson Crusoe, sailed away from
95 the island, never to return.

c He is made a slave.

d He returns to England.

e He manages a plantation.

f He sees an English ship on the horizon.

g He rescues the ship's captain.

h He builds a home on the island.

i He runs away to sea.

j He accepts his life on the island.

k He salvages things from the shipwreck.

9 Comprehension check

1 What future did Crusoe's father want for his son?

2 Even before the shipwreck, Crusoe had many adventures. What were they?

3 How did Crusoe feel when he realised he was all alone on the island?

4 What did he manage to do before the wrecked ship sank?

5 Describe Crusoe's way of life on the island.

6 What was the first sign that another human being had visited the island?

7 How did Crusoe finally manage to escape from the island?

8 Explain the meaning of the word *mutineer*.

10 Language study: Narrative tenses

To help the reader follow a story and understand how the events are connected, we use narrative tenses. Useful narrative tenses are the past simple, the past continuous, the past perfect and the 'future in the past'. *(I swam, I was swimming, I had swum, I was going to swim / would swim.)*

Study the tenses in the story of Robinson Crusoe with a partner. Underline each verb and decide which tense it is. Notice how the tense is formed. Add * if the verb is in the passive.

Ask each other why each tense is used.

With your partner, make notes for each narrative tense, like this:

The past simple
Typical examples in text

_____

Formed by

_____

Used in text because

_____

Finally, check your notes with a grammar book.

11 Beginnings and endings

Beginnings and endings are important in a story. How is our interest aroused at the beginning of the story of Robinson Crusoe? How satisfying did you find the ending?

What tenses are used at the beginning and end of the story? Why?

12 Discussion: Heroism

A What do we mean when we say someone is a 'hero' or 'heroine'? In what way do you think Robinson Crusoe could be described as a heroic figure?

B Can ordinary people living uneventful lives ever be called 'heroic'? Why/Why not?

C Who are your personal heroes or heroines? Share your ideas in your group.

D Crusoe changes a negative experience, being shipwrecked, into a positive one. What can we learn from our own negative experiences? How can the struggles and annoyances of daily life build our character and develop our understanding of ourselves and other people's problems? Do suffering and hardship ennoble the spirit or make people bitter and angry?

E Crusoe says he learned a lot from Friday, who came from a completely different, much simpler society. Give some examples of what he might have learned. Think about both survival skills and human values.

13 Continuing a story creatively

Try to imagine you are Robinson Crusoe, on your way back to England. Use these questions to help you continue his story.

■ What will you most miss about your island life?

■ What did you choose to take with you?

■ What have you learned from your experiences? Do you feel the hardships of the island have made you a better and more understanding person?

■ Who will remember you at home? Who will you want to see?

- How will you make your living?
- What might be the difficulties of fitting into a normal life again?

Share your ideas with your classmates.

14 Writing from notes

Most narratives use a variety of past tenses. The following paragraph describes Crusoe's return to England. Write the paragraph in full using the past simple, past continuous, past perfect, future in the past and past perfect continuous tenses.

We be / stand / deck / ship / when captain say /

English coast be / sight. I feel / very strange. Be I /

really go / see England again? After so many years /

solitude / noise / bustle / crowds / dock / almost

overwhelm me. I be / walk / towards town / when I

hear / voice / call my name. I turn / and see / sister. She

embrace me / warmly. I know / from tears / her eyes /

she forgive me / for hurt / our parents. She tell me /

she wait / me / since day / I leave. She almost /

give up hope / when she get / message / I be alive.

15 Comparing cultures

What stories in your culture have a sea theme? Think carefully about a story you know well and like. Then retell it to your group.

16 Showing surprise: Stress and intonation 🔊

Listen to the intonation patterns in these *wh-* questions and answers. When does the intonation rise? When does it fall?

1 Who arrived on the island in a rowing boat?
   Some mutineers.
   Who arrived?

2 What did Crusoe use to make a calendar?
   A wooden post.
   What did he use?

3 How long was he on the island?
   Twenty-eight years.
   How long was he there?

4 Why did Crusoe call the man 'Friday'?
   Because that was the day he saved his life.
   Why did he call him Friday?

Listen again and repeat the pattern.

Practice

Work in pairs. Ask each question with the falling tone. Then repeat the question showing surprise.

Try to continue with some questions and answers of your own.

8.2 Adrift on the Pacific

17 Pre-listening tasks

You are going to hear the true story of a couple, Maurice and Vita, who were attempting to sail across the world when their boat sank. They survived on a life raft for four months before they were rescued.

Narrative questions

A narrative should answer these questions:

Who…?	Why …?
What …?	How …?
Where …?	When …?

Write a question about the story beginning with each word.

Example: *Where did the boat sink?*

Try to make your questions grammatically correct.

Vocabulary check

Match these words which you are going to hear with their definitions.

1	emigrate	A	extremely thin
2	adrift	B	floating without purpose
3	counter-current	C	to make something using whatever materials are available
4	improvise	D	unaware of, not noticing
5	emaciated	E	a sea current running in the opposite direction
6	malnourished	F	to go to another country to live there permanently
7	oblivious to	G	unwell from lack of food

18 Detailed listening 🔊

Listen to the interview with the couple who survived. Try to note down answers to the questions you wrote.

19 Checking your answers

Did you find answers to your questions? Why/Why not?

20 Listening and note-making 🔊

Listen again and complete the notes.

a   Reason for the trip _____

_____

b   Where and why the boat sank _____

_____

c   Immediate reaction to the accident _____

_____

d   Rowing towards the Galapagos Islands was a mistake because _____

_____

e   Conditions on the raft _____

_____

f   What they ate _____

_____

g   Length of time adrift _____

_____

h   How they attracted the attention of their rescuers ___

_____

i   Length of time to recover _____

_____

j   How they coped emotionally during their experience

_____

21 Discussion: Motivation and adventure

A   What makes people want to become involved in risky projects such as sailing across the world in a very small boat, climbing a dangerous mountain, trekking in polar regions, or going into outer space? Discuss these ideas in your group.

- Are adventurers and explorers motivated by fame and money? Or a desire for risk and adventure? Or the competitive spirit?

- Is it a need to discover their potential and find out what they are capable of in the most testing circumstances – a kind of 'spiritual quest'?

Do you think people who undertake this kind of thing have greater 'inner strength' than others?

153

B   Is it right that each year large sums are spent rescuing people whose expeditions have gone wrong?

Could the urge for adventure be channelled more constructively into doing voluntary work on projects such as helping refugees? Or is this too 'tame' and over-organised?

When conditions on a dangerous expedition become very difficult, is it braver to accept defeat than to risk everything for success?

22 Ordering events

Put these statements about the couple on the life raft into the correct order by numbering them. Then link them using time expressions and conjunctions where appropriate. Choose from:

first, then, when, eventually, finally, before, until, next, after that, after many days

and conjunctions like *and, but,* etc.

- ☐ The *Sandpiper* was damaged by a sperm whale.
- ☐ They rowed towards the Galapagos Islands.
- ☐ They attempted to get to the Central American coast.
- ☐ The boat sank.
- ☐ A hostile current dragged them back out to sea.
- ☐ They tried to attract the attention of passing ships.
- ☐ They were rescued by South Korean fishermen.
- ☐ They returned to Britain.
- ☐ They sailed by unaware of the couple's situation.
- ☐ They escaped onto a life raft.
- ☐ They left England for New Zealand.

Check whether the order of events is correct by listening to the recording again.

23 Expressing emotions

In the interview Vita says, 'We continued towards that coast for three weeks. Then, to our horror, a hostile current dragged us out to the middle of the ocean.'

'To our horror' expresses the drama and emotion of the situation. Look at these similar expressions:

➕ **VOCABULARY**

to our amazement	to her disappointment
to our (great) relief	to their alarm
to my astonishment	to her concern
to their joy	to our sorrow
to his annoyance	to our delight

These expressions highlight the responses of the people involved in the events.

Study the following situations. Use a suitable emotional phrase to add to each description.

Example:
*We were waiting outside the operating theatre when, **to our great relief**, the surgeon came out and told us the difficult operation had been a success.*

1   I was looking through the TV guide when I realised I had missed my favourite programme.

2   We feared the worst when our son disappeared driving in the desert but yesterday he telephoned to say he was safe.

3   The racing driver was driving at top speed when he noticed his brakes were not working.

4   I was just going to have dinner when the telephone rang and I learned I had won first prize in a competition.

5   Jo was enjoying fishing for salmon when he saw a grizzly bear emerging from the forest.

6   I was looking forward to eating my favourite cake at the café when I found that the previous customer had ordered the last one.

Tenses

Examine the uses of tenses in the sentences. What tenses are used and why? Some sentences use more than one tense. Why, do you think?

24 Dictionary work: Prefixes

The prefix *mal-*

Maurice says that during their ordeal on the raft they became *malnourished.* The prefix *mal-* means 'badly' or 'wrongly'.

Replace the word(s) in italics in the sentences below with one of these words beginning with *mal-*. Work with a partner and use a good dictionary to help you.

➕ **VOCABULARY**

malfunctioning	malevolent	malpractice
malignant	a malingerer	
malicious	malnutrition	

1   The high-energy biscuits saved thousands of refugees who were suffering from *lack of food.*

2   The surgeon said the growth would have to be removed as it was *cancerous.*

3   To his horror, the pilot realised that one of the engines was *not working properly.*

4 The doctor was taken to court for *failing to care properly for his patients.*

5 Children's fairy stories often contain a character who is *very evil.*

6 This little boy is *deliberately hurtful* towards other children.

7 She's not really ill, you know. In my opinion she's *staying away from work for no good reason.*

The prefix *counter-*

In the interview you heard that Vita and Maurice had hoped to get to the equatorial *counter-current.* The prefix *counter-* means 'opposite', 'contrary' or 'reverse'.

Complete each sentence below with one of these words beginning with *counter-*. Continue using your dictionary if you need to.

✚ VOCABULARY

counterbalance	counterpart
counteract	counterargument
counterproductive	counterattack

1 Weights of the same size on this machine should be used to _____ each other.

2 If our aim is to make the workers do a good job, paying them less would surely be _____ .

3 In spite of heavy casualties, the soldiers launched a determined _____ against the enemy forces.

4 The doctor gave the child some medicine to _____ the poison she had swallowed.

5 The Danish Prime Minister met his Swedish _____ in Stockholm today for urgent talks on the fishing crisis.

6 Dominic came up with good reasons for continuing the journey on foot, but Celine put forward equally strong _____ s.

25 Revision of reported speech

When we are telling a story, we may want to change someone's actual words to reported speech.

For example, Maurice might have said to Vita, 'It's absolutely silent here. You can't have heard the engine of a boat. No one is coming to rescue us. You must be going mad.'

If this speech were reported it would change to:

Maurice told Vita it was absolutely silent there and she couldn't have heard the engine of a boat. No one was coming to rescue them. She must be going mad.

Study the example carefully.

What has happened to the verbs? What is the rule for **tenses** when direct speech is reported?

What has happened to *must?* Do other **modals** (*would, could, should, might, need, had better* and *ought to*) stay the same when speech is reported?

How have the **pronouns** changed? What usually happens to pronouns in reported speech?

What has happened to the **infinitive**? Do infinitives in direct speech change when the speech is reported?

26 Reporting verbs

Verbs such as *admit, promise, declare, invite, ask, explain, reflect, remind, mention, suggest, insist* and *refuse* are often used when we change direct speech into reported speech. Using them is a good idea because it brings breadth and variety into your writing.

Example: 'Remember to send your aunt a good luck message,' said their mother.

Their mother reminded them to send their aunt a good luck message.

What other reporting verbs do you know?

The following comments were made by a young woman, Silvia, who is planning to sail around the world single-handedly.

Change her actual words to reported speech, using suitable reporting verbs from the box. Some of the verbs are similar in meaning, so decide which you prefer.

✚ VOCABULARY

acknowledge	declare	reveal
add	explain	say
admit	insist	
confess	mention	

Example: 'I'm a yachtswoman and a loner. I would rather go sailing alone than in a group.'

She declared (that) she was a yachtswoman and a loner. She insisted (that) she would rather go sailing alone than in a group.

1 'I'm attempting to break the world record for sailing non-stop east to west the "wrong way" around the world.'

2 'I'm being sponsored on the trip by security firms and credit agencies.'

3 'I suppose my worst fear is personal failure. But I'm not trying to prove myself by sailing alone around the world. I've always been involved in challenging projects.'

4 'Yes, I'm doing it because I'm hoping to beat the present world record of 161 days.'

5 'I'm taking food and drink to last me up to 200 days.'

6 'The food includes 500 dried meals, 150 apples, 144 bars of chocolate, 36 jars of jam and marmalade and 14 tubs of dried fruit and nuts.'

7 'When I'm thousands of miles from shore, and if I'm injured, then I'll be scared.'

8 'I've been taught to stitch my own flesh in an emergency.'

9 'If there's a crisis, as long as danger is not imminent, I think the answer is not instant action, but to make a cup of tea and think about it.'

10 'I know I can handle the boat and I'll find out whether I have the strength to beat the world record.'

27 Writing a report of an interview

Imagine that you are a journalist. You have been asked to interview the yachtswoman. Write a report of the interview for your newspaper. Invent extra details to make your report convincing. Aim for a balance between reported and direct speech.

8.3 A remarkable rescue

28 Pre-reading tasks

Have you ever lost anything that was important to you? In pairs, ask each other questions using these prompts:

Where / be you?

Be you / alone?

What / be you / do / when you realise / it be lost?

What / you do / when you realise / what happen?

How / you react?

How / other people react?

What / happen / in the end?

INTERNATIONAL OVERVIEW

AN OCEAN OF FACTS! TEST YOUR KNOWLEDGE

1 The largest of the world's oceans covers more than a third of the earth's surface. Which is it?

   a   the Atlantic Ocean

   b   the Pacific Ocean

   c   the Arctic Ocean

   d   the Indian Ocean

2 The Arctic Ocean is the world's smallest ocean. True or false?

3 The world's largest inland sea has an area of 371,000 square kilometres. Which is it?

   a   the Baltic Sea

   b   the Black Sea

   c   the Caspian Sea

4 Which country of the world has the longest continuous coastline (37,653 km)? Choose from:

   a Australia   b Canada   c Russia

5 One country in the following list is the world's largest archipelago, with over 13,500 islands, of which about 6,000 are inhabited. Which is it?

   a   Indonesia

   b   the Philippines

   c   the Seychelles

6 The world's oceans contain about 10 billion tons of a precious metal, but nobody has worked out how to collect it. Which metal is it?

   a   silver

   b   gold

Predicting

You are going to read a newspaper article about an Irish farmer who lost his sheepdog while out walking on the cliffs near his home. Look carefully at the headlines and picture. What do they tell you about the story you are going to read?

Do you think the story will have a happy ending? Why/Why not?

Language and audience

Do you expect the language to be chatty and colloquial? Or formal and serious? Why?

Who do you think would enjoy reading this story?

29 Reading for gist

Read the newspaper article carefully, trying to guess any unknown words from the context. Most of the story is told using past tenses. As you read, underline examples of the past simple, past continuous and past perfect tenses.

30 Vocabulary check

Find words in the article and headlines to match these definitions. To help you, the definitions are in the same order as the words.

A REMARKABLE RESCUE

STRANDED SHEEPDOG REUNITED WITH OWNER AFTER 30-METRE CLIFF PLUNGE

WHEN Shadow the trainee sheepdog spotted a stray sheep, he did what comes naturally. The one-year-old set off in pursuit across several fields and, being a
5 young, inexperienced animal, somehow lost his sense of direction. He rounded the edge of a cliff and plummeted 30 metres, bouncing off a rock into the sea and, everyone thought, oblivion.
10 His owner, farmer Aidan McCarry, was very upset and immediately called the coastguard. Six volunteers abseiled down the cliff but gave up all hope of finding him alive after a 90-minute
15 search.

Three days later, a hurricane pounded the coast near Ballybunion, in south-west Ireland, and a resigned Mr McCarry was convinced he would
20 never see or hear of Shadow again.

Then, two weeks later, the phone rang and a man asked him if he would like his dog back.

The area is famous for birdlife,
25 including falcons and ravens, which can be seen on the cliff's narrow ledges. Two days earlier, a birdwatcher, armed with a telescope, had been watching some rock doves when he spotted the
30 dog sitting forlornly on a rock. While he raised the alarm, a young student, Brendan O'Connor, climbed down the cliff to collect Shadow.

The black and white collie had
35 initially been knocked unconscious but had survived by drinking water from a fresh stream at the base of the cliff. It was, as Mr McCarry admitted yesterday, 'a minor miracle'.
40 He recalled how he had left his farmhouse with his 16-year-old niece Keira, and set off on a coast walk.

'It was a beautiful day, with just a light breeze. Keira had got her camera
45 with her because she wanted to take photographs of the seals which come close to the shore. Shadow, who was a little in front of us, was running in a field full of wildflowers. Then he spotted a
50 sheep and began chasing after it. To my dismay, he forgot all the training I'd been giving him and completely ignored my whistles ordering him to come back to us. We tried to run after him but he was
55 too fast for us.'

He ran for about half a kilometre and fell head first down the cliffs and bounced off jagged rocks into the sea. 'We just stood there in stunned silence.

60 I was distraught. I had no idea how I would manage on the farm without him. We couldn't get down the cliffs because they were so sheer. I ran back to the village to get help, while Keira
65 phoned the coastguard. They turned up in seconds and a rescue party abseiled down the cliff, but they could not find him.'

Paddy Quin, who was in charge of
70 the rescue, said the dog was emaciated, a bit scratched and bruised, but otherwise healthy. He said: 'It was an extremely lucky dog.'

Vet Teresa Kelly, who was looking
75 after Shadow yesterday, said he had survived because of a plentiful supply of fresh water.

'He was also a well-fed dog before and still had his puppy fat – it was
80 probably those few extra pounds that saved him,' she added. 'He is very thin and hungry. But considering he had been there two weeks, his condition is very good.'

157

1 unable to get back

2 a sudden fall

3 noticed

4 fell quickly and suddenly

5 accepting the situation

6 looking lost and sad

7 a breed of dog

8 extremely upset

9 sharp

10 very steep, almost vertical

11 extremely thin

31 True/false comprehension

Decide whether the following statements about the story are true or false.

1 Shadow was used to working with sheep.

2 He followed a sheep over a cliff.

3 He lost consciousness when he fell.

4 His owner climbed down the cliff to find him.

5 The rescue party arrived very quickly.

6 His owner continued looking for him.

7 Shadow was identified by a student.

8 He was a little overweight before his fall.

9 He was in poor health when he was rescued.

10 He had survived because of access to fresh water.

32 Narrative structure

Like many newspaper accounts, the story is not reported in chronological order. It begins by explaining how Shadow got lost and the failed rescue attempt. We are then told that a second rescue attempt was successful. Halfway through the report the events of his fall and safe return are repeated, with more detail.

Why do you think the story is told like this? Consider the following:

- to provide a dramatic opening which is not slowed down by too much detail

- to enable us to hear actual spoken comments from the people who were involved

- to make the narrative as varied, moving and personal as possible.

33 Writing a summary from notes

Write a summary of the story describing how the dog got lost, what the owner did and felt, and how they were reunited. Use these notes to help you.

Farmer Aidan McCarry walk / with his sheepdog Shadow near Ballybunion / Shadow start / chase sheep. Unfortunately he fall over / cliff / towards the sea. His owner contact / coastguard / and rescue team / abseil down the cliff. However, Shadow cannot / found / and owner return home / feel / distressed. Two weeks later / man / ring. He say / birdwatcher / notice Shadow / on a rock. Student / rescue him. The dog / be thin / but well. Vet say / Shadow probably survive / by drink / fresh water.

34 Vocabulary: Adjectives

Shadow is described as a *well-fed* dog who becomes *emaciated*. His owner is *distraught* when he loses him.

The following adjectives describe emotion and appearance. With a partner, try to rank them in order. Use a dictionary as necessary.

Emotion

heartbroken   indifferent   distraught   happy irritated   pleased   satisfied   ecstatic   miserable

Appearance

slim   emaciated   skinny   plump   scrawny   thin fat   obese   overweight

35 Homonyms

Homonyms are words which have the same sound and spelling but different meanings. There are a number of examples in the article 'A Remarkable Rescue'.

1 'Two days earlier, a birdwatcher, armed with a telescope, had been watching some rock doves when he had *spotted* the dog sitting forlornly on a rock' (line 29).

   Spotted in this sentence is a verb which means 'noticed'.

   What does *spotted* mean in the following sentence? What part of speech is it?

   'He had a green and white *spotted* scarf around his neck.'

2 'We couldn't get down the cliffs because they were so *sheer*' (line 63).

   In this sentence *sheer* means 'extremely steep'.

   What does *sheer* mean in the following sentence? What part of speech is it?

'Driving fast on a motorway without a seatbelt is *sheer* madness.'

Practice

Work with a partner to check the meanings of the following homonyms. Use a dictionary if you need to. Then write example sentences to show the different meanings each word can have. Indicate whether the word is being used as a noun, verb, adjective, etc.

1	mine	4	dash	7	light
2	sound	5	file	8	match
3	stamp	6	book		

What other homonyms do you know? Share your ideas in your group.

36 Revision of defining relative clauses

Study this sentence from the text:

'Keira had got her camera with her because she wanted to take photographs of the seals *which come close to the shore*.'

The clause in italics is important to the meaning of the sentence. It is called a defining clause, because it defines or makes clear which person or thing is being talked about. Here are some more examples:

1 The vet *who treated Shadow* was very efficient.

2 They interviewed the man *whose dog had been rescued*.

3 Have you read the leaflet *which/that explains what to do if you have an accident?*

4 This is the house *where they live*.

A defining clause is essential to the meaning of the sentence. If it is left out, the sentence does not make complete sense or the meaning changes. No commas are used before defining clauses. Remember that the pronoun *that* can be used instead of *which* to refer to things in defining clauses.

Practice

Complete these sentences with suitable defining clauses.

1 They prefer stories _____ endings.

2 The man _____ has donated a lot of money to charity.

3 The student _____ received an award for bravery.

4 The watersport _____ on holiday has become my hobby.

5 The factory _____ is now a tourist hotel.

6 The doctor _____ comes from Guatemala.

37 Revision of non-defining relative clauses

Non-defining relative clauses give extra information about something. They can be in the middle or at the end of a sentence. Commas are used to separate them from the rest of the sentence.

Study these examples:

1 Paddy Quin, *who was in charge of the rescue,* said the dog was emaciated.

2 Pablo, *whose father is an ambulance driver,* is learning what to do in an emergency.

3 Forecasting the eruptions of volcanoes, *which can let off steam lightly for years,* is very difficult.

4 He gave the dog some water, *which she obviously needed.*

The pronoun *that* cannot be used in non-defining clauses.

Non-defining clauses 'round out' your sentences. Try to use them, as they make your writing more interesting and complex.

Practice

Add suitable non-defining clauses to these sentences. You should use *whose* in at least one of the clauses.

1 Rahmia Altat, _____, now does voluntary work.

2 We heard about the heroic acts of the rescue workers, _____.

3 Nurse Mara, _____, demonstrated the life-saving techniques.

4 Drowning, _____, can usually be prevented.

5 Smoke alarms, _____, should be fitted in every home.

6 My cousin Gina, _____, is being brought up by her grandparents.

Try to expand these simple sentences into more complex ones, using non-defining clauses to add extra information.

159

7   Mrs Nazir won a trip to the Caribbean.

8   Edward Smith left his fortune to the local hospital.

9   Our sailing teacher took us to an island.

Write some sentences of your own using non-defining clauses.

38 Functions quiz: Consoling and commiserating

Working in pairs, decide which is the most appropriate way to respond to the following statements giving bad news. Tick as many of the answers as you think are suitable.

1   *I've just failed my driving test.*
   a   What a shame.
   b   How horrific!
   c   That's sheer tragedy.
   d   You should have done better.
   e   Better luck next time.

2   *My grandma died recently.*
   a   Oh, I am sorry. Is there anything I can do to help?
   b   You must be really fed up.
   c   How sad. Was it sudden?
   d   Don't get too worried about it.
   e   What bad luck!

3   *I forgot my door key and had to wait outside for two hours until my father got back from work.*
   a   How annoying!
   b   That was forgetful of you.
   c   My heart goes out to you.
   d   I'd just like to say how sad I am for you.
   e   You must remember to put it in your bag in future.

4   *I thought I'd recorded 'Titanic' but when I sat down to watch it, I found I'd recorded the wrong programme!*
   a   Never mind. I can lend you the DVD.
   b   I bet you were furious.
   c   I'd have been really annoyed.
   d   You've got all my sympathy for what you're going through.
   e   Remember to follow the instructions next time.

Study the following comments. Write down some appropriate responses and then try them out on your partner.

5   I didn't get the job I applied for.

6   I'm really disappointed with my new haircut.

7   I broke my ankle on holiday.

39 Spelling and pronunciation: The suffix *-tion* or *-ion*

The suffix *-tion* or *-ion* is quite common in English. Examples in the text were *direction* and *condition*. How is the final syllable pronounced in these words?

Other examples are:

1   revision

2   fashion

3   occupation

4   demonstration

5   passion

6   invention

7   qualification

8   definition

9   recognition

10   ignition

11   exhibition

12   promotion

Listen carefully and try to mark the main stress in each of the words. Then practise saying them. 🔊

Question, *opinion* and *oblivion* are exceptions to the rule. How are they pronounced?

Now match ten of the words from the list to these definitions.

A   Will improve your chances of getting a job.

B   Another word for work.

C   A machine or gadget that is original.

D   Strong emotion.

E   A display of books or pictures.

F   The dictionary will give you this information about a word.

G   A better job with more money.

H   If this is turned off, the car will not start.

I   Artists can work for 20 years without getting this.

J   The latest styles in clothes and shoes.

40 Language study: Adverbs

Adverbs have a large number of different uses.

They can tell us more about a verb.

Example: *She walked slowly.*

They can be used before an adjective.

Example: *It was fairly difficult.*

They can be used before another adverb.

Example: *He drove terribly slowly.*

They can tell us when or how often something happens.

Examples: *occasionally, regularly, never*

They can give information about how certain we are of something.

Examples: *definitely, probably, perhaps*

They can connect ideas.

Examples: *firstly, however, lastly*

Formation of adverbs

Many adverbs are formed by adding **-ly** to adjectives. *Naturally, forlornly* and *initially* are examples from the text 'A Remarkable Rescue'.

Other examples are:

quick ~ quickly, cheap ~ cheaply

If the adjective ends in *-y*, you change the *-y* to *-i* before adding *-ly*.

Example: *angry ~ angrily*

If the adjective ends in *-ic*, you add *-ally*.

Example: *heroic ~ heroically*

If the adjective ends in *-le*, you drop the *-e* and add *-y*.

Example: *reasonable ~ reasonably*

Remember that some adjectives look like adverbs.

Examples: *lovely, elderly, friendly*

Notice also: *early ~ early, fast ~ fast, good ~ well*

Practice

Correct the report on jobs at sea on the next page, which is from a careers magazine for young people. Change the words in italics to adverbs. Ask your partner to mark it when you have finished to check that your spelling is correct.

CAREERS AT SEA

Working at sea sounds romantic but it can also be *surprising* hard work! Voyages on commercial merchant ships transporting cargo and passengers
5 last at least a week. Supersized cruise ships, which enable tourists to visit multiple holiday destinations during the voyage, can be at sea much longer. As you will see, it is *definite* not for the
10 *lazy*-inclined.

Here are some of the main jobs at sea.

The Captain

The captain is in overall control of the vessel. He or she (modern captains are not *necessary* male) is
15 *direct* responsible for the vessel, crew, cargo and passengers. It is essential that the captain can think *quick* in an emergency. The captain *normal* takes the vessel in and out of port.

Engineering Officer

20 Engineering officers are responsible for the ship's engines and all the equipment which is *electronic* operated. The equipment is checked *day* and

any faults must be corrected
25 *immediate*. Officers are *able* assisted by ratings – workers who maintain equipment in the engine room and elsewhere.

The Purser

The purser is responsible for
30 buying and storing food and making sure it is prepared and served *hygienic*. Pursers must make sure that all those on the vessel are fed *healthy* and *economic*. They
35 are also in charge of the cooks and stewards, who are *usual full* trained chefs and waiters.

Navigating Officer

The navigating officers are responsible for navigating the ship *proper* and
40 for making sure the loading and unloading of cargo is *total* safe. They respond *appropriate* to any changes in weather (in some areas the climate can change *dramatic* in seconds) and
45 adjust the ship's speed *according*. In difficult conditions, when it's snowing

very *heavy* for example, they may take over *temporary* from the helmsman.

Skills and qualities needed for work at sea

You must be:
50 ■ *technical* minded (for most jobs)
■ *suitable* qualified
■ able to work *capable* and *efficient* for long periods
■ able to get on *happy* with others as
55 part of a team
■ able to react *responsible* in times of crisis
■ able to stay calm even when *frantic* busy.

41 Look, say, cover, write, check

In the text 'A Remarkable Rescue' you saw the word *distraught.* The letters *aught* are a common combination in many words. The phonetic spelling is /ɔːt/.

Use the 'look, say, cover, write, check' method to learn these words. Make sure you understand the meaning of each one.

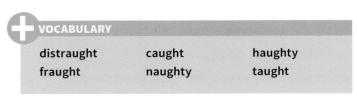

+ VOCABULARY

distraught	caught	haughty
fraught	naughty	taught

Ought is also pronounced /ɔːt/. Use the same method to learn to spell these words correctly.

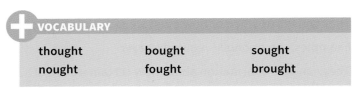

+ VOCABULARY

thought	bought	sought
nought	fought	brought

8.4 Reacting to the unexpected

42 Pre-reading task: Making notes

Read about these unexpected events that happened to various people.

> *I was walking home when a passer-by collapsed in the street.*

> *We had just gone to bed when the smoke alarms went off.*

> *I was chatting to my best friend when one of the party guests insisted I tried the dancing competition and I won first prize!*

> *My neighbour knocked on the door. She was sure her little girl had swallowed some poisonous berries.*

> *I was doing my homework when water started pouring through the ceiling.*

Have you ever had to cope with something, pleasant or unpleasant, that was completely unexpected? Think carefully about the event and then make notes under these headings.

The background to the event

Where were you? _____

_____

_____

_____

What were you doing? _____

_____

_____

_____

Who was with you and what were they doing? _____

_____

_____

_____

The event itself

What happened? _____
_____
_____
_____

How did you react? _____
_____
_____
_____

What did other people do? _____
_____
_____
_____

What happened then? _____
_____
_____
_____

The outcome

What happened in the end?_____
_____
_____
_____

What do you feel you have learned from the experience? _____
_____
_____
_____

How has the experience affected other people? _____
_____
_____
_____

Has the event had any other permanent effects? _____
_____
_____
_____

Compare your notes with your partner's. Look after them as you'll need them later.

43 Reading an example narrative

Read this narrative written for a school newsletter. Do you think you would react in the same way as the writer?

As you read, underline the tenses and the examples of non-defining relative clauses.

THE BIGGEST EVENT OF MY SUMMER
by Naila Khan Afza

It seemed like another ordinary day. My family and I had decided to spend the day on the beach. I sat in the sun watching the children throwing pebbles or paddling. I was thinking about having a swim when I noticed a strange object bobbing about in the sea. To my horror, I realised the 'object' was a child drowning. Without stopping to think, I plunged into the water and grabbed the child. With my free arm I swam back to the shore. The child, who was a boy of about five, was like a dead weight but I felt powered by a superhuman strength.

I laid the boy, who appeared to be unconscious, gently on the ground and gave him mouth-to-mouth resuscitation which revived him immediately. I was dimly aware that a large crowd had gathered and someone was telling me an ambulance was on its way. By the time the ambulance arrived, to my great relief, the boy was sitting up and talking.

Dale's parents were delighted with his quick recovery. They telephoned me later to thank me and we had a long discussion about the dangers of playing near water. They have arranged for him to have swimming lessons, which I think is a very good idea. I would definitely recommend that all the students in the school learn to swim. I'd also like to remind everyone to take care near the sea, rivers or swimming pools. You can drown much more easily than you think!

Comprehension check

1 What was Naila doing when the incident happened?
2 Did she have time to tell anyone else what was happening?
3 What helped the boy regain consciousness?
4 How did the boy's parents express their thanks?
5 What does Naila suggest everyone should do?

44 Analysing the narrative

A Openings are important in narratives. Does the story interest you immediately? Why/Why not?

B In the first paragraph, a number of different tenses are used. What are they, how are they formed and what are their functions?

C 'To my horror', 'Without stopping to think' and 'To my great relief' are used for effect. What other phrases could be used?

D Endings are important in a narrative. The reader should not feel there are unanswered questions. Do you think the story is brought to a satisfactory conclusion? Why/Why not?

E Remember, a narrative should answer these questions:

Who …?   Why …?

What …?   How …?

Where …?   When …?

How does Naila's narrative do this?

45 Dramatic expressions

My hair stood on end …

My heart missed a beat …

Your sentences can be made more dramatic by starting them with this kind of expression. Make complete sentences by matching the following openings 1–6 with the endings A–F. More than one option may be possible, so decide which you prefer.

1 With my heart in my mouth …
2 A piercing scream cut through the air …
3 I froze to the spot …
4 Panic mounted …
5 With trembling fingers …
6 Sweat poured from us …

A … as we fought to rescue the children trapped by the earthquake.

B … when flames appeared at the side of the plane.
C … as the hijacker produced a gun!
D …when the ghostly figure appeared in the graveyard.
E … I tiptoed past the sleeping kidnappers.
F … he struggled to open his parachute.

Now write four sentences of your own using dramatic expressions.

46 Pre-writing discussion

1 What does windsurfing involve?
2 What do you think is exciting about this sport?
3 Could it ever be dangerous? Why/Why not?
4 Does this hobby appeal to you? Why/Why not?

47 Ways of developing an outline

The following list of sentences is an outline of a story. It describes how a windsurfer was swept out to sea and what happened in the end. Read the sentences carefully. Make sure you understand all the points clearly.

I Fought To Stay Alive

I was sailing off the coast of Scotland.

It was a calm sunny day.

I'm a very experienced windsurfer.

Everything was going well.

The wind turned, forcing me offshore.

I tried for an hour to get back to the shore.

I began to feel weaker.

The wind started coming in gusts.

The sea was rough.

I clung hard to the board.

A helicopter flew over.

I thought it was coming to rescue me.

I waved and shouted.

It flew over me to the other side of the bay.

I was wearing a dark wetsuit on a blue and white board.

I was part of the sea and no one could see me.

When night fell, I lay down on the board, wrapped in my sail.

I was in my own little world.

Then I heard a helicopter.

I waved.

They saw me.

They rescued me.

Obviously, a list of events does not make a complete narrative. In fact, the pleasure of reading a good story often lies not in the plot, but in the details.

What details could you add to the outline above to produce an exciting, well-written story? With your partner, tick off the points which could make your story come alive.

a Beginning the story with some interesting details which set the scene, e.g. *It was a beautiful, sunny day and I was doing what I like best – windsurfing.*

b Describing the weather and the sea in a vivid way, e.g. *The wind was howling / The waves were crashing.*

c Using dramatic expressions, e.g. *My heart sank as the sailboard was carried far out to sea.*

d Using emotional expressions to add drama, e.g. *to my horror / to my intense relief* (See exercise 23.)

e Writing a clear conclusion to the story which expresses the feelings of the writer about the experience, e.g. *I am so grateful to the people who rescued me. I was not ready to die at sea!*

Don't forget!

Time expressions make the sequence of events clear, e.g. *Many hours passed, some time later, until, when, then, while, next, finally.*

Conjunctions connect clauses or show connections between sentences. e.g. *however, although.*

Non-defining relative clauses round out sentences and make them more interesting to read.

48 Building a story from a dialogue

In pairs, read this conversation about what happened during a school outing to the seaside.

Sophie: Where did you go for your school trip this year?

Miriam: We went to the coast. It was so hot that we all wanted to get out of the city.

Sophie: How did it go?

Miriam: Well, we had a great day, apart from one incident.

Sophie: Oh, what was that?

Miriam: Well, we all got to the beach without any trouble. We'd finished putting on sun cream and were just going for a swim when Mrs Kazan noticed that her purse, which had all our return train tickets in it, was missing.

Sophie: Oh no!

Miriam: Yes, she was dreadfully upset. She decided that the purse must have dropped out of her bag on the walk to the beach from the station. You see, Ethan had offered to carry the bag for her and she thought maybe it had fallen out then – but she wasn't really sure.

Sophie: So did you all go back to look for it or what?

Miriam: Well, I offered to go with her, but in the end she said she'd retrace her steps with Ethan and see if they could see any sign of it.

Sophie: Poor Ethan. He must have felt awful.

Miriam: I think he did. I mean, he was just going to have a swim when he had to put his clothes back on and go back to the station with Mrs Kazan.

Sophie: And did they find it?

Miriam: Well, they walked right back to the station without seeing it. At the station they asked at the information desk but it hadn't been handed in.

Sophie: Oh dear.

Miriam: On the way back to the beach they stopped at a café for a drink. They were talking about the purse and wondering what to do next when the owner came over. He asked if they'd lost anything. They mentioned her purse and the man produced it from under the counter. A passer-by had spotted it on the pavement outside and had handed it in at the café.

165

Sophie: Well that was lucky! And was everything still inside?

Miriam: Yes, it was, thank goodness.

Writing the story

You are Ethan. Write an account of the incident for the class newsletter. Before you begin writing, plan what you will say. Use these notes to help you.

- Give the story a clear **shape**: background details, main events and the outcome should be clear.
- **Tenses** and **pronouns** should be appropriate.
- Try to write **vividly**, using a range of vocabulary and expressions.
- Use clearly defined **paragraphs**.

GRAMMAR SPOTLIGHT

The interrupted past continuous

The interrupted past continuous is used to show that an action stopped at a specific point, when something else happened:

I was packing for my trip when the police knocked at the door.

We use *when* to link the two tenses. If we want to emphasise two things happening at just the same time, we may choose *as*:

It was snowing as he climbed higher up the mountain.

The interrupted past continuous is often used to set the scene and to make the beginning of a story more dramatic or interesting.

In the text in exercise 43, you have seen:

I was thinking about having a swim when I noticed a strange object bobbing about in the sea.

Look back at the speech bubbles in exercise 42 and underline any examples of the interrupted past continuous. Which actions were interrupted, and by what event?

Now complete the sentences below setting the scene for exciting stories.

1 I was alone at home late at night _____ a scary movie when I _____ the sound of footsteps on the stairs.

2 Anton was _____ a sandwich on the busy evening train when the elderly man opposite him _____ his newspaper and _____ a gun.

3 Lorna was desperately _____ for her mobile phone when, to her horror, she felt a large hand _____ her mouth.

4 Mr Greene was _____ a milky drink before bed when he _____ a strange face at the window.

5 The class were _____ quietly to Mr Hamsun's science lecture and _____ notes when the teacher suddenly _____ his hand in his pocket and _____ a fistful of fabulous diamonds onto the desk.

6 Alan was walking with his children in the woods when, to his amazement, he _____ a mysterious, veiled woman dressed in golden robes.

EXAM-STYLE QUESTIONS

Writing

1. You were walking on the beach with some friends when you discovered a valuable object. You decide to write an account of the incident for your school magazine.

   In the account you should describe:

   - how you felt
   - what you did about the object
   - what happened in the end.

   Write about 150–200 words (or 100–150 words for Core level).

2. You and your family were on a ship when a storm blew up. Fortunately, you were able to return to the coast unhurt. Write an email to your cousin, describing what happened.

   In your letter you should:

   - explain what you were doing when the storm blew up
   - describe how people reacted
   - explain how you felt afterwards.

   Write about 150–200 words (or 100–150 words for Core level).

3. You were on a school outing when one of the younger children got lost. You helped your teacher find him or her. Write an account of the incident for the school newsletter. In the account you should:

   - explain how the child got lost
   - explain how you managed to find him or her
   - say what you learned from the incident.

   Write about 150–200 words (or 100–150 words for Core level).

Speaking

1 Coping with setbacks

Some people are able to overcome difficult situations more easily than others. Discuss this topic with the assessor. In your conversation, you may like to discuss ideas such as:

- the kind of situations that cause us to feel disappointed or upset
- a time in your life when something went wrong for you
- what you learned from this difficult situation
- the view that modern teenagers are less capable of solving their own problems than previous generations
- the idea that coping with setbacks and disappointments helps us grow into stronger people.

You are free to use any other related ideas of your own. You are not allowed to make any written notes.

2 A job aboard ship

There are many different kinds of job opportunities at sea. Discuss the idea of a career aboard ship with the assessor. In your conversation, you may like to discuss ideas such as:

- whether a job at sea appeals to you
- the benefits and disadvantages of working on a large cruise liner
- the challenge of working on a small boat
- whether a job with the merchant navy is more attractive than being part of the military navy
- whether you would ever like to have a boat of your own, and why.

You are free to use any other related ideas of your own. You are not allowed to make any written notes.

KEY ADVICE

1. When asked to write a **narrative**, students sometimes say they don't know what to write about. The ingredients for stories are all around us: in the incidents that happen in everyday life; in the stories your friends tell you about things that have happened to them; in newspaper articles; in the letters read out on radio talk shows and so on. With a little ingenuity, you can rework intriguing ideas into your own writing.

2. The plot isn't everything. Many wonderful stories do not have particularly original plots. The main interest in a story often lies in the beauty of the writing. Giving **attention to detail** in your writing is as important as having an original plot.

3. **Planning** your composition before you start composing will help you structure it. Narratives usually start with background information. The story then develops and you explain what happened. Finally there should be a definite rounding off so the reader isn't left wondering what happened in the end.

4. Aim to **make your writing interesting** so the reader really wants to read on and find out what happened next. Here are some ways you can do this:
   - Use a mixture of short sentences and longer, more complex sentences.
   - Use vivid language and a range of emotional and dramatic expressions.
   - Try to set the scene at the beginning in a powerful, unusual way if you can.
   - Endings are important too. Try to make the ending satisfying and logical.

5. If you enjoy reading and have any favourite authors, try to work out what you particularly like about their books. Study their style. What techniques do they use to help you 'picture' the story in your mind? Could you adopt any of these techniques in your own work?

   Remember, regular readers usually do much better in exams than those who don't read very often.

6. Try to get into the habit of punctuating as you go along, by 'hearing' the prose in your mind.

Exam techniques

7. Where you are completing sets of notes in listening examinations you may be able to sets of notes in listening examinations you may be able to use the words exactly as you heard them, but at other times you might need to change the word order or use words and phrases of your own to complete the gaps.

   You will hear each exercise twice. Use the second listening to check your answers for complete sense.

UNIT FOCUS

In this unit you have learned to write a **narrative composition**. You have studied narrative tenses, and how to write strong openings and endings. You have learned to add interest to your writing by using **relative clauses**, and **emotional and dramatic expressions**.

You have read a detailed newspaper text and answered true/false questions. You have listened to an interview and **made notes**.

Unit 9:
Animals and Our World

9.1 A fresh look at zoos

1 Animal vocabulary

Working with a partner, match six of these words with the pictures. Make sure you know the meaning of all of them. Then decide whether each creature is a *mammal*, *reptile*, *fish* or *bird*.

+ VOCABULARY

bear	lion	parrot
rhino	snake	camel
crocodile	elephant	salmon
lizard	penguin	dolphin
vulture	leopard	monkey
gorilla	shark	wolf
cheetah	eagle	kangaroo

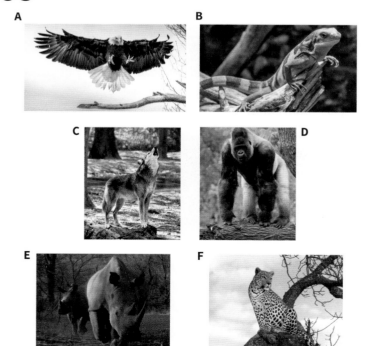

2 Definitions

Choose the correct word or phrase to match these definitions. Work with a partner and consult a dictionary if necessary.

1   A person in a zoo who looks after animals is known as:

   a   a carer

   b   a keeper

   c   a warder

   d   a poacher

2   The natural surroundings of an animal are called its:

   a   habitat

   b   location

   c   home

   d   enclosure

3   Animals which hunt and kill other animals for food are known as:

   a   scavengers

   b   beasts

   c   predators

   d   prey

4   Animals which may die out altogether are known as:

   a   endangered species

   c   indigenous wildlife

   b   animals in captivity

   d   migrating herds

5   Animals which once lived but have now died out are known as:

   a   domesticated

   b   extinct

   c   fossils

   d   amphibians

3 Pre-reading discussion

A   How do you feel about zoos? Talk to your partner about a zoo you have visited. Which aspects did you find particularly interesting?

   Think about:

   ■   the range of animals and birds

   ■   the conditions under which they were kept

   ■   whether they seemed contented

   ■   the atmosphere of the zoo in general.

B   Was there anything about the zoo that you did not enjoy?

C   If you have never been to a zoo, would you like to visit one? Why?

Keep a record of your views to use later in the unit.

4 Reading a school magazine article

Hammerton High School paid a visit to a zoo. After the visit, Michael wrote about the trip for his school magazine. Read his article below. How does his impression of the zoo compare with your own experiences?

As you read, underline the opinion words and phrases he uses.

Can Zoos Ever Be Animal-Friendly?

The theme of our last class discussion was 'How can zoos provide animals with a decent life?' Everyone except me (I just wasn't sure) believed it was impossible for zoos to give animals a decent environment. Mr Hennessy suggested
5 that, now the exams are over, actually visiting a modern zoo might give us a wider perspective.

I went to the zoo with an open mind and I was pleasantly surprised by what I found. In our debate, many people said that zoos are full of smelly cages containing animals with
10 miserable, hunted-looking expressions. Metro Park Zoo, however, was set in an attractive, open environment. Trees and bushes had been planted around the enclosures. Small ponds had been dug out so the animals had access to water. In my opinion, the animals, rather than seeming depressed
15 or frustrated, were peaceful and contented.

As we entered, we were given information packs about the origins and habits of the animals. The zoo takes a lot of trouble to keep the animals' diet, living quarters and social groupings as natural as possible. Expert veterinary
20 attention is on hand if they become ill.

At school, some people accused zoos of exploiting animals for profit but at Metro Park, as I see it, nothing could be further from the truth. Most of the profits are ploughed back to improve conditions at the zoo or donated to charities
25 for endangered species.

Before I visited Metro Park Zoo, I wasn't sure about the rights and wrongs of zoos. It was difficult to say how a zoo could really compensate animals for their loss of freedom. On balance, I feel that, although zoos can't
30 provide the stimulation and freedom of the wild, they can be animal-friendly by giving animals a safe, secure and caring environment where they are well fed and protected from predators. As long as they do this well, to my mind they make a positive contribution to animal
35 welfare. They also play an important part in educating us about wildlife. I think lots of my friends changed their minds, too.

On the bus back to school we all agreed that what we liked most was the zoo's atmosphere and we would definitely
40 recommend it for next year's group.

5 Comprehension check

1 Why did Michael's class visit the zoo?

2 What was his first impression of the zoo?

3 What did he find out from the zoo's publicity?

4 What kind of role does he think zoos have in modern society?

5 What do you think are the bad points about zoos which Michael has not mentioned?

6 Analysing the article

A Does the first paragraph form a good opening to the article? Do you feel you want to read on? Why/Why not? How is it obviously intended for an audience of school pupils?

B Paragraph 2 questions the attitudes many people have to zoos by contrasting their opinion with the reality (as Michael sees it) of Metro Park Zoo. Find the words and phrases which do this.

C Paragraphs 3 and 4 continue the theme of disagreeing with other people's opinions about zoos. Underline the phrase which expresses disagreement.

D Paragraph 5 sums up Michael's view of zoos. Which phrase tells us that he has thought about both sides of the argument before coming to a decision? Which connector is used to develop his argument and link his ideas together?

E Does the final paragraph round off the article effectively? How do we know that the writer is aware of his audience?

7 Typical opinion language

In paragraph 2, Michael introduces an opinion with *In my opinion*. What other opinion words and phrases does he use? Make a list.

_____

_____

What other opinion words and phrases do you know? Add them to your list.

Disagreeing with other people's views

In explaining his views, Michael thinks about and rejects the ideas other people have about zoos. Study the list and tick off the phrases Michael used. Can you add any phrases?

A common misconception is that …
Contrary to popular belief, …
It is believed that … , yet …
People think … but …
Some people accuse them of … but nothing could be further from the truth.
Many people say that … . However, …
It's unfair for people to say that …
People make the absurd/ridiculous claim that …
Despite claims that … ,

8 Making your mind up

Here are ways you can show that you have thought carefully about a variety of opinions before making up your mind. Can you recognise the phrase Michael used? Which do you prefer?

Now that I have considered both sides, I feel …
After weighing up the pros and cons, I would say that …
On balance, I feel that …
There are points in favour of each argument but overall I believe …
I tend to come down on the side of …

9 Writing a paragraph

Choose one of the following topics and write a short paragraph giving your own opinions on the subject. Don't forget that you need clear reasons to back up your views. Try to select appropriate phrases from exercise 7 to help frame your views.

Animals – healthy and happy in the wild, bored and fed-up in the zoo?

Pets – treasured companions or dirty nuisances?

Eating meat: vital for health or unnecessary and unfair to animals?

10 Reading aloud

When you are ready, take turns reading your paragraphs aloud. This will give you a chance to get an overview of your classmates' opinions. Does hearing other students' paragraphs make a difference to your own views? If so, you may like to choose a 'making your mind up' phrase to express your feelings.

11 Expressions of contrasting meaning

In his article, Michael says people think of zoos as full of 'smelly cages' but in fact the animals were kept in 'an attractive, open environment' – the opposite, you could say, of what was expected.

For each idea below, try to develop an expression which conveys a contrasting meaning.

Example: *a bare, cramped room*
a comfortably furnished, spacious room

Work in pairs or small groups, and take time to check words in a dictionary when you need to.

1. a dull, uninformative lesson
2. a scuffed, down-at-heel pair of shoes
3. a whining, sickly child
4. an overcooked, tasteless meal
5. an awkward, clumsy dance
6. an untidy, neglected garden
7. ugly, illegible handwriting
8. a rusty, battered bicycle
9. a loud, aggressive person
10. a hard, lumpy bed

When you have finished, compare your answers with the other groups. Which expressions do you think were most effective?

12 Before you listen

You are going to listen to a radio talk about the concept of an electronic zoo. Modern technology is used to portray the animals in natural settings.

Write down three things you would like to find out about this type of zoo.

13 Vocabulary check

Make sure you know the meaning of these words and phrases.

 VOCABULARY

audio-visual	live exhibits
filmed on location	natural history

14 Listening for gist 🔊

Now listen to the radio talk. Does the speaker answer your questions about electronic zoos?

15 True/false comprehension

Decide whether the following statements about the electronic zoo are true or false.

1 Visitors to the electronic zoo will gain a greater insight into animal behaviour.

2 The large animals will be allowed to wander freely, watched by cameras.

3 The technology at the zoo will help people feel they are watching a particularly good film show.

4 Ninety-five per cent of the world's species will be represented.

5 The pre-recorded film of live exhibits will be produced by staff at the electronic zoo itself.

6 Visitors will be disappointed if animals at the electronic zoo are asleep.

16 Post-listening discussion

A If you could choose between a visit to a 'real zoo' and an electronic zoo, which would you prefer? Try to explain your reasons.

B Do you think the electronic zoo will become popular with the public? Would it appeal more to one target group than another? Discuss your views in groups.

17 Functions 🔊

Have you ever been to a circus? Tell your partner what you thought of it.
Now listen to the dialogue. Silvia is expressing disappointment. Does her voice go up or down?

Malik: What did you think of the circus?

Silvia: Well, to be honest, I was just a bit disappointed.

Malik: Why was that?

Silvia: The trapeze artists weren't very exciting and I didn't like seeing large animals performing tricks.

Malik: Surely the jugglers were good fun to watch?

Silvia: As a matter of fact, they weren't as skilful as I thought they'd be.

Malik: But wasn't seeing a real live fire-eater amazing?

Silvia: To be frank, I've seen better things on television.

Malik: Sounds like a waste of money, then.

Silvia: It was! In fact, we left before the end.

Expressing disappointment

I was just a little bit disappointed.

It didn't come up to my expectations.

It wasn't as interesting / enjoyable / well done / polished as I thought it would be.

I've seen better things on television.

It was a let-down.

Expressing disagreement informally

Surely the clowns / costumes / performances / songs were amusing/intriguing/absorbing/spectacular?

But wasn't a real live fire-eater / film star / pop singer / famous athlete amazing/superb/unforgettable to watch?

Wasn't it wonderful to see the real thing?

Introducing personal opinion

As a matter of fact, / In fact,

To be honest, / If you want my honest opinion,

To be frank, / Frankly,

Actually,

Commenting

It sounds like a waste of money, then.

It sounds as if it wasn't worth going to.

It sounds as if you'd have been better off at home.

18 Practice dialogues

Try to make a complete dialogue from the prompts. Make sure the person expressing disappointment sounds disappointed!

A: What / you think / electronic zoo?

B: Frank / just bit / disappointed.

A: Why / that?

B: Most exhibits / asleep / interactive video / not work.

A: Surely / sounds / elephants / African waterhole / fascinating?

B: Actually / not be / realistic / thought / it be.

A: But / not be / Magic Windows / fantastic?

B: Matter / fact / be / let-down.

A: You / be / better off / home.

B: That's right! And saved my money, too.

Try to create similar dialogues around the following situations.

- A disappointing visit to an animal sanctuary where injured animals are cared for before being returned to the wild.

■ A disappointing visit to a theatre or concert to see well-known performers.

■ Some other disappointing event you have personally experienced.

9.2 Animal experimentation

19 Pre-reading discussion

Experiments on animals play a large part in medical research. Scientists say they hope to find cures for many human diseases by finding out how animals react to being given drugs or having operations.

Animals are living beings. Experimenting on them raises ethical questions. Ethical questions ask if something is right or wrong.

Ethical questions

Here are some ethical questions to discuss with your partner. Use a dictionary to check unfamiliar language.

Try to back up your answers with reasons and opinions.

1   Is it ethical to experiment on animals without painkillers or anaesthetics?

2   Is it acceptable to give a laboratory animal a human ear or heart?

3   Minor illnesses like colds and sore throats usually get better by themselves. Should animals be subjected to experiments to find cures for unimportant illnesses like these?

4   Genetic engineering can mean that laboratory animals are given genes which cause birth defects. When they reproduce, their young will be born with genetic problems. How justifiable is this?

5   Some serious illnesses are caused by overeating or smoking. Should animals suffer because of our bad habits?

6   Laboratory animals are used for non-medical experiments too. Is it fair to use animals to test the safety of luxury products such as perfume and aftershave?

Overall, what is your view of animal experimentation?

■ *It doesn't trouble me at all.*

■ *It's cruel and unjustifiable. I am totally opposed to it.*

■ *It's a necessary evil – all right so long as animals are not exposed to unnecessary suffering.*

It has been said that the average pet has more stress from living with its owner than the laboratory animal ever suffers.

Do you think that's a reasonable view? Why/Why not?

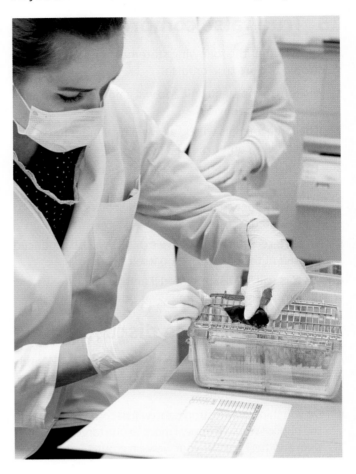

20 Predicting content

You are going to read an article written by a doctor who is a campaigner for medical experiments on animals. Would you expect the opinions expressed in the article to be:

a   balanced?

b   a bit extreme?

c   undecided?

21 Vocabulary check

Make sure you understand the meanings of these phrases.

VOCABULARY

an *emotive* issue

a *controversial* issue

22 Reading for detail

Read the article carefully and try to find answers to these questions. The questions reflect the opinions of the writer and not everyone would agree with them.

1   What does finding a cure for cystic fibrosis depend upon, according to the writer?

2   List the advances in medical understanding which have come as a result of animal research.

3   Why are particular diseases given to laboratory animals?

4   What dilemma is faced by researchers?

5   How might medical experiments on animals help animals?

Laboratory Animals: A Doctor's View

Each year, millions of animals are used in laboratory experiments. Can their suffering be justified? Dr Mark Matfield, Director of the Research Defence Society, defends testing.

The use of animals for research is an emotive, controversial issue – many people oppose their use on the grounds that the experiments are cruel and unnecessary.

Sixteen-year-old Laura thinks differently. Although she appears healthy, she has to take 30 different drugs each day to stay alive. Every year, hundreds of children are born, like her, with cystic fibrosis. There is no cure – at least not yet.

Laura may, just may, be one of the first cystic fibrosis children to be saved. A few years ago, scientists developed a new mouse – the cystic fibrosis mouse – with the same genetic defect as Laura. This made it much easier to develop new treatments. There may soon be ways of curing Laura, as long as that research, using those animals, continues.

There are plenty of emotional arguments both for and against animal testing, but let's start with the most obvious facts. If you examine the history of medicine, you find that experiments on animals have been an important part of almost every major medical advance. Many cornerstones of medical science – the discovery that blood circulates through our veins, understanding the way lungs work, the discovery of vitamins and hormones – were made this way.

Most of the main advances in medicine itself also depended on animal experiments. In 1988 there were an estimated 350,000 cases of polio in the world, causing paralysis or death but, thanks to the polio vaccine, the disease has been eradicated in most countries. Modern surgery would be impossible without today's anaesthetics. The list goes on: organ transplants, heart surgery, hip replacements, drugs for cancer and asthma – animals played an important part in these medical advances.

Animal experimentation wasn't the only type of research crucial to the medical advances that save human lives. Studies on human volunteers were also essential, and test-tube experiments were vital in many cases. But the history of medicine tells us that animal experiments are essential if we want to tackle the diseases and illnesses that afflict people.

If we are going to carry out research into serious diseases such as cancer or Aids, at some point in the process we are going to have to give those diseases to animals so we can study them.

This is the dilemma we face. We want to prevent suffering. The crucial issue is how we use animals in research. Modern science has developed humane experimental techniques. It is possible to do animal experiments using methods that the animals don't even notice. The worst these animals have to put up with is living in a cage with regular food and water, with animal handlers and vets looking after them.

The golden rule of laboratory animal welfare is to minimise any distress involved using the principle of the three Rs. First you reduce the number of animals used in each experiment to the minimum that will give a scientifically valid result. Then, whenever possible, you replace animal experiments with alternatives – experiments that don't use animals but will give equally valid results. Finally, you refine the animal experiments that you do, so they cause the least possible harm to the animals. If an experiment involves surgery on the animal, give it an anaesthetic.

175

When it comes round, give it pain-killers and antibiotics to combat infection.

The principle of the three Rs has been the basis for animal experimentation in many countries for the past ten years or more. It has been written into the law and is enforced by strict codes of practice, government guidelines and inspections. As a result, the number of animal experiments in the UK was reduced from more than 5.2 million in 1978 to 2.7 million in 2002.

People who experiment on animals are just the same as the rest of us – they know it's wrong to cause suffering if it can be avoided. But just because we like animals, we can't avoid the difficult decisions that have to be made in medicine and science. Sometimes, however, those decisions actually benefit animals. Distemper used to kill 500,000 puppies every year. Scientists believed they could find a vaccine but to succeed they would have to experiment on several hundred dogs, killing almost all of them. Not an easy decision. It took years to produce a vaccine that worked but now, every single year, 500,000 dogs are saved as a result.

23 Vocabulary

Try to match these words and phrases from the text with their definitions.

1	cornerstones (*line 35*)	**A**	worthwhile in terms of science
2	crucial (*line 56*)	**B**	reduce to the smallest amount
3	humane (*line 75*)	**C**	showing kindness
4	minimise (*line 84*)	**D**	improve
5	scientifically valid (*line 89*)	**E**	extremely important, vital
6	refine (*line 94*)	**F**	fundamental elements

24 Post-reading discussion

How sympathetic do you feel to the writer's view that medical experiments on animals are humane and necessary? Try to explain your views to your classmates.

25 Note-making

Make notes from the text of the reasons for carrying out medical experiments on animals, the achievements that have come about through animal research, and the steps that are taken to make medical experimentation as humane as possible. Try to find at least six points.

_____

_____

_____

_____

_____

_____

26 How the writer achieves his effects

A The writer achieves a calm, objective-sounding tone and style. He tries not to sound biased.

How do you think he achieves this? Write down your ideas.

_____

_____

_____

Compare your ideas in your groups.

B The following list shows techniques the writer uses to help him achieve the impression of being fair. How do the points compare with your list?

One of these points is incorrect. Try to find it and cross it out.

- He says the animals are well cared for.
- He uses a lot of statistics.
- He gives a lot of facts.
- He says researchers care about animals.
- He makes us laugh at people who campaign against animal experiments.
- He seems to try to understand the point of view of his opponents.

Try to find examples of these points in the text and circle them.

Compare your findings with the other groups. Is there anything you disagree about?

176

27 The angle of the argument

The writer suggests that the real issue is not whether you should be for or against animal experiments but HOW animal research can be as kind as possible to animals. This is an important change in the angle of the usual argument. Why, do you think?

28 Understanding bias in an argument

A Not everyone would agree that the writer is completely fair or unbiased. What points against animal experiments did the writer, as you see it, choose not to include? Write down some ideas.

_____

_____

B Study these opinions, which view animal experiments from a different perspective. Make sure you understand each one. Compare them with your own ideas and tick off any points which appeared on your list. Are there any ideas which you did not note but which you think are important points to consider? Tick them off too.

1 *'Animals are physically different from people so they react differently to drugs and medical experiments. You can't always extrapolate* from animals to people. As a result, many animal experiments are a waste of time.'*

2 *'Many members of the public think of medical research scientists as torturers and murderers.'*

3 *'Not all laboratories are wonderful. An American laboratory was taken to court recently for its disgraceful treatment of animals.'*

4 *'It's difficult for the public to see behind the closed doors of a laboratory. So scientists have a lot of freedom in the way they work and what they say they do.'*

5 *'Great improvements in health and life expectancy have come since the development of clean water systems and sanitation. This had nothing to do with laboratory animals.'*

6 *'Health education has helped people avoid disease. People have learned about a good diet, not smoking, being hygienic and taking exercise. Laboratory animals are irrelevant.'*

7 *'Research studies using human volunteers have been responsible for major advances in medical understanding. For example, the link between cancer and smoking came from studying people's behaviour and their reactions.'*

8 *'Advanced technology such as lasers and ultrasound is improving our understanding of the causes of disease. We could make more use of advanced technology and less use of living creatures in research.'*

**extrapolate:* to make predictions based on what you know

29 Writing an article for the school newsletter

'Is animal experimentation really worth it?'

Your school debating club has been discussing the rights and wrongs of animal experimentation. You feel that medical experiments on animals are useful and necessary but it is important to consider alternative techniques too.

Write an article for your school newsletter explaining:

- how animal experimentation has contributed to medical understanding
- why animal experiments do not always give useful results
- the alternatives to medical experiments on animals.

The angle of the argument

Get the angle clear. You are not writing a composition which is totally against animal experimentation, because you accept the need for it. Your aim is to show that medical experiments on animals, while sometimes helpful, do not always produce useful results. You want to explain how our health can be improved using alternative methods.

Planning the content

What points do you want to include? Can you give any explanations or examples to develop your points? How can you relate your content to the interests of the readers of the newsletter?

Structure and language

Use a strong opening for your article: get the reader's attention and keep it. Use a closing paragraph which clearly rounds off what you write. Don't let your composition 'tail off' so that the reader wonders what you really believe.

Structure your composition so the argument you are presenting is clear and easy to follow. Using opinion language and linking words will help you do this. Some of the expressions in exercise 7 will be helpful.

30 Prepositions after verbs

There are many examples of prepositions following verbs in the article about animal experiments.

Examples:

Hundreds of children are *born with* cystic fibrosis.

Let's *start with* the most obvious facts.

Blood *circulates through* our veins.

You *replace* animal experiments *with* alternatives.

People who *experiment on* animals are just the same as the rest of us.

Practice

Try to fill the gaps in the following sentences. Choose from these prepositions.

about   at   from   of   on   to   with

1 Is it right to experiment _____ animals?
2 Why bother _____ animal suffering when children are dying _____ incurable diseases?
3 I am surprised _____ you.
4 I object _____ all this animal rights propaganda.
5 Alan decided to contribute _____ an animal charity.
6 I won't quarrel _____ them.
7 Elephants depend _____ their keepers.
8 He died _____ a broken heart, so they say.
9 Can you provide him _____ an information pack?
10 Baby rhinos respond well _____ human contact.

What other verbs do you know followed by these prepositions? Discuss with a partner and try to make a list.

31 Spelling and pronunciation: Regular plurals

Most regular plurals in English simply add **-s**.

Look at this list of regular plurals. Check the meaning of each word and write a translation if necessary.

1 cats
2 hens
3 insects
4 cages
5 wasps
6 dogs
7 spiders
8 faces
9 horses
10 goats
11 birds
12 cows
13 houses
14 monkeys
15 bees
16 roses

The **-s** at the end of the noun plural can be pronounced /s/ or /z/ or /ɪz/. Listen to the list of words and write each word in the correct box, according to the sound of its ending.

/s/
cats

/z/
hens

/ɪz/
faces

Now say the words aloud to your partner. Does he/she agree the sound of each ending is clear?

32 Spelling and pronunciation: Irregular plurals

The following rules show how irregular plurals are formed. Say the examples aloud clearly, checking your pronunciation with a partner.

1 Nouns which end in *-ch, -s, -sh, -ss or -x* add **-es** to form the plural. The *-es* ending is pronounced /ɪz/.

   Examples: *bench ~ benches   bus ~ buses*
   rash ~ rashes   pass ~ passes   box ~ boxes

2 Nouns ending in *-f* or *-fe* replace the ending with **-ves** to form the plural. The *-s* is pronounced /z/.

   Examples: *calf ~ calves   leaf ~ leaves   wife ~ wives*

3 Some nouns form the plural simply by changing the vowel. The pronunciation changes too.

   Examples: *goose ~ geese   mouse ~ mice*
   tooth ~ teeth   man ~ men

4 Nouns which end in *-o* usually form the plural by adding **-es**, which is pronounced /z/.

   Example: *tomato ~ tomatoes*
   Common exceptions: *photos   pianos   rhinos*

5   Nouns ending in a consonant and -*y* form the plural by changing the -*y* to **-ies**. The -*s* is pronounced /z/.

Examples: *fly ~ flies   lady ~ ladies*

Nouns ending in a vowel and -*y* just add **-s**, which is pronounced /z/.

Example: *donkey ~ donkeys*

6   Some nouns are always plural.

Examples: *trousers   scissors   spectacles*

7   Some nouns are the same in the singular and the plural.

Examples: *sheep   deer   fish   salmon   bison*

33 Vocabulary

Work with a partner to fill the gaps with the plural forms of the nouns in brackets. Make sure you understand the meaning of each sentence. Check your pronunciation too!

1   The _____ have just given birth to several _____.   (*sheep, lamb*)

2   Watch out for _____, _____ and _____ if you go camping in the wild.   (*bear, wolf, wildcat*)

3   If you're lucky you'll be able to see _____, _____ and _____ in the park.   (*deer, goose, fox*)

4   A pet mouse needs a friend. The problem is you might soon have lots of baby _____.   (*mouse*)

5   _____ and _____ have the most amazing _____.   (*crocodile, rhino, tooth*)

6   Tropical _____ need special care but make interesting pets.   (*fish*)

7   It's strange to think that ugly _____ can turn into lovely _____.   (*caterpillar, butterfly*)

34 Look, say, cover, write, check

Are you confident you know the meaning of these words? You have already met some in the unit; you will come across others in later exercises.

Check any meanings you are unsure of in a dictionary. Then use the 'look, say, cover, write, check' method to memorise the words.

Finally, why not ask your partner to test you?

potato	anaesthetic
potatoes	elephant
clothes	leopard
calf	laboratory
calves	innocent
leaf	benefit
leaves	terrible
vaccine	veterinary
scissors	rhino

9.3 Animals in sport and entertainment

35 Discussion

A   Horse racing, camel racing and dog racing are popular sports for many people. In addition, circuses which use performing animals draw large crowds. Do you feel it's fair to animals to involve them in human pursuits in this way?

B   How are animals used for sport or entertainment in your country?

C   Sports in which animals are hunted are called *field sports*. Are these sports popular in your country? Have you ever seen or taken part in this form of sport? How did you feel about it?

36 People's opinions

Here are some reasons why people say they like animals to be involved in human pursuits. Discuss them with your partner and give them a ✓ or ✗ depending on whether they reflect your own views.

'I admire the skills and fearlessness of performers at the circus who ride bareback on horses or control savage animals.'

'What I find most awesome about bullfighting is the total concentration needed by the matador – without it he'll be dead or maimed.'

'Shooting birds demands a steady aim and perfect eye-hand coordination. What makes me cross is people who criticise me for shooting but think nothing of eating meat.'

'What I love about horse racing is the thrilling atmosphere as the horses approach the finishing line.'

37 Letter completion: My views on animal charities

The following text is a letter written by a student to a newspaper giving the reasons why she is against giving money to an animal charity. The blanks need to be filled with words and phrases which link her ideas and show her opinions and attitudes.

Working in pairs or groups of three, choose the most appropriate suggestions from the ones given. Then compare your answers to those of other groups.

Dear Editor,

I read in your newspaper that there are plans to give a large amount of money raised through our town's annual charity appeal to the Green Pastures Horses' Home. The home is a place where racehorses can live in comfort when they retire from racing. I am writing to say that (1)_____ this is a very (2)_____ idea.

I am not against spending on animal welfare, but what makes me really angry is the thought of money being spent on giving animals a happy retirement when many old people in our country are neglected and live lonely, poverty-stricken lives.

It is (3)_____ that racehorses have provided people with sport and entertainment, (4)_____ I can't see how this justifies spending so much on them. After all, they are only animals and humans should come first.

People (5)_____ that animal cruelty is wrong, (6)_____ they ignore the cruel treatment the elderly receive. I think money raised through charity should benefit human beings. The care of aged animals is the responsibility of those who own them, and it is (7)_____ to expect us to support them. (8)_____, people who own racehorses are rich and have the resources to fund a good retirement for their animals. Wouldn't it be more sensible for the owners to save a percentage of the big profits they have made (9)_____ use that for their animals' welfare in old age?

Our senior citizens have worked hard in their lives. People say their pensions are adequate but (10)_____. In fact, many old people have hardly enough money for food and bills, let alone luxuries such as horseracing.

At my school, I am starting a campaign to increase young people's awareness of the purpose of charity fundraising. I know we will not be in time to stop the funds going to the horses' home this year. (11)_____, we shall do all we can to ensure charitable funds are not squandered on useless projects in future.

Yours faithfully,
Bella Balkano

1 a for instance	**b** naturally	**c** I think	**d** personally
2 a unhealthy	**b** cruel	**c** misguided	**d** insincere
3 a argued	**b** denied	**c** appealed	**d** expected
4 a definitely	**b** but	**c** of course	**d** so
5 a shout	**b** demand	**c** insist	**d** expect
6 a on balance	**b** In other words	**c** yet	**d** surely
7 a unfair	**b** puzzling	**c** upsetting	**d** surprising
8 a It's all very well	**b** As I see it	**c** Nevertheless	**d** Even
9 a also	**b** and	**c** as well	**d** moreover
10 a nothing could be further from the truth	**b** on the contrary	**c** nonsense	**d** it is a fact
11 a Despite	**b** In addition	**c** Furthermore	**d** Nevertheless

When you have filled the gaps correctly, re-read the letter to get a sense of the flow of the argument.

Do you agree that the opening is clear and gets straight to the point? In your opinion, is the ending of the letter a firm way to round it off?

38 Vocabulary: Words for feelings

Bella expresses her feelings and attitudes in a forceful, impassioned way. The following exercise shows how adjectives of similar meaning can be used to describe feelings and attitudes. Can you complete each group of synonyms with an appropriate word chosen from the box?

1 I am disgusted / appalled / horrified / _____ by your actions.

2 He is worried / uneasy / fretful / _____ about the lack of clean water for livestock.

3 It is wicked / immoral / depraved / _____ to use animals in medical experiments.

4 He is remorseful / apologetic / regretful / _____ about the harm he has done.

5 It is absurd / ridiculous / ludicrous / _____ to say animals are as important as people.

6 They are soft-hearted / tender / caring / _____ towards injured animals.

7 I feel emotional / distressed / upset / _____ when I hear about children being unable to get proper medical care.

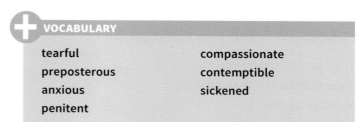

VOCABULARY

tearful	compassionate
preposterous	contemptible
anxious	sickened
penitent	

39 Language study: Adding extra emphasis

What ... clauses

We can use a clause beginning with *what* to give extra emphasis. For example, Bella says:

What makes me really angry is the thought of money being spent on giving animals a happy retirement.

This is another way of saying:

The thought of money being spent on giving animals a happy retirement makes me really angry.

Restructuring the sentence, using *what*, makes Bella sound more emphatic.

Contrast the structure of these pairs of sentences. Which one is more emphatic? Why? How has the structure been changed to achieve this?

She loves the idea that the safari park will provide jobs for people.

***What** she loves is the idea that the safari park will provide jobs for people.*

We doubted that the water was clean enough to drink.

***What** we doubted was that the water was clean enough to drink.*

I respect organisations that campaign to raise awareness of animal welfare.

***What** I respect are organisations that campaign to raise awareness of animal welfare.*

The person who ... , the place where ...

Consider these two similar constructions for adding emphasis.

The keeper understands the animals best.

***The person who** understands the animals best is the keeper.*

Polar bears thrive best in their natural habitat.

***The place where** polar bears thrive best is (in) their natural habitat.*

So + adjective

Consider the use of *so* before an adjective.

Their attitudes were caring.
*Their attitudes were **so** caring.*
He was thoughtful.
*He was **so** thoughtful.*

Do + main verb

Consider the use of *do* before a main verb. Are any other changes necessary?

I like your project work.
*I **do** like your project work.*
We're late. Hurry up!
*We're late. **Do** hurry up!*
Take a seat.
***Do** take a seat.*
He enjoys his work with orphaned elephants.
*He **does** enjoy his work with orphaned elephants.*

Look back at the comments in exercise 36 and underline any examples of emphatic forms. Why are they effective in that context?

40 Practice

Rewrite these sentences beginning with the words in brackets, to make them more emphatic.

1   She admires attempts to alleviate human suffering. (*What …*)
2   We need better fences to stop animals wandering onto the road. (*What …*)
3   The safari park wardens worry about animals escaping. (*What …*)
4   You can see owls, eagles and hawks in a falconry centre. (*The place where …*)
5   We didn't understand that animals are adapted to live in certain habitats. (*What …*)
6   I didn't realise how people depend on each other. (*What …*)
7   Hunters are responsible for the reduction in rhino numbers. (*The people who …*)
8   The golden eagle prefers to nest in treeless, mountainous country. (*The place where …*)
9   Endangered species in our own country ought to concern us. (*What …*)

10 I want the right to object to things I think are wrong. (*What …*)

41 More practice

Add *so* or *do* to these sentences for greater emphasis. Make any changes to the sentences that you need to.

1   Having a purpose in life has made her happy.
2   We all shouted, 'Tell us more about your adventures.'
3   Take lots of photos when you visit the wildlife park.
4   I never realised that baby rhinos were affectionate.
5   Raising funds for charity is worthwhile.
6   Your granny enjoys her garden, doesn't she?
7   You look tired today.
8   Thirsty animals are miserable.
9   Gordon felt sorry for the animals he saw at the circus.
10 I worry about you, you know.
11 Turn off the tap properly when you have finished washing.
12 Come in, Sophie. I'm pleased to see you.

42 Comparing languages

How do you add emphasis in your own language? Share words or structures you use with your group.

43 Writing sentences

Make up some sentences of your own using emphatic forms.

9.4 Animals at work

44 Thinking about working animals

A In what ways do animals 'work' in your country?

For example:

- ☐ on farms producing milk
- ☐ being raised for meat
- ☐ being raised to provide skins, leather, wool, etc.
- ☐ as guard dogs or police dogs
- ☐ as rescue dogs
- ☐ being used for transport
- ☐ as blind dogs or hearing dogs

Are animals used for work in any other ways?

_____

_____

_____

B People who keep animals have a responsibility to feed them. What other responsibilities do they have?

_____

_____

_____

_____

_____

45 Discussing ethical issues

A Generally speaking, do you feel working animals in your country get a decent life? Try to explain your opinions to your friends.

B People who are cruel to their animals may be prevented by law from keeping them. This might mean the loss of a business or family income. Do you think this is right? Why/Why not?

46 Building a letter from prompts

Using the prompts below, try to build up a complete letter to the editor of a national newspaper.

Why it is wrong to accuse farmers of cruelty

Dear Sir,

I write / response/recent articles / say / people / keep / animals for profit / be 'cruel and heartless'. My family make / living from / keep / sheep. In my view / our life / be harder / the animals'!

In lambing time / example / there be / no day off / no rest. My father get up / as soon as it / be light / and hurry out / to first task / of day / without even bothering / to have / drink. He work / for several hours / without break. He check / lambs that / be born / in night / or attend / ewes that have difficulty / give birth. He bring / sickly lambs indoors / be bottle-fed.

He try / get round the flock / four or five times / day / often in driving snow / cruel winds. If there be / specific problem / he have to / go out several times / night / with flash light. Although / expensive / vet / always call / when he be / needed.

It be / true that every ewe or lamb that / die / be a financial loss / us / so it be / in own interest / care for / sheep. Sheep / eventually be sold / at market. How / we can live / any other way? But we be / certainly not / 'ruthless exploiters' / of your article. In fact, nothing be / further from truth.

Yours faithfully,
Gillian O'Connor

183

47 Assessing the argument

When you have written the complete letter, re-read it to get a better sense of the argument. Has Gillian convinced you that her family provide a high standard of care for animals?

48 The closing paragraph

Study the closing paragraph of the letter carefully. Closing paragraphs of opinion arguments should draw the argument to a clear end; the reader should be sure what you think. The language you use to end the letter depends on what you said before.

Do you think Gillian's final paragraph is effective?

49 Vocabulary: Young animals

Humans have children; sheep have lambs. Choose a word from the box to match with each animal/bird. You will need to use some words more than once.

✚ VOCABULARY

calf	foal	pup/puppy
kitten	kid	cygnet
cub	chick/chicken	duckling

1	bear	7	goat
2	duck	8	horse
3	hen	9	elephant
4	cow	10	whale
5	cat	11	swan
6	dog	12	lion

50 Comparing languages

Does your language have special words for young animals? Discuss the expressions you use.

51 Vocabulary: Collective nouns

Decide which of the words in the box can follow these collective nouns. Sometimes more than one answer is possible.

✚ VOCABULARY

bees	elephants	ants
dogs	wolves	goats
fish	sheep	deer
cows	locusts	

1   A herd of _____
2   A flock of _____
3   A shoal of _____
4   A pack of _____
5   A swarm of _____

52 Discussion: Intensive farming

Consider these issues related to food production.

Many farmers are using modern technology to rear their animals intensively. Some kinds of animals and birds (calves and hens, for example) can be reared inside, in very small spaces. Feeding can be provided artificially and controlled very carefully. Some animals are given hormones to increase their growth. This is sometimes called 'factory farming'.

Pesticides are widely used by farmers to keep crops free of disease.

Why people object

Some people object to modern farming methods because they think they are cruel to animals. Also, they are increasingly worried about the effect of hormones and pesticides in the food chain.

Because intensive farming relies on machines, not people, this has resulted in fewer jobs for agricultural workers.

What the farmers think

Farmers using intensive systems argue that they are an efficient method of producing food cheaply.

Some farmers are reluctant to change to 'organic' farming because they have invested a lot in new technology. Also, they feel organic methods will be less reliable, will involve higher costs, and might lead to higher food prices for the consumer.

In some countries, farmers receive a subsidy (money from the government) for using intensive methods.

What are your views? How do you think food should be produced? Work in groups and note down your ideas.

53 Punctuation

Read the following letter for meaning. When you feel you have understood it, rewrite it with punctuation and paragraphs so that the sense is clear.

Remember to use a comma after an introductory linking word or phrase such as *Nevertheless, … , In fact, … , Despite claims to the contrary, … .*

Fair methods of food production

dear sir like many of your readers i want to buy healthy food which is produced in a way which is fair to farm workers and animals furthermore i don't believe food production should damage the environment many farmers in our area say that it is cheaper to rear animals under intensive conditions than it is to give them a decent life however if farmers were given subsidies they would be able to afford more space and comfort for animals farmers get subsidies for intensive methods so why not pay them for a kinder approach similarly many of the farms around here use harmful pesticides which can get into the food chain farmers say it is less expensive to use pesticides than to use more natural or 'organic' methods which require a bigger labour force and so would be more expensive what is more expensive in the end subsidies to the farmers for organic farming or a damaged environment in my view we have a right to know what is in our food tins packets and fresh food should be labelled by food companies as free-range* or factory farmed or whether pesticides were used so that we know exactly what we are eating i realise my ideas might lead to higher food prices but i have no doubt at all it would be worth it

yours faithfully shahar rishani

Free-range eggs and meat come from animals which live in natural conditions.

54 Checking the text flow

When you have punctuated the letter correctly, read it through, as always, to get a sense of the way the text flows. Are the beginning and ending clear and decisive?

55 Further thoughts

How far do you agree with Shahar's view that it's worth paying more for food that is produced ethically?

In what ways do you think intensive methods of food production could be unfair to farm workers? Try to give some specific examples.

56 Rhetorical questions

A rhetorical question is a special kind of question, to which you do not expect an answer. It's a device to get more attention for your opinions when presenting an argument.

Study the following rhetorical questions. What is the opinion of each speaker?

1 'Don't you think it's about time people showed more sympathy to farmers?'

2 'Who can honestly say they would enjoy eating a battery hen?'

3 'Which is worse: to pay a tiny bit more for food or to make innocent animals suffer horrors under intensive systems?'

4 'Wouldn't we all be happier knowing our food was ethically produced?'

5 'Do we really need all this food from thousands of miles away?'

6 'Who can worry about animals when little children are starving?'

7 'The theory is that pets are safe and happy with their owners, but is it the whole truth?'

8 'How can you put a price on a child's life?'

57 Restructuring statements into rhetorical questions

Try to rewrite these statements in the form of rhetorical questions.

1 A vegetarian meal is not always healthy.

    Is _____?

2 No one can say the farmers are wrong.

    Who _____?

3 We can save an animal or save someone's life.

   Which is _____?

4 No one knows the extent of the problem.

   Who _____?

5 We buy fur coats and leather handbags. I am not sure we really need them.

   Do we _____?

6 I think we would all be happier knowing that our food was free of chemicals.

   Wouldn't _____?

7 I think it's about time we remembered endangered species at home.

   Isn't _____?

8 I think we should consider farm workers before worrying about animals.

   Shouldn't _____?

Look back at the letters in exercises 46 and 53 and underline the examples of rhetorical questions.

You may like to use the rhetorical question device in your own arguments. One or two are usually enough.

9.5 Helping animals in danger

58 Discussion: Could you help animals?

Many species are being endangered by human activity. Hunting, overfishing and poaching, for example, reduce animal numbers. In addition, forests are cut down for agricultural or commercial purposes and wildlife loses its habitat as a result. Similarly, when cities expand, new roads and buildings mean wild animals and birds lose their homes and sources of food.

Do you know of any examples in your own country of wildlife being affected in this way?

Which endangered species in the world do you know about? Which do you care most about? How could you help endangered species in your own country or overseas? Write down your ideas.

The chart below shows the approximate numbers of selected big cats still in existence in the wild. Which three species on the chart are the most endangered?

Asiatic lion
African lion
Jaguar
Cheetah
Snow leopard
Clouded leopard
Tiger

0   10 000   20 000   30 000   40 000

■ Endangered big cats – estimated wild populations

59 Reading for gist

Skim-read the following leaflet which gives information about two ways of helping to protect endangered animals. A lot of the vocabulary should be familiar from previous exercises. Try to work out the meaning of unfamiliar words from the context.

Wild Action Appeal

The adoption scheme

King's Park Zoo, as well as being a great place to visit, plays an important part in protecting endangered species. The Zoo is often the last sanctuary and breeding ground for these animals. We have 160 different species of animals, birds and reptiles, many of which are endangered in the wild. We need your support to help these animals win their battle against possible extinction with breeding programmes funded by the adoption scheme.

Most animals in the zoo are available for adoption. Many individuals and families, as well as groups, take great pleasure in adopting their favourite animal. Companies, too, can benefit from the scheme and find it a worthwhile and cost-effective form of advertising.

What adopters receive

All adopters will receive an adoption certificate and regular copies of 'Zoo Update', the zoo's

exciting newsletter. For a donation of £50 you will receive four free entry tickets; for a donation of £100 or more you will receive eight free entry tickets and a personalised plaque on the animal's enclosure.

Our **Wild Action** appeal was launched in 2013 to support work with endangered species in their threatened natural habitats. Donations to the appeal will go directly towards the following projects:

Rainforest Action Costa Rica

Costa Rica's tropical forests contain a wealth of wildlife – 200 species of mammals, 850 species of birds, 220 species of reptiles and 160 species of amphibians. All these are at risk, including the jaguar, ocelot, margay and jaguarundi. **Rainforest Action Costa Rica** is securing a biological corridor of rainforest that is intended to stretch throughout Central America, providing a safe haven for indigenous wildlife. Just £30 will save half an acre of Costa Rican rainforest.

The Tiger Trust

The Tiger Trust is creating two natural habitat sanctuaries in Thailand for the Indo-Chinese tiger, which is facing the threat of extinction. Tiger Mountains I and II provide a near-natural existence for tigers orphaned by poaching.

Only 3,000 tigers remain in the wild and hundreds are being trapped and shot by poachers for an appalling trade in tiger bones and body parts. A donation of £40 will go towards looking after Sheba, a two-year-old Indo-Chinese tiger, who was found next to the body of her mother. She now lives with other rescued tigers on Tiger Mountain II in Thailand. You will receive a colour photo of Sheba and a tiger T-shirt.

187

60 Reading comprehension

Now answer these questions.

1 Which animals are available for adoption?

2 How does the zoo use the adoption money it raises?

3 What does a £50 donation to the adoption scheme give you?

4 What is the aim of Rainforest Action Costa Rica?

5 Where are Tiger Mountains I and II, and what is special about them?

61 Building a newsletter article from a first draft

Ramon wanted his school to support the zoo's conservation work. He decided to write an article for the school newsletter, explaining why it was a good idea and how the school could benefit.

Try to rewrite his rough draft of main points in the form of a finished article. The final paragraph is missing: try to think of a strong way to close the article.

How We Can Help Endangered Species

We could adopt a zoo animal. We could visit it on school trips. The zoo would send us a regular newsletter which would give us information about breeding programmes for endangered species. We could even get a plaque at the zoo with the school's name on it. The adoption scheme is a way of raising the zoo's income. The money helps the zoo with its breeding programmes. The breeding programmes encourage the animals to reproduce. The zoo is also running an appeal called Wild Action. Money from the appeal will help to preserve the Costa Rican rainforest. The money will also support two groups working to protect tigers. Only 3,000 tigers still survive in the wild. Poachers kill the tigers and sell the skins, body parts and even the bones to make cosmetics and manufactured goods. The groups set up reasonably natural sanctuaries for tigers orphaned by poaching. These natural sanctuaries protect the tiger cubs.

Structure

Structure the article into paragraphs. Use a strong opening and definite final paragraph. Use defining clauses to make sentences more complex. Would you like to use some emphatic structures or rhetorical questions as a way of adding emphasis?

Link ideas with linking words and expressions, and use opinion language to introduce your views.

Content

Ramon makes several very interesting points. Could you provide any extra examples or explanations of your own? Can you show any further audience awareness in the letter? Think, perhaps, about your own school. How might the schemes be of particular interest to pupils? Try to show some audience awareness in your final paragraph.

Proofread your work for punctuation and spelling errors.

Feedback

When you feel you have produced a reasonable draft, why not show your work to a friend? Listen carefully to his/her comments. Would you like to add anything or change anything?

✸ GRAMMAR SPOTLIGHT

1 The past perfect passive

The **passive form of the past perfect** is used to describe something which was completed in an earlier past, when the action is more important than who or what did it:

Trees and bushes had been planted around the enclosures. (exercise 4, paragraph 2)

(We do not need to know who had planted the trees and bushes.)

Underline another example of the past perfect passive in the same paragraph of exercise 4.

The past perfect passive is formed with **had + been + past participle**.

The negative is *had not been* (or *hadn't been* in informal English):

*In spite of the methods the farmers had introduced, the wolves **had not been driven** away.*

2 Passives with two objects – revision

In Unit 3 Grammar Spotlight you looked at verbs in the passive with two objects:

Marianne was offered *a place at Oxford University.*

This construction is often used with the verb *give*. In exercise 53 of this unit you saw:

If farmers were given subsidies *they would be able to afford …*

Can you find an example of a passive with two objects in paragraph 3 of exercise 4?

EXAM-STYLE QUESTIONS
Writing

For each of the following questions, you should write 150–200 words (or 100–150 words for Core level). The comments in *italics* may give you some ideas, but you should also try to use some ideas of your own.

1 There are plans to build a small safari park close to your town. Visitors will be able to see animals from all over the world. Here are some comments from letters in newspapers on the topic.

   'It will be so exciting and attract tourists too.'

   'Wild animals should stay in their natural habitat.'

   Write a letter to your local newspaper giving your views.

2 Your school ecology club is trying to persuade people not to use products that have been tested on animals. Here are some comments made by your friends.

   'Animals should not suffer for our health or vanity.'

   'If we don't buy these products, people will lose their jobs.'

   Write a letter to your school magazine giving your views.

3 Local farmers are trying to persuade people to buy food in their local farmers' markets, and not in modern supermarkets. Here are some online comments from readers to newspapers.

   'Our local farmers work so hard and produce lovely food.'

   'I want the freedom to shop wherever I like.'

   Write an email to your local newspaper giving your views.

4 Your headteacher has asked for students' responses to the following idea:

   The school would like to start supporting a charity. We are considering a charity doing research into animal diseases.

   Here are some comments made by your friends.

   'How wonderful! Animals deserve to be healthy and happy.'

   'I would prefer to support a charity that helps poor people.'

   Write an article to your school magazine giving your views.

Speaking

1 The role of science in modern life

Scientific research has brought many benefits, but also causes controversy. Discuss this topic with the assessor.

You may wish to use the following ideas to help develop the conversation:

- what you have enjoyed, and found challenging, about studying science subjects
- whether you would choose science as a career
- how life has changed for good or bad, as a result of scientific and technological discoveries and developments
- whether it is right to use animals and human volunteers in medical research
- the idea that some scientific research is a waste of money or has caused harm to people.

You are free to consider any other related ideas of your own. Remember, you are not allowed to make any written notes.

2 Animals in a human world

Animals share the planet with us, and are often used by us for our convenience, business or pleasure. Sometimes conflicts arise because we disagree about the rights of animals. Discuss this topic with the assessor.

You may wish to use the following ideas to help develop the conversation:

- animals you find interesting or exotic
- whether or not working animals are properly treated
- the view that hunting wild animals should be banned
- the suggestion that using animals in sport and entertainment is unfair
- the idea that the plans or desires of human beings are always more important than the needs of animals.

You are free to consider any other related ideas of your own. Remember, you are not allowed to make any written notes.

3 Pets

Pets are very important in some people's lives, whereas for others, pets are of no interest at all.

Discuss this topic with the assessor.

Here are some possible ideas for developing the conversation:

- why people enjoy having a pet
- animals which make good pets
- the responsibilities people have towards their pets
- whether everyone has the right to keep a pet
- why a pet may not be suitable for every home.

You are, of course, free to use any other related ideas of your own. You are not allowed to make any written notes.

Listening 🔊

You will hear six people talking about wildlife. For each of Speakers 1–6, choose from the list A–G which idea each speaker expresses. Write the letter in the box. Use each letter once only. There is one extra letter which you do not need to use.

You will hear the full recording twice.

Speaker 1 ☐
Speaker 2 ☐
Speaker 3 ☐
Speaker 4 ☐
Speaker 5 ☐
Speaker 6 ☐

A   I am keen to help people in my area live with wildlife.

B   We no longer worry about having dangerous wildlife nearby.

C   When I was camping, I met a grizzly bear near the campsite.

D   Human food attracts wild animals.

E   Wild animals can give people financial problems.

F   Safe crossings to protect wildlife from traffic are unlikely to be a success.

G   Human activities have had a negative impact on wildlife.

Form-filling

Susi Minap, who has just had her sixteenth birthday, is very interested in ways to care for our natural world. She attends school in Mumbai, where she is studying for IGCSE exams. She lives with her family at Bungalow 2000, Banyan Road, Cocora, Mumbai, India. Susi's email is sus@meandyou.com and even though her internet connection is occasionally unreliable, this is the way she likes to keep in touch with people. Her mobile number is 7506000592.

She is close to her older brother Amjad, who is training as an ecologist at university, and he has inspired Susi's love of nature and wildlife. Susi has already written articles for her local newspaper on the plight of baby elephants which are orphaned when their parents are shot by poachers. Susi was delighted to receive letters from the readers who were moved by her articles, especially as some readers have decided to support sanctuaries for orphaned elephants.

Susi is interested in all wild animals, but is most fascinated by sea creatures, and is keen to do more to help protect vulnerable species. She has heard about Wild Aid, a charity which helps people start wildlife clubs. She would love to start a club at school, and thinks that if she can use resources, such as video clips, quizzes and leaflets, then the meetings could be made very lively.

Susi has asked her headteacher, Mr Mhanda, if she can start a Wildlife Club for students in her year at school so they can all explore ways to take better care of wildlife. At first, Mr Mhanda was not supportive of the idea as he was worried that attendance at the club would be a distraction for students. He also felt there were enough after-school recreational clubs. However, Susi has convinced him that the club will be different from the other clubs and will be very educational, so, finally, he has agreed to the idea.

Her form tutor, Mrs Sunil, supports her plans and has said that now Susi has permission from Mr Mhanda, she will be a point of contact. Susi's father, Asrif Minap, who is a keen amateur wildlife photographer, says he would be happy to be a guest speaker at the club and show the photographs of reptiles, tigers and birds he has taken.

Imagine you are Susi. Read the information about Wild Aid, and then fill in the membership application form.

FREE MEMBERSHIP OF WILD AID!

Would you like free membership of one of the world's most active wildlife protection societies? Wild Aid is an international organisation which campaigns to protect wildlife, including some of our most endangered species. For the next three months, Wild Aid is offering free membership to young people who can convince us they are genuinely concerned about protecting wild animals and birds and their habitats. Young people who are enthusiastic about spreading the message of animal conservation throughout their community will be given priority for membership.

Membership privileges include a Starter Information Pack, which contains educational leaflets, badges, a DVD, stickers, posters and a set of 15 printed T-shirts. You'll also be invited to participate in our internet discussion forums. If you prefer, we can keep you informed by post.

If you would like to have free membership, all you have to do is complete both sections of the application form and return it to: The Secretary, Wild Aid Foundation, Head Office, Anse Aux Pins, Seychelles. Don't delay!

MEMBERSHIP APPLICATION FORM

SECTION A

Please give your name and address in BLOCK CAPITALS.

Full name: _____

Home address: _____

_____

_____

Male / Female (*Please delete.*)

Age: _____

Email: _____

Which of our FACT PACKS would you like to receive? (*Please circle a, b or c.*)

(a) Our Planet's Disappearing Butterflies

(b) Birds of South-East Asia

(c) Go Wild Together – 20 ideas for involving your school in protecting wildlife

We can send you regular updates on the progress of our wildlife campaigns. How would you like to receive information from us? (*Please tick.*)

☐ By post

☐ By email

☐ I have no preference.

Which area of wildlife are you personally especially interested in?

_____

Please give the name of one person we could contact in support of your application for membership, and state his/her relationship to you.

_____

_____

SECTION B

In one sentence describe any actions you have taken so far to raise awareness of wildlife issues in your community.

_____

_____

_____

Write one sentence explaining what use you could make of the Starter Information Pack.

_____

_____

_____

191

KEY ADVICE

1 Plan your **opinion essay** first. Think about content. Try to have enough interesting ideas to expand fully: don't run out of ideas halfway through. Engage with the subject and try to make the argument sound serious and important. Come across as convincing and you will convince other people.

2 Structure your essay so that it is clear and logical. Try not to 'backtrack' halfway through to ideas you mentioned earlier. Use paragraphs and linking words.

3 Use an appropriate tone. Opinion arguments are often quite measured, and you may want to give consideration to what other people say.

4 Devices such as rhetorical questions or restructuring sentences for greater emphasis will make your writing stronger and more persuasive.

5 Try to use a mature and varied vocabulary which is appropriate to the topic.

6 Punctuate carefully, using commas, full stops, question marks and so on. Proofread your work for punctuation errors.

7 Check your spelling carefully, especially words you know you usually misspell or words which present special problems such as plural forms, silent letters and suffixes.

8 Try to give attention to your **handwriting**. If your composition is interesting and well structured, and your handwriting is attractive, your work will be a pleasure to read. If you feel you have particular difficulty forming certain letters or keeping handwriting on the line, try practising using special handwriting worksheets.

9 Try experimenting with different kinds of pens in order to find one which helps you write better. A good quality pen is a good investment if you can find one that is not too expensive.

Exam techniques

10 In an exam, many students stop while writing a composition to count the number of words they have produced so far. This is a waste of time. Get used to seeing what 150 words, for example, look like in your handwriting. You will then be able to see whether you are writing to the right length. The lines on the exam paper are also there to help you.

The **word limit** given is a guide to the required length. Don't worry if you write a few words more or less than this.

UNIT FOCUS

In this unit you have learned to write letters and articles putting forward **formal arguments and opinions**.

You have listened to a radio talk and answered true/false questions.

You have produced a set of notes on a detailed magazine text.

You have completed a **form based on a scenario**.

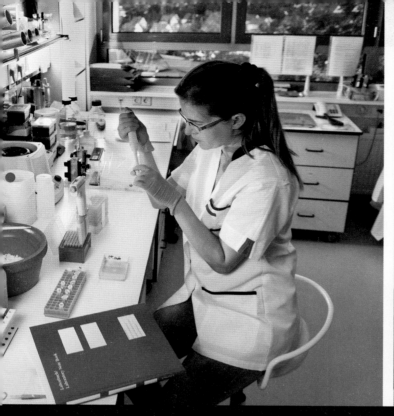

Unit 10:
The World of Work

10.1 The rewards of work

1 Discussion

Why do people work? Earning money is one reason. What other reasons are there? With a partner, try to add four or five more ideas to the list.

Reasons why people work

They get a sense of achievement.
They feel good about themselves.

_____

_____

_____

_____

_____

2 Skills and qualities for work

Match the following skills and qualities to the occupations you think they are essential for.

1	patience	A	novelist
2	good communication skills	B	dentist
3	artistic flair	C	nursery teacher
4	an ear for languages	D	firefighter
5	business acumen	E	interior designer
6	physical stamina	F	cellist
7	courage	G	labourer
8	musical talent	H	tycoon
9	dexterity	I	linguist
10	imagination	J	journalist

3 Pre-reading tasks

A Think of any new products you have tried in the last year. Why did you try them? If you saw them advertised, did they live up to the advertiser's promise? What was the 'image' of the product conveyed in the media? How were the new products you tried different from similar products already available?

B You are going to read about how a totally new chocolate bar is produced. What challenges do you think are involved in this process?

Examples:

You have to make it taste delicious.

You have to have the right equipment to make it.

4 Predicting

Look carefully, without reading, at the pictures in the text 'A Bar Is Born'. What do you think the pictures show?

5 Reading for gist

Now read the text for general meaning. Try to work out the meanings of any unfamiliar words from the context.

A Bar Is Born

Despite trends towards healthy eating, many people still love eating chocolate. The Swiss consume the most (almost 12 kilos per person per
5 year) followed by the Irish, with the British not far behind. An average chocolate bar weighs about 40–45 grams, which means that the average Swiss person eats about 240 bars in one
10 year. The demand for chocolate in other parts of the world, including China and India, is growing, creating exciting new markets for the manufacturers of chocolate.

15 Many of the mass-produced chocolate products on sale are variations of the basic ingredients of chocolate, caramel, nuts, raisins and biscuit. With popular new ingredients so hard to find,
20 manufacturers are forced to look for new ways of combining the old favourites into new products.

1 Opportunity

All chocolate manufacturers have marketing departments to think up
25 ideas for new products. These departments analyse consumer fashions and lifestyles and try to identify opportunities for new products. One major chocolate company
30 introduced mini-bars when they discovered that many parents cut up a full-size bar into smaller portions for their children.

Some new products come about
35 through new technology rather than marketing. In these cases, scientists or engineers will have invented a machine that can do something new to chocolate which is noticeably
40 different from anything that has been produced before.

It might take anything from six months to a number of years to conduct all the necessary research to
45 assess whether the proposed new product is likely to succeed.

In the UK alone, each research exercise may cost more than £100,000. For every ten ideas for new products,
50 only one will get beyond research assessment, so the real cost of getting a new product to the development stage is approximately £1 million.

2 Product development

One of the key criteria for producing a new chocolate bar is that it should be difficult for rival companies to replicate. No manufacturer wants to spend a great deal of money developing a brand that will quickly attract stiff competition.

Creating a new bar may involve making minor adjustments to existing machinery, or it can mean investment in a whole new factory costing millions of pounds. So it is vital that the new bar can be produced economically.

Chocolate is a price-sensitive product. Even though a manufacturer might come up with a delicious formula for a new bar, it would not go ahead with production unless it could be made for the right price.

Sometimes new products cannot be made at all. One manufacturer found that, in one bar it was developing, it was unable to stop the wafer becoming soggy, and another found that the raisins always sank to the bottom of the bar. Both these projects were abandoned.

The chocolate bar must also be consistent; even the smallest change in the balance of ingredients can affect the taste significantly. Manufacturers want consumers to buy the same brand over and over again, and if a bar cannot meet this requirement it will not go into mass-production.

The process of development is one of constant refinement. Manufacturers rarely make their ideal product first time round, and it is not unusual for them to have up to 30 attempts at getting it right.

3 Packaging

Care is taken to ensure that the packaging is consistent with the type of bar produced. A bar aimed at teenagers may well be packaged in a red and yellow packet to appear cheap and cheerful. Blue is considered to be a sophisticated colour and is often used to package top-of-the-range brands. Whatever the design, manufacturers will make sure that it stands out enough to be noticed on the sweet counter, where it will have to compete with 50 other brands.

The name of the bar must also reflect the right image.

4 Advertising

Most new chocolate bars are launched with a press and TV advertising campaign. Advertising companies begin planning their campaigns by deciding what message they want to convey about the product. For example, is it a luxury or is it a snack? They then work on a number of advertisements before deciding which one is likely to work best.

This process may take between 3 and 18 months. Filming the advert may cost over £250,000, and buying the television airtime to screen it may cost over £3 million.

5 Testing

Manufacturers and advertisers conduct extensive testing at all stages in the development and launch of a new product. Groups from different parts of the country are asked to give their opinions on either the taste of the chocolate or the impact that an advert has had on them. These comments then form the basis for future refinements.

6 The launch

Many new brands do quite well initially, as it is comparatively easy to get people to try a new chocolate bar once. However, for a launch to be successful, sales must be sustained over a long period of time. Achieving this is extremely difficult. Nine out of every ten new products launched fail to reach full production.

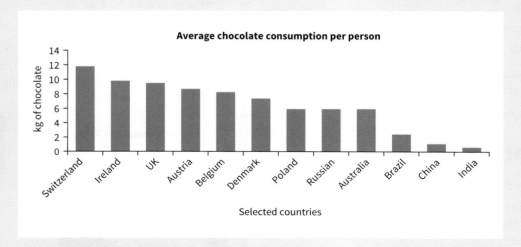

Average chocolate consumption per person

6 Reading comprehension

1 Explain why marketing departments study people's behaviour, habits and way of life.

2 Why is it important that a new chocolate bar should be difficult for other companies to copy?

3 What kinds of information does a company want to find at the testing stage? Name two things.

4 According to the chart, which countries consumed about half the amount of chocolate consumed by Switzerland?

5 Write a paragraph of about 75 words explaining why many new chocolate bars made in the factory never reach the stage of being packaged, advertised or sold.

7 Post-reading discussion

Has the article surprised you in any way? Why/Why not?

Do you think the way new chocolate is launched could apply to other products?

8 Vocabulary

Look back at Section 2 of the text, Product development. Make a list of all the words in this section which are connected with making and selling a product.

Examples: *companies, manufacturer*

Put a **?** against words you don't understand. Look these up in a dictionary.

Collocations

Find these collocations in Section 2 of the text:

stiff competition

price-sensitive product

delicious formula

What other collocations could be made with the adjectives *stiff*, *sensitive* and *delicious*? Make a list with a partner.

Examples: *a delicious cake, a sensitive child, a stiff breeze*

9 A rewarding job?

Work in pairs or groups of three.

How do you think the people involved in developing the new chocolate bar might feel about their work? Write down your ideas.

Examples: *excited, frustrated*

What skills and qualities do you feel would be necessary for working on a new product, such as the one described in the article? Make a list.

Examples: *enthusiasm, determination*

10 Sharing ideas

Look back at the notes you made in exercises 1 and 2 about reasons for working and the skills and qualities needed for specific occupations. Do any of them apply here? Add them to your lists above.

Share your ideas with the other groups. Listen carefully and add any other interesting ideas.

11 Understanding visual data

As you already know, visual data, graphs, charts, etc. are often included in newspaper and magazine articles, especially those of a factual type. The information in the chart often mirrors information in the text in a different format and may also add extra information.

Re-read the opening paragraph of 'A Bar Is Born'. Then study the chart in the article. How does the chart:

a reflect information in the first paragraph?

b give extra information?

12 Role play: Product development meeting

It is 10 a.m. You are a member of the Product Development and Marketing team, which is meeting to discuss the production of a new bar of chocolate. At the end of the meeting you need to decide:

■ who the chocolate will be aimed at

■ the name and packaging

■ your advertising strategies.

In groups of four, choose from the roles. Study your role carefully. Make sure you understand the information so that you can express it during the meeting.

DESIGNER

You think there is a need for a new chocolate bar. It should be aimed at young children as this is where the market is strongest.

You specialise in the design of the wrappers. You prefer a bright red, green or yellow wrapper, something which will stand out and catch children's attention – definitely not anything which looks grown-up or is too subtle. You would also like images of animals and their young put on the wrappers. This will encourage parents to buy the chocolate for toddlers.

You want the name 'Choccie' or 'Chic-Choc'. You think this will encourage parents to buy it for their children's lunchboxes or as a treat after school. You think the taste should be very sweet and milky, which will not appeal to more sophisticated palates.

You are rather forceful in meetings. Give your opinions firmly and clearly. (You may want to look back at the opinion language in Unit 9.) You also hate to be interrupted.

MARKETING EXECUTIVE

You expect that the market research you are carrying out will show there is a need for chocolate that will appeal to older teenagers and adults. In your opinion, people are rather bored with the taste of the chocolate bars you already produce and want something which tastes more of chocolate and less of sugar and milk.

You think the name and image should be as sophisticated as possible. The colour of the wrapper should be black, blue or gold. The advertising should suggest the chocolate is a luxury. Eating it is a pleasure and makes an occasion special. It is not a quick snack or an item for children's lunchboxes.

You are not happy with any of the names suggested for the product. You think consumers will confuse these names with other brands.

The chocolate market is extremely competitive so the advertising budget needs to be high enough to cover the cost of advertising on TV.

SALES EXECUTIVE

You are convinced there is a need for a new chocolate bar aimed at families, to include adults and children of various ages. You have some ideas for names for the product: 'Golden Bar', 'Delight' and 'Soft-Centred'. You dislike childish-sounding names which suggest the chocolate is for young children.

The advertising should suggest the chocolate is an all-round family choice, not something too sophisticated or very child-orientated. The advert could show people eating it at work, on trains, or just enjoying it on holidays, family outings, etc.

You are going to suggest that the product is advertised in magazines and on the internet rather than on television. TV advertising is too expensive and will not necessarily increase sales.

You are a good listener. You do your best to get on with everyone and calm 'ruffled feathers'.

HEAD ENGINEER

You are very unhappy with the plans to produce a new chocolate bar. You have been working on many different kinds of formulas and each time the product is unsatisfactory. It goes soft easily, it's too sweet or isn't sweet enough, it's too dry, or it crumbles very easily.

The most satisfactory result so far was a bar that tasted very similar to one you already make. You think that if the factory invested in a new machine that could produce the chocolate in a different shape and size from the original, then the new product would seem different enough to be successful.

One possibility would be to cut the chocolate into small circles and sell it in large, family-size bags.

10.2 Facts and figures

13 Approximations

Study the following exact amounts. Say them aloud carefully, checking the pronunciation with a partner. Where does the stress fall in *per cent*?

1   4.9%

2   10.4%

3   52.3%

4   74.7%

5   98.8%

6   19.2%

7   23.8%

8   32.9%

Now match the exact amounts to these approximations.

A   getting on for three-quarters

B   a good half

C   over one in ten

D   under one in five

E   almost a quarter

F   practically all

G   nearly a third

H   about one in twenty

When facts and figures are presented, both exact amounts and approximations might be used. For example, you may hear '*19.8% of the town's population, that's getting on for one in five men and women of working age, are unemployed.*'

What are the advantages of using approximations to present information? Are there any disadvantages?

14 Questioning statistics

A   Statistical information looks authoritative but you need to treat it with caution. Pressure groups, for example, may use statistics to influence public opinion.

What has the following survey found out? How does it compare with your own experience?

A recent survey found that children who come from homes where the mother works have half as many absences from school as the children of non-working mothers. Working mothers seem quite prepared to send their children to school when they are unwell.

B   Before deciding whether the above conclusion is valid, you need to ask more questions. For example:

- Who asked for the survey to be carried out?
- Why was it carried out?
- Who took part in the survey?
- What was the size of the sample?
- Exactly what kind of questions were asked?
- Were the groups of children closely matched in terms of age, background, social class, etc?

Why are these questions important? What kind of answers do you think you might get?

C   With your partner, make notes on the questions you would want to ask before accepting the validity of the following 'facts and figures'.

The majority of the population thought that young people under the age of 18 should not be allowed out after 9 p.m.

_____

_____

A survey found that the Rio School was much better than the other schools. It had by far the best exam results.

_____

_____

15 Criticising statistics

Study the statement below and then read the reactions to it. Make sure you understand the expressions in **bold** type.

A survey of young people found the majority were not going to bother to get a decent job when they left school or college.

It's **a total distortion of the truth**. *The teenagers I know would do anything to get on a good training scheme.*

They're **fudging the facts**. *We all want a good job.*

I can't stand surveys which **bend the truth**. *I'd like to know exactly who they asked and the questions they used.*

They're **twisting the results** *so they don't have to give us careers guidance.*

Who dreamed that up? *It's rubbish!*

Look back at the statistical information given in exercise 14C. Practise criticising the statements with your partner. Do you both sound indignant enough?

16 Young lives: Good or bad?

A survey of young people produced the following results. Read each statement carefully and decide with a partner whether it gives a good or bad impression of teenagers. Mark each statement **P** if a positive impression is being given, and **N** if the impression given is negative. Underline the words which help you decide.

1   23% valued spare-time jobs more highly than their school studies.

2   Over three-quarters were concerned the schools did not arrange work experience.

3   Over a fifth said that working at casual, part-time jobs was the only way they could pay for ordinary everyday things they needed, or buy treats such as sweets or magazines.

4   18% objected to the amount of pocket money they received but were not prepared to work to earn extra spending money.

5   Over a quarter of teenagers were dissatisfied with the amount of freedom their parents allowed.

6   74% were happy with the amount of freedom they were allowed.

7   Reading was a popular activity for two out of three of those interviewed.

8   A third never pick up a book outside school.

9   The majority do nothing to help their community.

10   One in three teenagers do voluntary work for their community.

Decide which statistics you would choose to present if you were:

a   an employer who feels teenagers are a bad employment risk

b   a youth leader encouraging firms to develop training schemes for young people.

17 Rewriting in a more formal style

The following letter was written to a newspaper by a teenager who disagreed with a report it had published. Discuss the letter with your partner and try to decide whether it is written in an appropriate tone and register for its target audience.

Consider the use of:

- slang
- colloquialisms
- contractions
- rhetorical questions, question forms, and question tags.

Underline those aspects of the letter both you and your partner are unhappy with.

199

> Dear Editor,
>
> Hi! It's me again! Ollie Debeer from your go-ahead high school just outside town. Your report 'Young Lives Shock!' just got me mad! You, too, I bet! I mean, the report says 'We are unconcerned about employment'. Talk about fudging the facts, eh? All my mates are dead worried about getting a decent job. I also read 'teenagers value their spare-time jobs more than their studies'. Who dreamed that up? My dad's a single parent and there's no way he can afford to buy me the trainers or kind of phone

I want. No way! So I work for them, right? I work in a café twice a week after school and, yeah, I do find it hard to concentrate the next day, but I do extra homework to catch up. Nothing wrong with that, eh? That stuff about teenage entertainment was kind of distorted too, wasn't it? 'The youth of today show a strong preference for the company of their peer group over that which their parents can offer.' I mean, who wouldn't rather be down at the youth club than stuck at home watching the old man snore? But it didn't say we dislike our parents, did it? I reckon you were pretty upset about that report in your paper, too, mate. Anyway, write me back. It's gonna be great hearing your views!

Love,

Ollie

When you are ready, try to rewrite the letter in a more formal style, and divide it into suitable paragraphs. Remember: a letter to a newspaper can include some aspects of informal style, such as the occasional idiom or colloquialism. However, the general impression should be formal.

Show your finished letter to your partner. Does he/she agree that the 'balance' of your style (neither too formal nor too informal) is about right?

10.3 Job stereotypes

18 Pre-listening discussion

What kinds of shops do you usually like visiting? Which shops do you enjoy the least?

How would you rate the service in most shops?

If you could improve shops in one way, what would you do?

INTERNATIONAL OVERVIEW

The graph shows the average worldwide take-up of tertiary education by young people within five years of leaving secondary school, as a percentage of the relevant age group. (*Tertiary* means college- or university-level.)

1   What percentage of young people worldwide were enrolled in tertiary education in 2005, 2008 and 2012?

2   Is the trend up or down?

Why do you think this change may have happened? Discuss your ideas in your group.

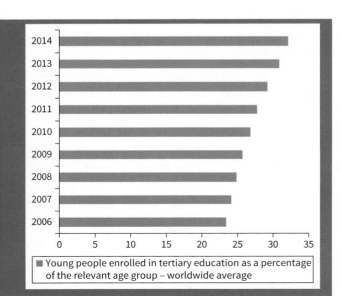

Young people enrolled in tertiary education as a percentage of the relevant age group – worldwide average

19 Predicting content

You are going to listen to Zoe, a human resources officer who works for a chain of electrical stores, talking in an informal way about her job. She aims to help the stores run more efficiently and profitably.

What aspects of her job do you think Zoe might be going to mention? Tick off the points on this list.

- ☐ Making suggestions about new products the stores could sell
- ☐ Helping managers decide whether they need full-time or part-time members of staff
- ☐ Suggesting that shop staff have extra training to improve their skills
- ☐ Encouraging managers to go for promotion
- ☐ Disciplining staff who are performing badly
- ☐ Advising sales managers if their sales are falling

20 Vocabulary check

Before you listen, make sure you understand the meaning of these words and phrases.

VOCABULARY

| personal sales targets | influential | wide spectrum |

21 Listening for gist

Listen to the recording. Which of the points that you ticked are mentioned?

22 Detailed listening

Now listen for detail and try to complete each statement correctly.

1 Zoe visits stores in
   a shopping malls.
   b out of town centres.
   c high streets.

2 A common problem is that sales staff
   a do not look professional.
   b fail to reach sales targets.
   c lack interest in working hard.

3 Zoe suggests that staff should have
   a more training and development.
   b more training and better pay.
   c more training and longer hours.

4 Staff may be given a camera to take home
   a as a reward for doing a good job.
   b so they can learn how it works.
   c to practise selling it.

5 Staff often lack the ability to
   a display goods effectively.
   b relate to the customers.
   c find goods in the store.

6 Zoe feels that
   a a wide variety of people can do well as sales assistants.
   b only people of a certain type will succeed.
   c sales staff should have a similar background to their manager.

7 Zoe
   a tries to make the managers work harder.
   b lets managers blame her when things go wrong.
   c is sympathetic and helpful to the managers.

23 Post-listening discussion

A Zoe says she finds managers want to recruit people who are '*just like themselves*'. What kind of people do you think she has in mind? How do you think they would look and behave, and what way of life would they have?

B Stereotypes often form around particular occupations. What would you expect a 'typical' person doing each of the following jobs to be like?
   ▪ labourer
   ▪ pop star
   ▪ prison governor
   ▪ scientist

C Do you think the stereotype of an occupation helps you when you are choosing which career to follow? Why/Why not?

D Can you think of someone who doesn't fit the norm for their job? Try to explain your views.

24 Common work-related expressions

Zoe describes store managers as being 'on a treadmill'. What do you think she means?

Can you work out the meaning of the following expressions from the context?

1   I meet friends from work socially but we never *talk shop*.

2   The new assistant is hard-working and enthusiastic – *a real go-getter*.

3   He got *a golden handshake* worth $20,000 when he retired.

4   Although the policeman was *off-duty*, he arrested the thief.

5   I'm called an 'office assistant' but really I'm just a general *dogsbody*.

6   Not liking the structure of big companies, I got work where I could *be my own boss*.

7   He's not *a high-flyer*; he doesn't have any brilliant ideas, but you can depend on him.

8   Because of their working conditions, *blue-collar workers* are more likely to have accidents at work than *white-collar workers*.

25 Pronunciation: Linking sounds

Practise reading this advert aloud, checking your pronunciation with a partner. Does he or she feel you are reading smoothly and naturally? Notice that if a word ends with a consonant and the next word begins with a vowel, the sounds are linked.

BRIGHTEN UP YOUR SUMMER – GET A JOB WITH US!

If you need extra cash and are 16+

WE NEED YOU!

Lots of vacancies in our seafront restaurant.

It's fun, it's easy, hours to suit!

Ring Ian on 01774 456156

Now mark the linked sounds in this advert and practise reading it aloud to your partner.

HEADLIGHTS HAIRDRESSING

CAREER OPPORTUNITIES FOR SCHOOL LEAVERS

Trainees needed. Learn in a leading salon. If you've got energy and enthusiasm, we can take you to the top.

Contact Elma Telephone 01223 569432

26 Writing a job advert

You work in a laboratory. One morning you find this note on your desk from your boss.

Hendrik

The lab is getting so messy that I've decided to advertise for someone to come in on Saturdays to wash the glassware, sweep up and keep the area tidy. We can pay £8.00 per hour and travel expenses as well. It might interest a student. Can you draft an advert for the Evening News? Call it a general assistant or something. Use the lab telephone number. Amy Jones will take the calls.

Thanks.

Joanna

Write a suitable advert based on the note. Then mark the linking sounds and show it to a partner. Does he/she agree with the word linking?

Ask your partner to read it aloud. Correct the pronunciation if necessary (tactfully, of course!).

10.4 Recruitment with a difference

27 Pre-reading task

A   Do you enjoy 'fast food'? When (if ever) do you visit fast-food restaurants?

What do you think are the strong points of these restaurants?

B You are going to read an article about a fast-food restaurant which is run by deaf staff. Write down four questions you would like to see answered in the article.

Example: *How do customers communicate with the staff?*

_____

_____

_____

_____

28 Vocabulary check

Make sure you understand the meaning of these words and phrases, which you will meet in the text.

VOCABULARY

hearing impairment recruiting agile criteria mentor

29 Reading for gist

Now read the article. Are any of the questions you wrote down in exercise 27 answered?

Work Without Limits

When Aly Sarhan, 28, was asked to head a new branch of the Kentucky Fried Chicken restaurant chain in Egypt, run by deaf people, he didn't
5 know what to expect.

'Working in the midst of 30 deaf youths is like working in a foreign land,' says Sarhan, who took a crash course in Arabic sign language.

10 For Sarhan, however, the experience has been an eye-opening one, and has changed his attitudes towards people with disabilities. 'My staff's hearing impairment does not stop them from
15 doing anything a hearing person can do. They certainly have a whole load of determination in them,' he says.

The idea for a deaf-run KFC — the first in the Middle East — was born
20 when KFC's top management decided to 'pay their dues towards society,' according to Sarhan. 'We found that deaf people existed in large numbers in Egypt, so we decided to do some-
25 thing for them,' he explains.

The obvious place to start recruiting from was the Deaf Society in Heliopolis. The KFC board used the same criteria they apply when choos-
30 ing hearing applicants. Successful candidates had to be tactful, presentable, agile, and no older than 25 years of age. 'It was very difficult turning people down, so we decided to pick the
35 most eligible applicants, in addition to drawing up a long waiting list,' Sarhan says. For KFC, this was groundbreaking work.

Sarhan, one of the youngest store
40 managers working at KFC worldwide, says his biggest concern in the beginning was how to communicate with his employees. 'I did not know a single sign, so I had to use an interpreter.
45 Whether the kids got to like me or despise me depended on the interpreter. I was determined, however, to learn the language and remove any barriers between us,' he says.

50 That was easier said than done, he remembers. 'Arabic sign language is one of the most difficult languages you can learn, because it is mainly composed of movements rather than dis-
55 tinct signs,' Sarhan explains. Having worked with his staff for only 11 months, he is still a weak signer, but he knows enough to help him get by and gain the trust and acceptance of
60 his employees.

So far, the restaurant has been a big success and has helped create a supportive environment for the employees. 'What made the kids so enthusi-
65 astic about our new endeavour was the fact that they get to be in a place where being deaf is the norm. Most of them have been through bad work experiences in which they were the
70 only person with hearing impairment in the place, which made them feel lonely and left out.'

This supportive environment, Sarhan says, has made many of the deaf
75 employees depend on themselves more. 'Many of the employees had been spoilt and pampered all their lives by their parents, out of pity, which made them rather bad-tem-
80 pered and lazy. Once they began to like us, it was as if we had tapped a well of undiscovered energy.'

At the branch in Dokki, pictures on the menu and light signals compensate

85 for the lack of verbal communication. Customers simply have to point to the picture of the food item they want on the picture-menu. 'Despite that, lots of people come in with the feeling of 90 being at a loss written all over their faces. They start making signs, and are relieved to find out I can talk. I start carrying out the customer's role with-

out signing, to show them how easy it 95 all is,' Sarhan says.

The newly married Sarhan says that he considers his staff part of his family now. He has become some-thing of a mentor for them and has 100 helped to create a friendly environ-ment. 'This place has helped the deaf employees psychologically, not just

financially. I hope more companies will think of embarking on similar 105 adventures. It truly is exhilarating to help make a difference to people's lives,' he says.

by Manal el-Jesri

30 Comprehension check

1 Why did the restaurant choose to employ deaf people?

2 How did the management decide what would be the right criteria for selecting applicants?

3 Contrast the way employees felt about work before they began their jobs at the restaurant with their feelings about work now.

4 Describe the personality changes the employees undergo.

5 What does Aly feel he has gained from this work? Name two things.

31 Post-reading discussion

A Aly hopes other companies will follow the example of his restaurant and employ staff with disabilities. How can companies be encouraged to recruit a wider range of types of people? Share your ideas.

B Aly says, '*It truly is exhilarating to help make a difference to people's lives.*'

Jobs which are 'people-orientated', such as nursing, teaching, human resources, or the hotel trade, bring different rewards and stresses from 'product-orientated jobs' such as those in engineering, carpentry or design.

Which kind of work would you find rewarding, and why?

C Aly is described as being a '*mentor*'. He supports and inspires his employees.

Many schools and colleges have 'mentoring schemes' whereby students are matched with highly successful

adults of a similar background. The mentors give hope, encouragement and practical advice to their students. Sometimes students spend time at the mentor's workplace, 'shadowing' him or her, or doing some work experience. Do you think this is a good idea? Why/Why not?

Who would you choose for your mentor and why?

32 Vocabulary study

A Try to put these adjectives into order, from most active to least active. Use a dictionary to check unfamiliar words.

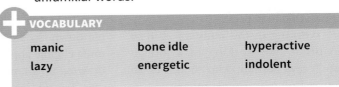

VOCABULARY		
manic	bone idle	hyperactive
lazy	energetic	indolent

B Now put these adjectives into order, from most positive to most negative.

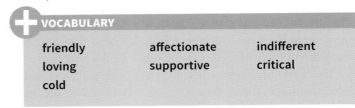

VOCABULARY		
friendly	affectionate	indifferent
loving	supportive	critical
cold		

C Which word is the odd one out?

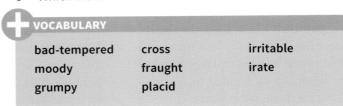

VOCABULARY		
bad-tempered	cross	irritable
moody	fraught	irate
grumpy	placid	

33 Similes

Similes are descriptive forms of comparison which enrich your writing and make it more sophisticated. Study these examples from the reading text:

'(It) is **like** working in a foreign land.'

'It was **as if** we had tapped a well of undiscovered energy.'

Notice that *like* is followed by a noun or gerund:

It's **like a fridge** in here – let's turn the heating on.

It was **like being** on holiday.

As if/as though are followed by a verb clause:

He looked **as if he had** seen a ghost.

Similes include traditional expressions such as: *as good as gold, as thin as a rake, as flat as a pancake, as white as snow, like talking to a brick wall* and many more.

Complete the following sentences with suitable similes.

1 The room was so hot. It felt like _____
2 Her hands were as cold as _____
3 The house was so dirty. It was as if _____
4 Samira was thrilled with the news. She reacted as though _____
5 We're not allowed any freedom. It's like _____
6 I was so depressed when I couldn't get a job. It was as if _____

34 Spelling: *-able* or *-ible*?

A In the text you met the adjectives *presentable* (line 32) and *eligible* (line 35). The adjective endings *-able* and *-ible* are often confused. From the word *depend* we get *dependable,* but *convert* gives us *convertible.*

Complete the adjectives in these sentences, using a dictionary if necessary. Then learn by heart the spellings you find most difficult.

1 I'm afraid I won't be avail_____ until after the 13th.
2 The house was almost invis_____ in the fog.
3 Fortunately, the disease was cur_____.
4 I'm sure she'll make a respons_____ parent.
5 I found Ken's story absolutely incred_____.
6 This is a sens_____ idea.
7 Let's take your car – it's more reli_____ than mine.
8 Cheating in exams is not advis_____.
9 Heavy snow made the house inaccess_____.
10 Tiredness tends to make him irrit_____.

B Now complete these adjectives with the endings *-able* or *-ible* and then use each one in a sentence of your own.

1 wash_____
2 ined_____
3 digest_____
4 desir_____
5 approach_____
6 excit_____
7 bear_____
8 incomprehens_____

35 Phrasal verbs

Notice how these phrasal verbs are used in the article in exercise 29. Then use them in a suitable form in sentences 1–5.

turn down (line 33)
leave out (line 72)
draw up (line 36)
carry out (line 94)
get by (line 58)

1 Gavin earns so little money, I don't know how they _____.
2 She was careful to _____ all the instructions exactly.
3 We're going on holiday next week, so I'm afraid I shall have to _____ your invitation.
4 All the children in my son's class were invited to the party as we did not want to _____ anyone _____.
5 The management have _____ new guidelines for staff interviews.

36 'Eye' idioms

Aly says the experience of working with people with disabilities has been *'an eye-opening one'* (line 11). What do you think he means by this?

Match the first parts of these sentences (1–8) with their endings (A–H).

1 Jim wanted to paint the room green, but Vera wanted blue,
2 As she had to do the ironing,
3 The bride looked wonderful in her wedding dress. She really
4 When I first saw the Pyramids, I thought they were so amazing that
5 Although it was very late, we walked home,

205

6 The children weren't supposed to be eating sweets

7 Visiting a foreign country for the first time

8 The new manager was so much more astute than the old one that it was impossible

A I couldn't keep my eyes off them.

B is quite an eye-opener.

C keeping an eye out for a taxi all the way.

D to pull the wool over his eyes.

E but I decided to turn a blind eye to it.

F was a sight for sore eyes.

G I kept an eye on the baby.

H so I'm afraid they didn't see eye to eye.

10.5 Preparing for work

37 How well does school prepare you for work?

A What kind of career would you like to have when you leave school or college? What general things do you feel you have learned at school which will help you?

Write down any ideas which seem relevant, even if you don't have a clear picture in your mind of the exact career you want to follow.

Examples:
I've learned how to use my initiative when I do projects.

I've learned foreign languages which will give me international opportunities.

I've learned to be more punctual, which is essential in most jobs.

I want to be an engineer and my school arranged some work experience for me.

B Have you held any positions of responsibility at school (e.g. helped run a club or society) which might be useful when you apply for college or work? What have you learned from 'working' at school? Note down your ideas.

Examples:
I've learned how to get on with different kinds of people.

I've become more mature.

_____

_____

_____

Keep your notes, as you'll need them later.

38 Before you read

Many schools have a prefect system. Students who are prefects help the school run smoothly by keeping a check on other students' behaviour, doing litter patrols, helping in the dining room, etc.

Do you think this is a good idea? Could there possibly be any drawbacks?

Students who show special abilities are chosen as Head Prefect or Head Boy or Girl. In many schools, one of their main tasks is to represent the opinions of the students to the teachers.

Do you have a Head Prefect in your school? What are his/her duties? How is he/she chosen?

39 Reading, analysing and writing

Read this article from a school newsletter. What is its purpose?

> ### HEAD PREFECT ELECTIONS by Luke Adams
>
> I know you all have your own ideas about the best candidate for Head Prefect, but if you can spare a minute to read this I'll explain why Matthew Okoro is the strongest and most experienced candidate.
>
> Matthew, who is the youngest senior prefect in his year, has shown the most fantastic negotiating skills. Do you remember when we were banned from the swimming pool at lunchtime? Matthew was the one who persuaded the teachers to let us use it by offering to supervise it himself. The fact that we can go on school trips is due to Matthew's hard work, too. He worked round the clock to raise funds for a reliable minibus to take us on outings. He might not be as keen as some of us on playing team sports, but he is a regular supporter at all our matches.
>
> Outside school, Matthew helps at a home for disabled teenagers. His experience has made him much more understanding of people's problems, which makes all the difference in a large, mixed school like ours.

Read the article again and underline examples of:

- complex sentence constructions, including defining and non-defining relative clauses (revised in Unit 8, exercises 36 and 37)
- comparisons, including comparative/superlative constructions
- collocations describing qualities and skills
- idioms
- audience awareness.

Now write the closing paragraph to Luke's article, trying to use the same style.

Matthew is _____

_____

40 Comparing two styles

Now read this second newsletter article. What are the main differences between this article and Luke's? Make a list.

Example: There are no paragraphs.

> ### HEAD PREFECT ELECTIONS by Leila Masoon
>
> You've got to vote for Nicola Wilson. It's not fair if she isn't made Head Prefect. She set up a social club. She worked after school every day. She worked on Saturdays as well. Before that we didn't have a club. Now we have a club. Everyone goes to the club. It is good. She has stopped the bullying. The bullying was happening a lot. She spoke to the bullies. She made them stop. Now everyone is nice to each other. She started a 'Welcome Day' for new students. Now new students are happy. They are not lonely. We had to wear skirts in winter. It was horrible. We were cold. Nicola explained we wanted to wear trousers. Now we can. That was because of Nicola. The other prefects talk about themselves. They say how good they are. But Nicola doesn't. She works in a hospital on Saturdays. She visits patients. They are patients who have no visitors. She knows more about people now. You must vote for Nicola.

41 Rewriting in a more mature style

Try to rewrite Leila's article so that the style is more fluent and mature. Look back at Luke's article for an example of a more sophisticated style.

When you've finished, show your letter to a partner. Listen carefully to his or her comments. How far do you agree with them? Will you change anything?

42 Brainstorming

Work in small groups. Make notes about unemployment under the headings below, using the prompts to give you ideas. Remember: brainstorming allows you to write down anything you think of at the time. Don't worry about relevance at this stage.

Try to think about your own country. Note examples of problems and remedies which are relevant to your own situation.

Looking for work

Why are people unemployed?

- *Industries such as … have closed down because … and so …*
- *We import goods such as … and people prefer to buy these rather than the similar products we make at home, because …. This results in … in our own industries.*
- *Modern technology has …*
- *The level of education and training is …*
- *Industries have moved out of city centres because … and now city centres are …*
- *People are leaving their farms in the countryside, which means … and going to the towns, which results in …*

What would help people get jobs?

- *Government money could be given to …*
- *Industries such as … could be encouraged to set up in our area.*
- *Training schemes such as … could be organised.*
- *Industries which use old, out-of-date equipment could …*

Other ideas

- *The school-leaving age is now … and it could be changed to … which might help …*
- *Colleges should offer more courses in … because …*
- *Unemployed people could visit advice centres to find out …*
- *Schools should arrange work experience in …*
- *Careers guidance at school could …*

When you have finished, compare your notes with those of other groups and add any useful ideas. Keep your notes carefully, as you will use them later.

208

43 Reading an example letter

Study this letter which was written to a local newspaper. The writer makes four separate points. What are they?

1 _____

2 _____

3 _____

4 _____

Unhappy to be jobless

Dear Editor,

I do not usually write to newspapers but when I read your report which suggested that young people were happy to be unemployed, I felt I had to respond.

I am a school leaver, and in my opinion school leavers need much more detailed careers guidance. Moreover, I think schools should start a 'mentoring scheme' which would match pupils with successful career people. Spending one day a week with a mentor would be a real eye-opener and provide us with the work experience companies say they want but which students find so hard to get!

Furthermore, the majority of the firms in our area are 'hi-tech', whereas some school leavers around here are not computer-literate. Firms should form a partnership with schools to develop training schemes which would enable us to learn the skills needed for the job.

I would also like to add that the statistic in your report '85% of pupils had no idea what life without a job is like' is a complete distortion of the truth. Many of us have parents who are out of work and we definitely do not want to be in the same boat.

When you are at school, getting a good job is like a high wall you have to climb over. Young people need all the help they can get, not criticism.

Yours faithfully,

Jennifer Aziz

44 Analysing the letter

When you are writing a composition, you should aim for a mature style. The following checklist shows some aspects of verbal sophistication. Re-read Jennifer's letter and find examples for each item on the list.

Defining clauses _____
Comparative structures _____
Idioms _____
Similes _____
Linking devices _____
Opening sentence _____
Conclusion _____
Style and register _____

45 Writing a letter of reply

Write a letter to Jennifer describing the employment situation in your country and explaining what you think would help people in your country get jobs.

Remember:

- Try to use an appropriate, mature style.
- Keep to the topic.
- Start a new paragraph for each new topic.
- Open and round off the letter sensibly.

46 Choosing appropriate vocabulary

When you read an exam question, you need to identify the topic as clearly as you can and think of language connected to it. As always, try to choose language which is lively and varied and really conveys a sense of occasion.

This also helps you avoid 'rubric error'. This means answering the question in a way which is not relevant to the topic. For example, a question about medical experiments on animals should not produce a composition about taking your pet on holiday!

Read the exam-style questions below and the vocabulary which follows. Working in small groups and using dictionaries, decide what vocabulary is unlikely to be connected to the topic. Make sure you all agree.

Question 1

You had an important test and left home in very good time. However, something extremely unexpected happened on your journey. You arrived at the test only just before it was due to begin. Write an account of what happened for your school newsletter.

What language is unlikely to be connected to this topic? Delete it from the following list.

decide my future	emergency services
with seconds to spare	dawdled
panicked	invigilator
hasty	not a moment to lose
yelled	indifferent
shoved	alarmed
budget deficit	stampede
anxious	strolled
grabbed	broke out in a sweat
absolutely desperate	loudspeaker
snatched	announcements
sales figures	share prices
darted	sheer despair

Question 2

Despite your expectations, you have been selected for a special training scheme which will help you get the job of your dreams. Explain the way you felt when you heard the news and how this training scheme will help bring you closer to your chosen career.

Delete the inappropriate language.

sarcastic	aggrieved
bitterly disappointed	over the moon
relieved	ecstatic
thrilled	challenge
walking on air	develop new skills
repelled	isolated
practical experience	cast down
delighted	disenchanted
amazed	subdued
many benefits	swelled with pride
breathed a sigh of relief	worthwhile
forsaken	huge burden off my shoulders
irritated	colleagues
golden opportunity	

Question 3

You have to move house because your parents have been promoted in their jobs. Although you will not be living very far away, you are sad to leave your old home. Write a letter of welcome to the new occupants of the house explaining what you particularly liked about the house and why.

Delete the inappropriate language.

hostile	*memorable*
treasured memories	*sense of history*
poison-pen letter	*contentment*
sick and tired	*unjust*
nostalgic	*macabre*
favourite hideaway	*know the place by heart*
light, airy and spacious	*charming*
deeply depressed	*outraged*
rambling garden	*quality of life*
security	*terrified*
sentimental value	*not of this world*
small, cosy, comfortable	*contemptuous*
ill at ease	*delightful*
disgusted	*ideal spot*

47 Timed writing

Choose one of the topics which you find appealing from the exercise above. Write about 150–200 words.

Allow yourself 15–20 minutes maximum to write the composition.

Reading aloud

Read your composition aloud to your group and pay close attention to the feedback. How far do you agree with the comments, and what would you change?

48 Listening: Four work scenarios 🔊

You will hear four short recordings. Answer each question using no more than **three** words for each detail. You will hear each recording twice.

1   a   Maria is ringing up to change the time and date of a job interview. What alternative is she offered?

    b   What is Maria doing on Tuesday?

2   a   According to the careers talk, what special qualifications are needed to enter training schemes for the police force?

    b   What two personal qualities are needed?

3   a   What did the headteacher think about your friend's idea of helping at the children's clinic?

    b   When does your friend want to visit the clinic?

4   a   Has the speaker received good news or bad news?

    b   What job does he want to train to do?

✳ GRAMMAR SPOTLIGHT

1   Superlatives of long and short adjectives

Superlatives of short adjectives are made by adding *-(e)st*:

> *the oldest   the cleverest   the largest*

With some words there are also spelling changes:

> *lazy ~ laziest   big ~ biggest*
>
> *She had **the happiest** smile of anyone I had ever met.*

For superlatives of longer adjectives, we use *the most* before the adjective:

> *I thought Mel's presentation was **the most interesting**.*

Note these irregular superlatives: *the best, the worst, the furthest*.

The article in exercise 39 contained this example:

> *Matthew Okoro is the strongest and most experienced candidate.*

Skim-read the article and underline other examples of superlatives.

2   Adverbs of degree

We can use adverbs of degree to modify or intensify an adjective. In exercise 12, the Head Engineer's opinion of the different kinds of new chocolate is:

> *… it's too sweet or isn't sweet enough.*

Notice that *too* goes before the adjective but *enough* goes after it.

Other adverbs of degree include *very, extremely, rather, quite, a little, a bit* (informal). These all go before the adjective:

> *Don't you think it's **a bit late** to start watching a film?*

Skim-read the roles of the Sales Executive and the Marketing Executive in exercise 12 and underline examples of adverbs of degree.

EXAM-STYLE QUESTIONS
Form-filling

Boris Maltsin is a student in Class 11R, Ellemere International School, 134 52nd Street, New York. He recently completed two weeks of work experience with Adnitt Couzens Creative, an agency which organises advertising campaigns for a wide range of industries. Boris's favourite subject at school is art, and his form tutor, Mr Gooch, has told him he has a good deal of artistic flair.

Boris wanted to work in a company where he could develop his artistic skills and where there would be opportunities to find out more about the commercial aspects of art. Normally, the school finds work experience placements for its students, but Boris, unlike most of his friends, organised his own. As soon as he arrived at Adnitt Couzens, he noticed the friendly atmosphere. The employees (six men and four women) sat at large tables in an open-plan studio. The owner was Mr Jim Couzens, a softly spoken, genial man who had spent his life building up the business.

Boris spent the first day working with two of the graphic designers to produce artwork for a brochure advertising a new range of CDs. He enjoyed using his imagination and was fascinated by the range of computer applications available. He also began to learn about working as a team – how it is not the individual alone who is so important, but the way he or she works with others to create the end product. He disliked some of the more mundane tasks such as filing, although he realised they had to be done.

Various members of staff were helpful to Boris. Juanita Sims, the data input clerk, was always patient when he was carrying out tasks for her. Alain Neflon, the senior designer, advised Boris on the psychological effects of colour. He suggested, for example, that a silver grey would be more appropriate for a brochure advertising music designed to appeal to older people, rather than the bright orange Boris originally wanted.

Boris especially enjoyed working with Marc Damina, a junior designer who always answered his questions carefully and explained what was important and what was not. They discovered they had the same sense of humour, and Boris found himself telling Marc about his hope that one day he could work as a photographer, travelling around America and taking the kind of pictures that would make people see life in a different way. Mr Couzens, despite being very busy, checked regularly on his progress and encouraged Boris to build up pieces he could include in his school portfolio.

Although there was no kitchen at the agency, employees were able to make hot drinks whenever they wished to. Boris usually went across the road to a local coffee shop for a sandwich at lunchtime, often with Marc. He began work at 9 a.m. and finished at 6 p.m. The day was much longer than a school day and he found himself wishing it ended at 5 p.m. However, Mrs Bianchi, the office manager, was very strict about punctuality and time-keeping in general. She had reprimanded Boris for being late on his second morning (due to missing his usual bus to the studio), so he knew better than to ask if he could leave earlier!

Boris's school asks students to complete a feedback form at the end of their work experience period. Imagine you are Boris and complete the form.

ELLEMERE INTERNATIONAL SCHOOL
WORK EXPERIENCE FEEDBACK FORM

SECTION A

Name: _____

Class: _____

Was a portfolio produced?   *Yes / No (Please circle.)*

Name of company or organisation: _____

Nature of company's business: _____

Number of employees: _____ Hours of work: _____

How was your placement arranged?
It was arranged by the school / I arranged it myself. (Delete as appropriate.)

Method of transport to work placement: _____

Were catering facilities provided?   *Yes / No (Please circle.)*
What were your first impressions of the company?

_____

_____

Give one example of something you liked about the work you did on the work placement.

_____

_____

Give one example of something you disliked about the work.

_____

_____

Who, if anyone, did you get on particularly well with?

_____

_____

What, if anything, would you change about your work experience placement?

_____

_____

SECTION B

Write one sentence of 12–20 words saying whether you would recommend this work experience placement to future students.

_____

_____

Writing

1   There is a proposal at your school to offer students two weeks of work experience locally after they finish their IGCSE exams. Here are some comments from students on the idea.

    'We will learn skills that will help us understand the working world.'

    'We would not benefit because work experience is not like doing a real job.'

Write an article for the school magazine giving your views. The comments above may give you some ideas but you should try to use some ideas of your own.

Write 150–200 words (or 100–150 words for Core level).

2   Reply to the advertisement below, describing the experience, qualities and skills you have which make you suitable for this position.

Spend the summer in Argentina!
Responsible students needed to help in children's holiday camp. Must have good organisational skills, be keen on sport and able to supervise children aged 8–11 years. Fares and accommodation provided.

Write 150–200 words (or 100–150 words for Core level).

3   A recent survey discovered the reasons why school leavers were still unemployed six months after leaving full-time education.

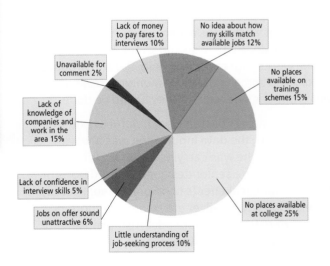

Lack of money to pay fares to interviews 10%
No idea about how my skills match available jobs 12%
Unavailable for comment 2%
No places available on training schemes 15%
Lack of knowledge of companies and work in the area 15%
Lack of confidence in interview skills 5%
Jobs on offer sound unattractive 6%
Little understanding of job-seeking process 10%
No places available at college 25%

Write an email to your local newspaper commenting on the information and suggesting ways **some** of these problems could be overcome.

Your email should be about 150–200 words long (or 100–150 words for Core level).

Speaking

1 Worthwhile work

What do you think is the most important and worthwhile work in the world today? Choose one or two jobs you think are particularly important. Say why you think these jobs are important and how society benefits from them.

In your discussion with the assessor you could consider such things as:

- the particular qualities and skills needed for such jobs
- how more people could be encouraged to do this kind of important and worthwhile work
- whether the pay received by people who do these jobs reflects the value of the work
- whether you, yourself, would like to do this work
- the sort of job you would ideally like for yourself in the future.

2 The shopping experience

Some people enjoy spending time in shops and exploring different stores. They spend a long time looking for just the right products. Discuss this topic with the assessor.

You may wish to use the following ideas to help develop the conversation:

- the kind of shops you enjoy visiting and why
- ways in which shops could be improved
- whether doing some work experience in a store interests you
- the advantages and disadvantages of internet shopping
- the view that we are too concerned with luxury designer products and brand names.

KEY ADVICE

Revision and practice

1 You can't, strictly speaking, 'revise' for the exam. However, you can refresh your memory by studying your vocabulary records, reading through good examples of your own work and looking at the examples in this book. Take regular, short breaks and do something relaxing. You probably can't concentrate effectively for more than 20 or 30 minutes at a time.

2 Ask your teacher for exam practice papers. Time yourself answering the questions. Why not practise with a good friend? It's less lonely and more encouraging than working alone.

Before the exam

3 Concentrate on staying relaxed and calm. Have a light meal, fresh air, exercise and a good sleep the night before. Visualise yourself completing the paper well and in good time, and imagine the good results you will receive. Avoid the company of people who enjoy agonising over exams. Laughter is good therapy so you may like to do something light-hearted the night before, like watching a humorous film.

Exam techniques

4 The order in which you tackle reading and writing papers is a matter of personal preference, but it's generally a good idea to answer those questions you feel most confident about first. Aim to complete the paper; gaining just a few extra marks on a question makes a difference to the overall score.

5 Make sure you don't run out of time because you have spent too long on answering one section of the paper. The number of marks for each individual question is shown at the end of the question.

6 Always read the questions very carefully. Don't be tempted to answer comprehension questions without reading the passage first. You will probably miss important links in the text. For summaries and compositions, make sure you understand the 'angle' of the question.

7 Never try to twist a pre-prepared essay to fit the topic of the composition if it really is not relevant. It's far better to tackle the question confidently and write something fresh which answers the question set.

8 Try to stay calm and relaxed during the exam. Flex your fingers so they do not become stiff, and stretch from time to time. Make sure you are sitting comfortably and in the correct posture.

9 If you get really stuck on a question, leave it, move on to another question, and go back to the question later.

10 Be prepared for the inclusion of a graph, chart, diagram, map or table of figures.

214

UNIT FOCUS

In this unit you have answered questions on a detailed reading text which included information in the form of **charts**.

You have listened to a detailed talk and answered **multiple-choice comprehension questions**.

You have practised writing letters and articles describing experience and giving your **opinions**.

You have completed a **form based on a scenario**.

Audioscript for Unit 5, exercise 5

Teacher: Sam and Carol, you've each chosen to talk about quite different films. Sam, you've chosen 'Crocodile Dundee' and Carol, you've selected 'The Hand that Rocks the Cradle'. May I ask why you chose these particular films?

Carol: I wanted to talk about a thriller because it's my favourite genre.

Sam: I wanted to say why I enjoyed a comedy adventure.

Teacher: They sound very interesting! Could you both tell me a bit about the plots?

Sam: 'Crocodile Dundee' is about an Australian outback hero, called Crocodile Dundee. An American journalist interviews him because she's heard about his reputation for defeating crocodiles. The film is set in two great places, New York and Australia, and it's basically about the hilarious adventures they have.

Carol: In 'The Hand that Rocks the Cradle', a normal, middle-class American family employ a nanny to look after their children. The nanny thinks, wrongly, that they are responsible for her husband's death. While she's working at their house, she's actually planning to murder them.

Teacher: Characters are extremely important in films. Carol, would you mind telling me about the nanny?

Carol: Well, she seems sweet-natured but underneath she's very bitter and revengeful.

Teacher: So her appearance is very deceptive! What's the hero of 'Crocodile Dundee' like?

Sam: He's a tough guy but I felt I could identify with him because he's honourable and he's got a great sense of humour. The character is played by Paul Hogan. He's ideal for the part, because he has a sort of rugged, outdoor appearance.

Teacher: Can you give me an example of how his personal qualities were shown in the film?

Sam: In one scene, he's visiting New York when he's almost mugged by a young man with a flick knife. Dundee says 'Call that a knife?' and pulls out a really huge knife he uses in the bush. You know he's not going to use it but the mugger is terrified. I couldn't stop laughing.

Teacher: I know 'The Hand that Rocks the Cradle' is set in America. Could you explain in more detail why you think the setting is effective, Carol?

Carol: Well, the setting is very suburban. This makes the atmosphere more sinister because it shows how evil and danger can come into the lives of ordinary people.

Teacher: You've said that 'Crocodile Dundee' has two fascinating locations, Sam – New York and the Australian bush. Something else I'd like to know is whether there are any special effects?

Sam: Yes. A really good special effect is when Dundee confronts an angry bull in the bush and is able to soothe it with his bare hands.

Teacher: Carol, thrillers should be full of tension. Were you personally in suspense?

Carol: It was so scary that I was on the edge of my seat! There's a really frightening scene where the nanny picks up a pillow to put it behind the baby's head and I really thought she was going to harm the baby.

Teacher: Do you think it's right that the film shows how evil people can be?

Carol: Yes, because the underlying message is that evil is overcome by the forces of good. The real suspense is waiting to find out how that happens.

Teacher: Sam, did 'Crocodile Dundee' have a message?

Sam: I think the message is that courage and caring for others is more important than the background you come from.

Teacher: Carol, why would you recommend the film?

Carol: It's an exciting thriller and it's interesting for anyone who wants to work in a position where trust is important – caring for children, for instance.

Teacher: Sorry, I don't quite understand why you say that.

Carol: In the film, you see how much nannies are trusted and what could happen if a nanny abuses that trust.

215

| Teacher: | Finally, why do you think other people would enjoy 'Crocodile Dundee', Sam? |
| Sam: | It's so relaxing and light-hearted. I've been working hard for my exams, and it's such an escapist film that I forgot about everything. It's fun for children as well as adults. |

Quiz scores

Unit 1, exercise 1: Are you living the life you want?

Mostly As

To be happy there has to be some momentum in your life, but you've hardly got off the launch pad! You're seeking first and foremost to protect and preserve your security. This involves a defensive approach and few risks. It's almost as if you're waiting for life to come and dish out the happiness. Try indulging a whim or two and see what happens.

Mostly Bs

Congratulations! You're probably as happy as a person can be. You've a strong sense of what your wishes, wants and priorities are, and you're prepared to live in a way that suits you, even though it may be unfashionable or present the wrong image. You try to strike a fair balance between your needs and those of others. You're at home with yourself, know your strengths and limitations and don't allow your failures or the failures of others to get you down.

Mostly Cs

You are trying hard to achieve happiness. What you don't realise is that happiness isn't an achievement but an attitude. You're striving for all the things we are told will make us happy, but may be disappointed because you're taking your values from outside. You often feel guilty about your supposed failures. Try being more tolerant of yourself and of others.

Acknowledgements

The author and publishers acknowledge the following sources of copyright material and are grateful for the permissions granted. While every effort has been made, it has not always been possible to identify the sources of all the material used, or to trace all copyright holders. If any omissions are brought to our notice, we will be happy to include the appropriate acknowledgements on reprinting.

Text permissions

p6 © www.timeincukcontent.com; p12 © Telegraph Media Group Limited 1996; p2 © www.timeincukcontent.com; p30 Josephine Fairley; p49 Sarah Farley; p58 © by kind permission of The Lady; p41 abridged article by Sally Smith in the TES; p57 from NUTURESHOCK by Po Bronson & Ashley Merryman, published by Ebury Press, reprinted by permission of The Random House Group Limited; p67 Friends of The Earth; p91 interview by PhilipGray in Springboard magazine; p106 Kingswood Camps; p126 Explore Worldwide; p115 © Good Housekeeping UK/Hearst Magazines UK; p134 © Good Housekeeping UK/Hearst Magazines UK; p157 adapted from article by Luke Harding, Daily Mail © Solo Syndication; p175 © Zest UK/Hearst Magazines UK; p194 Copyright Guardian News & Media Ltd 1996; p203 article by Manal el-Jesri, Egypt Today.

Image permissions

Cover SteveRussellSmithPhotos/Shutterstock; p2 (top left); p2 (top right) Steve Debenport / Getty Images; p3b © Image Source / Alamy; p3t © Blend Images / Alamy; p6 Denis Tabler /Alamy; p8 © AfriPics.com / Alamy; p10 Mint Images RF/ Shutterstock; p13 © Blend Images / Alamy; p14 Jack Hollingsworth/Thinkstock; p16 Topalov Djura / Getty Images; p21 (top) © Hill Street Studios/Eric Raptosh/Blend Images/Corbis; p23b canadastock/ Shutterstock; p23t © OJO Images Ltd / Alamy; p25 © Blend Images / Alamy; p27 Christy Thompson/ Shutterstock; p29 Image Source/ Getty Images; p30 © Arcaid Images / Alamy; p33 © Adrian Weinbrecht / Alamy; p34 Buccina Studios/Thinkstock; p40 (top) © imageBROKER / Alamy; p41 Monkey Business Images/ Shutterstock; p42 Krailurk Warasup/ Shutterstock; p46 Maxisport/ Shutterstock; p52 © W2 Photography/Corbis; p55 John Blanton/ Shutterstock; p57 © Hank Morgan - Rainbow/Science Faction/Corbis; p61 (top) weerapatkiatdumrong/Thinkstock; p61b © RooM the Agency / Alamy; p64 Judith Brown; p65 Monkey Business Images/ Shutterstock; p66 © RosaIreneBetancourt 4 / Alamy; p67 © UrbanLandscapes / Alamy; p68 Kanuman/ Shutterstock; p71b Laitr Keiows/ Shutterstock; p71t Ppictures/ Shutterstock; p73 Seqoya/ Shutterstock; p75 Hoberman Collection/Contributor/Getty Images; p76l Gwoeii/ Shutterstock; p76r ssuaphotos/ Shutterstock; p77bl FloridaStock/ Shutterstock; p77br Craig Lovell / Eagle Visions Photography p77tl anweber/ Shutterstock; p77tr 1000 Words/ Shutterstock; p82 © Eugene Sergeev / Alamy; p83 (top) © Pictorial Press Ltd / Alamy; p85 © Hero Images Inc. / Alamy; p87 © Photos 12 / Alamy; p90 Pavel L Photo and Video/ Shutterstock; p91l © Johnny Jones / Alamy; p91r © AF archive / Alamy; p94 Pavel L Photo and Video/ Shutterstock; p95 Dragon Images p97 © AF archive / Alamy; p105 (top left) RuthChoi/ Shutterstock; p105 (top right) Krzysztof Wiktor/ Shutterstock; p106-107 all Kingswood Camps; p109b © Fab Fernandez/Corbis; p109c © Image Source Plus / Alamy; p109t © Wig Worland / Alamy; p111 © Hero Images Inc. / Alamy; p114 © Stuart Forster / Alamy; p115 K. Roy Zerloch/ Shutterstock; p116 Angelo Giampiccolo/ Shutterstock; p117 © Anna Serrano/SOPA RF/SOPA/Corbis; p120b Susan Law Cain/ Shutterstock; p120t © Adrian Sherratt / Alamy; p121 © colinspics / Alamy; p126 E_K/ Shutterstock; p128 (top left) Brand X Pictures/Thinkstock; p128 (top right) © Marc Hill / Alamy; p130 © Cultura Creative (RF) / Alamy; p134 © Simon Grosset / Alamy; p134 © Blend Images / Alamy; p135 © Design Pics Inc / Alamy; p141 © Hero Images Inc. / Alamy; p143 © Martí sans / Alamy; p147 (top left) Lemonakis Antonis/ Shutterstock; p147 (top right) Rich Carey/ Shutterstock; p148bl alybaba/ Shutterstock; p148cl © Eye Ubiquitous / Alamy; p148cr Paulo Resende/ Shutterstock; p148tr hpbdesign/ Shutterstock; p149 S.m.u.d.g.e/ Shutterstock; p151 © Terry Mathews / Alamy; p153 Taras Kushnir/ Shutterstock; p155 © Roger Bamber / Alamy; p157 Ksenia Raykova/ Shutterstock; p157 © The Photolibrary Wales / Alamy; p161 © Buzz Pictures / Alamy; p164 © DBURKE / Alamy; p169 (top) Mickrick/Thinkstock; p169bl Albie Venter/ Shutterstock; p169br Sue Green/ Shutterstock; p169cl Waddell Images/ Shutterstock; p169cr Erik Zandboer/ Shutterstock; p169tl PhillipRubino/ Shutterstock; p169tr FlavoredPixels/ Shutterstock; p170 © Robin Weaver / Alamy; p174 anyaivanova/ Shutterstock; p175 Tooga/Getty Images; p179 © dbimages / Alamy; p180 racorn/ Shutterstock; p182 Goodluz/ Shutterstock; p183l Sirko Hartmann/iStock/Getty Images; p184r © Travel Pictures / Alamy; p184 old apple/ Shutterstock; p186l guentermanaus/ Shutterstock; p186r davemhuntphotography/ Shutterstock; p187 DeLoyd Huenink/ Shutterstock; p193 (top left) anyaivanova/ Shutterstock; p193 (top right) Dmitry Kalinovsky/ Shutterstock; p194l Sebastian Radu/ Shutterstock; p194r © Erik Tham / Alamy; p196 auremar/ Shutterstock; p199 © Juice Images / Alamy; p200 © Image Source / Alamy; p203 © conmare GmbH / Alamy; p206t Monkey Business Images p206b © Blend Images / Alamy; p208 Palle Christensen/ Shutterstock.